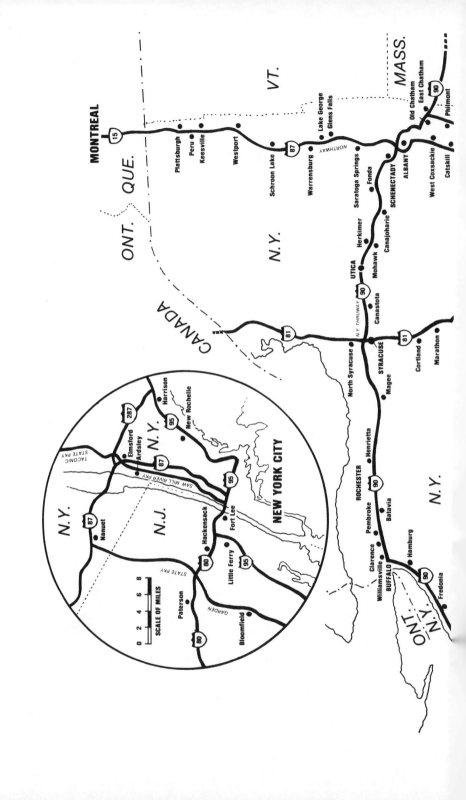

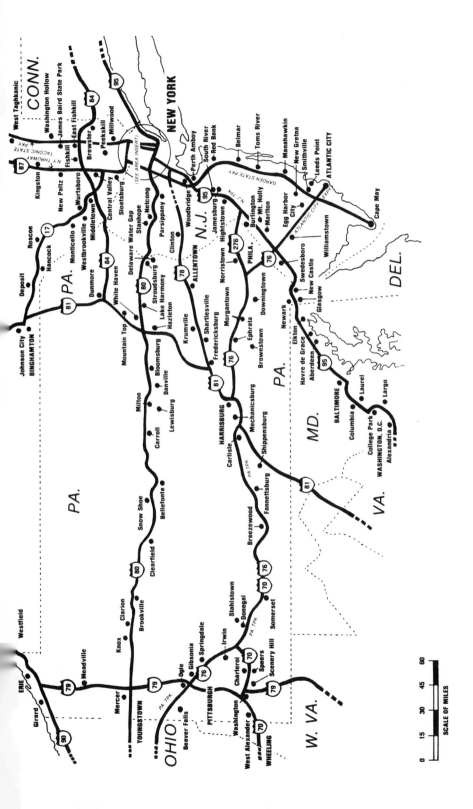

THE INTERSTATE
GOURMET

Mid-Atlantic

Neal O. Weiner and
David M. Schwartz

SUMMIT BOOKS

NEW YORK

The reader should be aware that the restaurant business is unpredictable. Restaurants change their menus, prices and hours; some even change their names or addresses. While we have made every effort to update this book over the past year, we would be most grateful to hear about any changes you have encountered in your travels so that we may keep future editions up to date.

Copyright © 1983 by The Interstate Gourmet, Inc.
All rights reserved
including the right of reproduction
in whole or in part in any form
Published by SUMMIT BOOKS
A Simon & Schuster Division of Gulf & Western Corporation
Simon & Schuster Building
Rockefeller Center
1230 Avenue of the Americas
New York, New York 10020
SUMMIT BOOKS and colophon are trademarks of Simon & Schuster
Designed by Eve Kirch
Illustrations: Kristin Funkhauser
Map: Robert MacLean
Manufactured in the United States of America

10 9 8 7 6 5 4 3 2 1

First Edition
Library of Congress Cataloging in Publication Data
Weiner, Neal O.
    The interstate gourmet—mid-Atlantic.
    Includes index.
    1. Restaurants, lunch rooms, etc.—Middle Atlantic
States—Directories. I. Schwartz, David M.
II. Title.
TX907.W437   1983   647'.9575   83-380
ISBN 0-671-44993-1

ACKNOWLEDGMENTS

So many people helped us in so many ways that no list could even remotely do justice to the extent of our appreciation. For this Mid-Atlantic edition we are especially grateful to the many friends who shared their homes with us during our wearying travels.

The greatest thanks must go to Mary Lou Brozena, Charlotte Sheedy, and Becky Nordstrom. But also: Elizabeth Boice; Glenn Cantor and Inge Eriks; Sue Carroll; Florance and Tom Cowan; John and Grace Crowley; Rose Crowley; Stan Duobinis; Jeffery Farrance; Enid Parker Fary; Lenny and Karen Fromkes; Charlie Gilbert; Debbie and Mike Oppenheim; Patricia Parker; Mary Piscotty and family; Don Ruggles; Morris and Diane Schwartz; Robin Stahl; Vera Stek; Renee Vorbach; Heidi Watts; D'Arcy Webb; Sylvia Weiner; and John Whelan.

Jessica Weiner's love and forbearance allowed the work to go forward. Mary Lou's assistance when called on, and her patience when not, spurred it to completion.

CONTENTS

INTRODUCTION

Long before either of us moved up to the front seat, we knew that there had to be a better way to eat than the way it's done on the New Jersey Turnpike. Unhappy memories of boyhood trips along that infamous highway have outlasted the indigestion they inflicted. *The Interstate Gourmet* is our attempt to conquer this universal dilemma—where to eat when you're on the road.

There you are at 55-plus miles per hour, trapped on a concrete corridor totally insulated from the world around you. Tractor trailers assault your eardrums, and a malodorous sea of oil refinery tanks greets your other senses. And when it's time for a break, you're herded into a service area to fight the crowds for prepackaged food at criminally high prices in a stockyard atmosphere.

Traveling doesn't have to be like this. You needn't choose between culinary abuse and heroic feats of highway endurance. But you don't have time to go poking up back roads looking for Ma's Diner.

What if there were a book that told you where to find good, interesting, local restaurants close to the interstate exits? Couldn't someone just go down the road, exit by exit, and find them? That's what we wondered, and then we decided to do it ourselves.

And we *did* find them! Did you know that within minutes of the New Jersey Turnpike in Burlington, there's an excellent French restaurant that doubles as an art gallery? That Swedesboro has a reasonably priced country inn? That a terrific diner in

Marlton serves award-winning cheesecake, and another in Hightstown has great chopped liver and pickled herring at its salad bar? Even industrial Perth Amboy has a superb Mexican restaurant just half a block from the exit ramp.

It doesn't raise your toll one nickel to exit for lunch and later return to the turnpike well fed. And the minutes it takes to reach these restaurants could be spent in the rest-room waiting line at the service area.

It's the same story on the New York State Thruway and the Pennsylvania Turnpike. And on the rest of the interstate system you must leave the highway to eat whether you like it or not, but where do you go?

In Clinton, New Jersey, there is a low-priced gourmet restaurant run by a 22-year-old woman whose cooking has been featured in three food magazines and a book. New Paltz, New York, has a funky omelet house that turns every egg it touches to gold. In Syracuse, you can get fabulous French food in a used-car lot, and in Westfield, near the Pennsylvania border, the same cuisine is served in a former speakeasy paneled with old slabs of bark.

There's wonderful Pennsylvania Dutch cooking near Ephrata in a down-home restaurant where half the customers are Amish and the prices are rock bottom. Or how about a magnificent "Dutch" feast of more than 30 dishes for just $6.25 at a hotel in Shartlesville, just half a minute from the interstate exit?

Pennsylvania Dutch isn't the only regional cuisine you can sample along the interstate system. North of Baltimore, I-95 skirts the shores of Chesapeake Bay, where blue crab is king. There's nothing in the world like peppery steamed crabs, Baltimore-style, and we found four places that specialize in them, along with crabcakes, crab soup, soft-shell crabs, hard fries, and fluff.

From the Garden State Parkway it's easy to sample the seafood of the Jersey shore. In Cape May you can even choose among oyster houses, continental cuisine, or superb Southern cooking served on verandas dripping with Victorian gingerbread and cooled by an ocean breeze.

The Buffalo area specializes in wings—chicken wings, that is, deep-fried and seasoned with Tabasco and pepper to three degrees of spiciness, sometimes described as "smoldering," "scorching," and "suicidal." Also popular in western New York is "beef on weck." "Weck" is Kümmelweck, a kind of hard roll that is piled with slices of roast beef and saturated with the meat's natural juices. Off the Northway, near Plattsburgh, New York, there's a place that does great things with dishes made from the local apple crop. Ever tried duckling à l'apple?

Ethnic restaurants of every nationality lie close to the highway —Chinese, Japanese, Italian, German, French, Greek, Jewish, Vietnamese, and more. In fact, an overview of the Mid-Atlantic interstate system can start to look like a blown-up dining guide to Manhattan. We even found an Ethiopian restaurant in Alexandria, Virginia, and an Armenian place in Fort Lee, New Jersey.

Then there are the diners, of course, those gems of Americana that always have low prices and often good food as well (we tell you which have which). And the soda fountain/luncheonettes, not nearly so celebrated as the diners, but beautiful in their own way and just as homey.

And in our travels we realized that a whole new genus of American restaurant has sprung up in the last decade. We call them brick-plants-and-oak cafés, after their decor, or BPOs for short. They're usually found in renovated downtown buildings, often right near the road, and they're invariably trimmed with Tiffany-style lamps, advertising mirrors, and pressed-tin ceilings. BPOs like to pun, so their sandwiches often get names like "Lady Chatterley's Liver" or "Uncle Monte's Cristo," but whether they pun or not, you can be sure of finding quiche, spinach salad, and Reubens—the ubiquitous QSR menu. These places discovered fried potato skins and are quick to melt a chunk of cheddar over almost anything. And they are convinced that carrot cake is a dessert whose time has come.

Add to all this the country inns, the old hotels, the natural foods restaurants, dairy bars, bakeries, and delis, and it's hard to find a reason to get stuck at a chain restaurant ever again.

All the restaurants in this book have one thing in common: we liked them. Something about each makes it worth a visit. In most cases it's good food, but since adventure is a part of eating on the road, we included a few places that were stronger on local color than cuisine. If your palate is fussy, you'll probably want to pass them by. With these restaurants, we flag your attention right at the top of the entry. The same for places we picked because of low prices, convenient hours, or some other purely practical reason.

But always we leave out the chains, the Polynesian palaces, the monotonous steak 'n lobster joints, and almost anything with a name like Beef 'n Brew, Burger 'n Bun, or Suds 'n Duds.

Within these limits we looked hard for variety, trying to please all palates, purses, and moods. In this book you'll find 80-cent hamburgers right next to $18 Chateaubriand, all treated with egalitarian respect, though we've borne in mind that most people aren't looking for costly culinary subtleties when on the road. And we've tried to space our choices so that wherever you are and whatever your taste, something you like will be less than 30 minutes down the pike.

Occasionally, we found slim pickin's. When this happened we put in a few marginal places so that you'd have something besides fast food for a hunger that just can't wait. Here too, we warn you, right at the top of the page, so you won't even bother reading about it if you're more interested in a marvelous meal than a bearable burger. We tell you which is which, never afraid to call a spud a spud.

We discovered all of these restaurants on a gargantuan, six-state odyssey. And we sampled the food in nearly every place in this book. A few restaurants were closed when we passed through, and there were a few times that we simply couldn't bear the thought of another bite. We get you to the front door of those places and leave the rest to your spirit of adventure. Let us know what you find. But 99 percent of the time you'll know just what lies beyond the highway signs.

When you stop for a roadside lunch, you're not just buying food. You're also renting space, and so we tell you how a place feels—what it will do to your day if you pass an hour there. Of course we also describe the menu, the prices, and the quality of the food without trying to sound as though we were reviewing Lutèce for *The New York Times.* And we've put an enormous effort into providing unmistakably clear directions, stop sign by stop sign, from highway to restaurant. Well we know the frustration of missed turns and missing street signs after a long, hard drive!

In these inflationary times we can't be sure that the prices you find will be the ones we saw. They may go up, but no matter what happens to the economy what we report here will be a good relative guide to the cost of your meal.

As with any directory, from *Who's Who* to *Consumer Reports,* this book will be subject to quarrels about who got in and who didn't. And surely we missed some very good places, sometimes even "the best in town." But our goal was to spare you the fast-food tedium. If you consider the restaurants in this book relative to the usual run of highway eateries, we doubt you'll argue too fiercely over the fine points.

If we did miss your favorite place, do let us know so that future editions of the *Interstate Gourmet* will be even more useful. In the meantime, we guarantee to change your perspective on the highway dining dilemma. It's true that getting stuck in a chain restaurant is but a minor misfortune, but it's one we've cured for good. Perhaps the little evils are the only ones that can be done away with once and for all.

Pennsylvania

THE BUTTERY, *Exit 1, West Alexander*

Way out here on the West Virginia border there's a tiny little place dedicated to quality in a straightforward, unpretentious way. The small rooms, bare floors, and oak furnishings of the Buttery occupy a row house on West Alexander's charming Main Street, where there are so many old wooden buildings we were reminded of New England, except that here they're painted in pastels. The bank and church are brick, however, and from the latter's belfry came a welcoming rendition of the "Ode to Joy."

It's a delightful town for a lunch stop, and the Buttery will please you with its soups from scratch (65 cents a cup, 95 cents a bowl), fancy sandwiches ($3.75 for a Reuben), salad and bread ($3.95), rarebit ($3.95), Brunswick stew ($3.95), or crêpes. Dinner is even better, but you can get it only on Saturday and Sunday. Then it's first-rate country cooking at moderate prices: chicken and dumplings or ham and yams for $5.95 and pan-fried trout for $6.95.

HOURS Tue.–Fri. 11 am–3 pm; Sat. 11 am–6:30 pm; Sun. noon–6:30 pm; closed Mon.

DIRECTIONS From Exit 1 turn right at end of ramp and go 0.3 mile to a stop sign. Turn left onto Main St. The Buttery is 0.2 mile up the street, on the right.

WASHINGTON RESTAURANT
SHORTY'S HOT DOG LUNCH, *Exit 4, Washington*

Washington just isn't a town for fine dining, or even fine lunching. But the Washington Restaurant will give you decent food and a glimpse of life in a pleasant little city where Marsh Wheelings are the standard after-dinner cigar and Mail Pouch chewing tobacco is displayed along with Life-Savers.

It's a clean, plain, plasticky lunchroom that seems to be the center of downtown life. All kinds of people fill it with lively chatter at lunchtime, producing a surprisingly urban feel, even though the jukebox plays country music.

The food is acceptable, though nothing special for this kind of place. Prices are modest—$1.10 for a hamburger, $4 for the average dinner. One egg, toast, and coffee go for a buck, and there are about 30 comparably priced sandwiches on the menu.

Just around the corner is Shorty's Hot Dog Lunch, where it's been for 50 years. Shorty's has the appeal of age—old, dark wooden booths and venerable woodwork behind the counter. A mixed crowd of businessmen in pinstripes and miners in cowboy hats can be found lunching here on hot dogs and burgers (65 cents each), but either the quality of Shorty's franks has declined or it doesn't take a whole lot to please these folks.

HOURS   **Washington:** Mon.–Fri. 6 am–7 pm; Sat. 7 am–7 pm; closed Sun.
Shorty's: Mon.–Sat. 8 am–5 pm; closed Sun.

DIRECTIONS   From Exit 4 turn right onto Chestnut St. (U.S. 40). Go 2.2 miles to Main St. **Shorty's** is on the right, ½ block before Main. For the **Washington,** turn right on Main and go ½ block; it's on the left.

CENTURY INN, *Exits for Bentleyville & Glyde (Routes 917 & 519), Scenery Hill*

* Far, but special

Whether you're weary of soulless motels or just looking for good country cooking in a pleasant, colonial atmosphere, the few extra minutes to the Century are well worth the trouble. Since 1794 this solid, stone inn has been serving travelers along the old National Pike (U.S. 40), and if you search the dusty guest registers you'll find such names as Lafayette and Andrew Jackson.

Warm, inviting, and comfy, the inn's 20 rooms are beautifully furnished with colonial antiques. Some are quite large, and all have private baths. Guests share the handsome downstairs living room with innkeepers Gordon and Megan Harrington, whose own quarters are on the third floor. For $35 that's an astonishing bargain, especially when you consider the alternatives.

Since the innkeeping tradition means good food, and lots of it, the Century's cuisine matches the charm of its lodgings. It's carefully prepared American fare, served in either the large dining room (colonial wallpaper, white tablecloths, print curtains, and fine antiques—more pretty, actually, than authentic) or the smaller and more rugged Keeper Room, with its mammoth fireplace from the original kitchen.

As with the rooms, meal prices are low, considering what you get—only $6.95 for a full roast turkey dinner, $7.95 for broiled fish, or $9.95 for beef Burgundy. Sandwiches at lunchtime run from about $2.25 to $4.25. Entrées like chicken à la king on waffles or ham rolled around asparagus and smothered beneath a cheese sauce are around $4 (salad included).

You just can't beat the Century for warmth and country friendliness.

HOURS　Mon.–Thu. noon–3:30 pm and 4:30–7:30 pm; Fri. & Sat. noon–3:30 pm and 4:30–8:30 pm; Sun. noon–6:30 pm. Breakfast for guests only. Closed from the Sunday before Christmas to mid-March.

DIRECTIONS　NOTE: You can mitigate the extra mileage to the Century by returning to I-70 7 miles farther along in the direction you are traveling. If eastbound, return by following westbound directions in reverse. If westbound, reverse eastbound directions for the return to I-70.

Eastbound: Take exit for Route 519 and go about 2 miles south to Glyde. Turn left onto Route 40 East. It's about 3½ miles to Scenery Hill and the inn, on the left.

Westbound: From I-70 take the Bentleyville exit onto Route 917 South. Follow this curvy road for 6½ miles until it ends in a T at U.S. 40 (if in doubt, follow the arrows at the turns). Turn left onto U.S. 40, following signs for Scenery Hill. Go 1.1 miles; the Century's on your left.

THE MEAT PLACE
LOUIE'S BAKERY, *Exit 17, Charleroi*

Exit 17 gives you the choice of fine dining at the Back Porch (see next entry) or wonderful meaty, greasy, spicy ribs at the Meat Place followed by an éclair at Louie's next door.

Classy the Meat Place ain't, but it makes up for its bright, plastic atmosphere by the succulent flavor of its Texas-style barbecue. They do up chicken, ribs, and "kabassi" here, in the rotisserie right behind the counter, and sell them for just over $3 a pound. The food comes to you instantaneously on plastic plates that you'll carry to the table in rapt anticipation. Licking your fingers is just fine at the Meat Place, so you may not want to use the little foil-wrapped towel that comes with the meal. The ribs are as crisply delicious on the outside as they are juicy within. They come with hot or sweet-and-sour sauce, but we thought it a travesty to mess around with perfection.

Louie's isn't quite so exciting, but it is a better than average bakery with colorful displays of everything from crusty Italian bread to cookies, Danish, and doughnuts. No place to sit, so you'll have to savor them on the go.

If you choose this pair of humble eateries, you'll get to drive two miles along the industrialized Monongahela shoreline and see something of the barge traffic, coal cars, and steelworks that are the lifeblood of Pittsburgh. Not the usual conception of scenery, but a bit of an education.

HOURS   **Meat Place:** Mon.–Sat. 10 am–10 pm; closed Sun.
        Louie's: Mon.–Fri. 6 am–4:30 pm; Sat. 6 am–4 pm; closed Sun.

DIRECTIONS From Exit 17 turn left onto Route 88 North. Go 1.6 miles if eastbound; just 1 mile if westbound. The **Meat Place** is on the left, in a shiny red and white building. **Louie's** is next door.

THE BACK PORCH, *Exit 17 (Charleroi/Route 88), Speers*

At the Back Porch you get two decors and a fringe benefit. The perk is that the restaurant is just a block from a barge towing service on the Monongahela River, where a few minutes' observation offers an education in the workings of modern-day river traffic.

Whether or not that interests you, once inside this fine colonial building you can dine upstairs amidst brick walls, paneled fireplaces, antiques, and white tablecloths; or downstairs, where the 18-inch-thick stone foundation encloses a labyrinth of small, dark, romantic rooms.

Whichever you choose, the food will be the same excellent fare that had been praised in print many times before we showed up. It'll cost you between $9.50 and $12.95 (dinners only, here), and what you get will be the likes of red snapper amandine, steaks, ribs, or spiedini (lightly breaded, stuffed roulettes of beef in Mornay sauce on a bed of white and wild rice, $9.50). Potato, vegetable, and salad bar come with the meal, and we were glad to see that the salad bar had spinach, endive, and Romaine to help the iceberg lettuce along.

A good place for a fine, slow dinner—and don't forget the river!

HOURS Tue.–Thu. 5–10 pm; Fri. & Sat. 5–11 pm; Sun. 4–9:30 pm; closed Mon.

DIRECTIONS Eastbound: Turn left from Exit 17 onto Route 88 and go 0.2 mile. Turn right just before the bridge, and go 1 block to Speers St. Right onto Speers, and it's 1 block to a large brick building on the right.

Westbound: From Exit 17 turn right onto Route 88. Go 0.4 mile, under the bridge, to the first left. Take this left and go 1 block to Speers St. Right onto Speers, and it's 1 block to a large brick building on the right.

I-76 (Pennsylvania Turnpike)

Pennsylvania *(INCLUDING I-276)*,
New Jersey *(I-276)*

Pennsylvania

GIUSEPPE'S RESTAURANT, *Exit 2, Beaver Falls*

Joe Pronesti's place looks touristy from the outside and glitzy within, but the fact is that most of his trade is local. And no matter what you think of fake brick and gilt-sprinkled statues, this is a comfortable, relaxing environment and a true family operation.

Most important, the food is great. Joe makes sure of that. He's almost always there, proudly presiding over every detail, from the homemade pasta to the wonderful buttery clam sauce that tastes like clams, not garlic. Or perhaps he's in the kitchen whipping the ricotta cheese. It's destined to join powdered sugar, crème de cacao, and bits of bitter chocolate on a bed of cinnamon graham cracker crumbs. Then it's dubbed "Giuseppe's Delight," a lovely, subtle dessert you won't soon forget.

Lunch at Giuseppe's is a relatively humble matter, mostly pasta specials ($2.95 with meatballs, salad, and bread) and a variety of sandwiches with Italian accents, like the "Pro-burger"— Italian sausage with onions, green peppers, mozzarella, and tomato sauce ($2.25).

It's at dinnertime that the more interesting Italian dishes come out: wedding soup (with heart-shaped bits of carrot), for example, at $1.75 a bowl, or the bracciole of which Joe is so proud. It's a rolled sirloin tip stuffed with Italian treats and simmered in sauce till tender ($12.95). Most pasta dishes are around $5, and fettucini in that delicious clam sauce goes for $6.50. There's a good selection of American dishes too, in the $8–$13 range. But even with these the accent is Italian, both in the flavorings and the names—instead of "surf 'n turf" it's "pésce e càrne." Sounds better that way, doesn't it? Tastes better too.

HOURS Mon.–Thu. 10 am–11 pm; Fri. & Sat. 10 am–1 am; Sun. 10 am–10 pm.

DIRECTIONS It's ½ mile south of Exit 2 on Route 18, toward Beaver Falls. Can't be missed, on the left, beneath a big sign.

EAST AND WEST INTERNATIONAL DINING, *Exit 3, Ogle*

Now here's a really unusual place. Two women whose church work brought them in contact with the wider world decided to start a business that would somehow blend the world's cultures in a celebration of the human community. Since they'd been learning all sorts of cooking by entertaining a steady stream of foreigners in their kitchens, a restaurant seemed the way to do it. The result is no ordinary place, not even an ordinary ethnic eatery. It's got a dinner menu divided into East and West. Italian, French, and American dishes are on the right. On the left are curries, sweet and sour shrimp, shish kebab, and kibbe Nayee (a Middle Eastern specialty).

All this has been packaged in a little red-brick house and solarium, set way back from the road and introduced by a long green canopy. It doesn't look like a restaurant, and even after you've assured yourself that it is, they still keep you guessing by decorating each of the three small dining rooms differently. The American room is close-feeling, with antiques, yellow tablecloths, and fireplace; the Moroccan room has walls and ceiling draped in a paisley print; and finally there's the light and breezy sun porch, gay as summertime, with white chairs and an abundance of greenery. Taped classical music or jazz plays throughout, and guests from far away are invited to stick a pin in the world map by the doorway.

Nothing is frozen here; no MSG is used, and special vegetarian dishes are gladly made up on request. Butter comes in delightful little curlicues, served with Irish soda bread. Dinners range mostly from $8.50 to $12.50, though some specials run as high as $20.

Although most of the midday menu was a fairly Occidental collection of sandwiches ($3.25–$4.25), quiche ($4.25), omelets ($3–$4.25), and salads ($3.75–$4.75), we went for the chow fu yung and found it delicately flavored, rich in crabmeat and scallions. You might also enjoy the salad Oriental, a mélange of dark chicken meat, water chestnuts, pineapple, chutney, and lemon juice.

East, west, north, or south, we think you'll like this place.

HOURS   Tue.–Fri. 11:30 am–3 pm and 4–9 pm; Sat. 6–11 pm; Sun. 10 am–3 pm for brunch and 3–9 pm for dinner. Closed Mondays and for two weeks in mid-January.

DIRECTIONS   Just 1.6 miles north of Exit 3, on U.S. 19. It's on the right.

HARTNER'S, *Exit 3, Ogle*

If it's straight domestic fare and moderate prices you're after, you'll do well at Hartner's. Their delicious, fluffy pancakes were a real relief from the usual flabby flapjacks of the highways, suggesting that Hartner's reputation for great baked goods and good country cooking is well deserved.

Don't be put off by the classy-looking white building. Though there's been an effort to fancy things up, the feel within is that of a better than average family restaurant—nothing more intimidating. Dinners are $8.95–$12.95, but lunchtime sandwiches are only $1.95 (more for clubs). Cheese plates are available from $2.50, and cheesecake is only a buck.

HOURS   Mon.–Fri. 11 am–9 pm; Sat. 9 am–10 pm; Sun. 9 am–8 pm.

DIRECTIONS   Just 0.7 mile north of Exit 3 on U.S. 19; it's on the right.

VENUS DINER, *Exit 4, Gibsonia*

* Not great, but always open

Looking a bit like a tour boat sailing a placid lake of asphalt, this stainless-steel diner with wraparound windows puts up decent food at quite modest prices, and does it 24 hours a day. The chicken noodle soup was hearty, and burgers sell for only 90 cents; $1.45 for a double burger with one pork patty and one of beef.

It's spiffier than most inside—wide and handsome with booths in British-racing-car green and a mirrored ceiling that runs its entire length (there's nothing kinky about it—it's left over from the days when you had to worry about what got slipped into the burgers; the mirror lets you see the goings-on behind the counter from any spot in the diner).

HOURS Always open.

DIRECTIONS On Route 8, just ¼ mile directly north of Exit 4.

CRYSTAL INN, *Exit 5, New Kensington*

* Color, not cuisine

We couldn't pass by Pittsburgh without finding at least one place like the Crystal, an unadulterated working-class bar specializing in Slovenian-style breaded chicken. To reach it you ride right along the industrialized shoreline of the Allegheny River and pass the huge, rusted building of the Stone Steel Company.

The Crystal itself is reminiscent of a scene from *The Deer Hunter*. A square, white-brick building with red awnings for trim, it's dark inside because life here is dominated by the TV, all eyes glued to its perch above the bar. Five booths, a few tables covered with red-checked vinyl, a Franklin stove off in one corner, and a large crocheted American flag make up the decor. It's the sort of neighborhood place you hate to enter for fear that every head will turn in your direction. But everyone was so intent on the TV that we were hardly noticed. When we did attract some attention, all were as friendly as folks can be.

Now the Slovenian chicken, we'll grant, tastes a lot like chicken in spiced-up Italian bread crumbs. All the same, it's a lot better than what you get from the Colonel. At $2.50 for half a dozen pieces ($5 for 15) it's also a lot cheaper. You can get Bar-B-Q chicken too (half a bird for $2.25), but more intriguing still was the Bar-B-Q lamb at $5.50 a pound. That exotic, however, is to be had only on weekends from 4 to 6 P.M.

Whatever your choice, you can wash it down with beer at 40 cents a glass!

HOURS   Tue.–Sat. 11 am–midnight; Sun. 1–8 pm; closed Mon.

DIRECTIONS   From Exit 5 follow signs for New Kensington, going straight north on Route 28 for 1.6 miles. It's on the left.

ISALY'S
COLONIAL GRILL, *Exit 7, Irwin*

Isaly's is actually a local chain of ice cream counters, but this one has its own bakery and deli. You can get a decent sandwich here and have your choice of ice cream or sweet roll for dessert. Irwin has a charming Main Street that boasts some pretty fancy brickwork. So even though the bakery is less than memorable and the deli doesn't offer a great selection, it's a good choice for a quick bite.

Hamburgers from the cafeteria setup are just $1.29. Ham or kielbasa sandwiches go for $1.49, and a Reuben is $2.19. If even that's too steep, try a fried egg sandwich for 65 cents. A single-dip cone is 47 cents, and the bakery prices are, as they say in the ads, too low to mention.

Decor isn't Isaly's strong point. The place is done up in fast-food yellow and pink, but the food is better than that.

Right next door to Isaly's is the Colonial Grill, closed, unfortunately, when we passed through, but promising. If you're looking for something a bit classier than Isaly's, it's worth a chance.

HOURS   Isaly's: Mon.–Sat. 7:30 am–9 pm; Sun. 8 am–9 pm.

DIRECTIONS   From Exit 7 go 1.3 miles west on U.S. 30 to a light. Turn right onto a street marked by a sign for "Downtown Irwin" and follow this until it ends at a T. Turn left here onto Pennsylvania Ave., go 2 blocks to Oak, right onto Oak, and continue 5 blocks to Third St. Turn left on Third, 1 block to Main, and left onto Main. It's ½ block to Isaly's, on the left.

P. P. CHABOT CHICKEN AND RIBS
THE PIE SHOP, *Exit 9, Donegal*

If you're heading east it's almost 100 miles from Donegal to the next really notable restaurant. So, here we went farther afield than usual to find three fine ones that are 5 to 7 miles from the exit (next entries). For a quick bite right by the road the only places worth trying are P. P. Chabot's open-air barbecue, which smells wonderful even when nothing's cooking, and the Pie Shop right next door. If not patisserie-quality, it at least provides an adequate dessert.

HOURS   **Chabot's:** Summer weekends only.
Pie Shop: Every day 7 am–8 pm.

DIRECTIONS From Exit 9 turn left onto Route 31 West. Go 1.3 miles; they're on the right.

THE ARK, *Exit 9, Stahlstown*

* Far, but worth it

The Ark has got to be one of the most delightfully unclassifiable, naïvely zany restaurants we've ever come across—well worth the 10 minutes it takes to find it. If we had to invent a category for this place, the best we could do would be to call it gourmet-cuddly, with a strong dose of old-time religion.

You know something's odd the moment you see the vinyl tile floor and the murals—schooling fish, the Matterhorn, and a *Fantasia* waterfall. If they don't fit your idea of a fine restaurant, how about the hundreds of cute stuffed animals that perch on every sill, rafter, and ledge in the place, including the balcony that rims this small room? A mirror tilted against one wall lets you see the monkeys cavorting above your head. There's also a statue of a primate contemplating the bust of Darwin, which you might take as a joke till you spot a good two pages of the Genesis flood story painted verbatim on the wall by the salad bar.

Disoriented but enchanted, we tried the mushroom soup, and from then on little else mattered. It was wonderful stuff—thick, rich, and tangy. So we went for a sherried shrimp with artichoke crêpe, which was almost as good as the soup, as was the sweet poppy-seed salad dressing.

Unfortunately, the Ark didn't steer a steady course. The peas were dull and the bread blah, but we were still delighted with our odd-ball discovery. Especially when we learned that it's a three-meals-a-day establishment with generally quite reasonable prices: beef Stroganoff and baked ham dinners for $4–$6.50 ($2.50 more with soup and salad bar). Steaks are $10–$11, but sandwiches only $1–$3.75. The "house sandwich" is a mélange of beef, ham, cheese, lettuce, tomato, and mayo graced with ample quantities of Ark sauce (pickley and unusual). It goes for only $2.40.

We never did quite learn the whole story behind the Ark, but it seems to have been mothered by a wealthy, energetic, religious-minded woman in her seventies who does things her own way and decided to pump some life into sleepy Stahlstown. It's her inspiration that guides everything here, and her "artistic" touch that created the decor.

Well, more power to her. We doubt Noah ate so well amidst *his* menagerie.

HOURS   Mon. & Wed.–Sat. 9 am–10 pm; Sun. 11 am–7 pm. Closed Tuesdays and from December 20 to March 6.

DIRECTIONS   From Exit 9 turn left onto Route 31E, following signs for Ligonier. Go 0.3 mile and turn left onto Route 711 North. Remain on 711 by bearing right at the fork ½ mile up the road, and then go 4 miles farther to Stahlstown. Turn right when you see a white house on the left and go 1 block. On the left.

NEPENTHE, *Exit 9, Donegal*

If you feel like retreating to an isolated mountaintop for good food and earthy elegance, then Nepenthe is the place for you. It's a renovated ski lodge, way off by itself up a mountain road. The walls of the large dining room are of chinked horizontal planks, the cathedral ceiling is bare wood, and in the center is a massive stone fireplace. But from there on it's all quite posh, in the best sort of modern good taste—quiet and dignified, with handsome place settings on yellow tablecloths and museum-framed modern art on the walls.

You can enjoy all this at lunchtime while choosing from sandwiches ($3–$4), burgers and French fries ($3.50), spinach salad ($4.75), soup ($1), or entrées like Oriental shrimp ($5.95) and chicken parmigiana ($4.25).

Dinners are mostly in the $10–$11 range, pretty much in an American vein, though you'll find chicken Cordon Bleu on the menu. And even though bouillabaisse isn't an official entry, it's one of the most popular dishes, made from fresh fish only, flown in from Boston.

Nepenthe, by the way, is Greek for "no sorrows," and you're quite as likely to forget yours in this lovely mountaintop retreat as at the more famous California wonderland of the same name.

HOURS Mon.–Thu. 11:30 am–3:30 pm and 5–11 pm; Fri. & Sat. till midnight; Sun. noon–9 pm.

DIRECTIONS From Exit 9 turn right onto Route 31 West. Go 5.6 miles and turn left at sign for Nepenthe. It's 0.7 mile up the mountain to their driveway.

NINO BARSOTTI'S, *Exit 9, Donegal*

Nino Barsotti's is a large commercial restaurant in barnboard, bentwood, Tiffany glass, and antiques. But here they do food right: soups and dressings from scratch, pastries baked daily, and meats cut on the premises. They also fly in their own fish two or three times a week and make the fettucini themselves. What's more, there are some nice touches usually found only in smaller restaurants—fruit for dessert, for instance, with nuts and cheese.

Nino does a great deal of the cooking himself, and he comes by an interest in Italian food naturally, since Barsotti's Italian Bakery was his father's operation in Pittsburgh. The results of his efforts will please you, we think. We sampled a full-flavored, but light and clear, tomato sauce on al dente pasta. The salad that accompanied it had nary a leaf of iceberg—always a good sign.

The dinner menu at Barsotti's is a mixture of American steaks and seafood ($10–$19), pastas in any of seven sauces ($5–$8), and half a dozen Northern Italian veal or chicken dishes at $10–$13. Lunches are pricey—$5 for a Reuben and $4.50 for a hamburger (both with French fries)—but you can get the salad bar for $2.95 and pasta for around $5. Seafood entrées are $6–$7 and soup du jour, $1.50.

The fruit and cheese dessert is $1.50. Sugar lovers can rest assured, however, that there's also an adequate supply of cheesecake and sundaes.

HOURS Tue.–Thu. 11 am–10 pm; Fri. & Sat. 11 am–11 pm; Sun. 11 am–10 pm; closed Mon.

DIRECTIONS From Exit 9 turn right onto Route 31 West and go 6.3 miles; it's on the left.

THE PINE GRILL, *Exit 10, Somerset*

The Pine Grill is just a spanking-clean family restaurant and it's right at the exit, oriented more toward the highway than the town. All the same, we found good food here and an atmosphere that was far beyond the fluorescent and plastic we expected. Its modest prices add the final touch and make the Pine Grill a likable choice for a quick bite.

We couldn't learn how it came about, but the place is quite handsomely designed—real pine paneling, scrollwork, old wooden booths, and indirect lighting. It was so pleasant, in fact, that we couldn't quite put it together with the typical family menu that the friendly waitress handed us.

We were more surprised still when the special, veal parmigiana, turned out to be quite tasty, even if not exquisite—crisp on the outside beneath a tangy sauce. The huge spaghetti side order was almost as good. Not so many points for the soup and rolls, but you're just not going to do much better for $4.25.

Most sandwiches here are around $1. BLTs go for $1.45 and clubs for $2.95. The 30 or so full dinners are $5.80–$9, but the specials are less expensive still and, to judge from our experience, decidedly the way to go.

HOURS   Every day 6:30 am–9:30 pm.

DIRECTIONS   Turn right at Exit 10, and then look immediately to the left.

THE COFFEE SHOP, *Exit 10, Somerset*

If the Pine Grill sounds good but you'd like to see more of the local life, then we've got the place for you. Where else are you going to get hamburgers for 95 cents, white tablecloths, and a mixed crowd in neckties and truckers' hats?

Classy it ain't. There's a long counter by the door and orange vinyl chairs sit before the white linen. But it's clean and pleasant enough, with good coffee, spicy sausage, and okay French toast. You can get an oyster sandwich for $1.20, a steak for $5.95, and 15 other dinners for not a whole lot more than $2.95.

There are added benefits to the half-mile drive into downtown Somerset. One is the wonderfully cluttered, old-fashioned men's store just four doors from the Coffee Shop. The other is the truly impressive county courthouse you'll pass. It's a magnificent, stately edifice, and if you take the time to walk in you'll find a delightful array of staircases, mezzanines, and ornate painted moldings beneath the central dome. We could only marvel at the civic pride it must have taken to build such a monument in so tiny a town.

HOURS   Sun.–Thu. 6 am–7:30 pm; Fri. & Sat. 6 am–8:30 pm.

DIRECTIONS   Turn right at Exit 10 onto Center Ave. and then go 0.6 mile to third light. Turn right onto Route 3W and it's 1 block up, on the left.

OVEN 'N GRILL, *Exits 11 & 12, Everett*

* *Color, not cuisine*

There are lots of touristy places at the Breezewood exit, and as tumbledown a diner as we've seen, but nothing that's both local *and* good. However, U.S. 30 stretches from Exit 12 almost to Exit 11, and it's as fast as the turnpike itself—without the trucks! With almost no loss of time, then, you can explore the town of Everett in between the exits.

If you do, you'll find the Oven 'n Grill, an unassuming village lunchroom with the virtue of a window-facing counter that lets you watch the world go by while sampling the BBQ pork or the carrot cake (not bad, either of them). You may also overhear bearded truckers in cowboy hats discussing their rigs or a suited businessman going over church affairs with a retired railroad worker.

HOURS   Mon.–Thu. & Sat. 6 am–6 pm; Fri. 6 am–8 pm; Sun. 6 am–2 pm.

DIRECTIONS   Eastbound: From Exit 11, use connector road to U.S. 30 and Bedford. Head east on 30 for about 8 miles to a light at Route 26. Turn right onto 26 South; go 1.3 miles. It's on the right.

Westbound: From Exit 12, bear left at the fork in the ramp onto U.S. 30 West. Follow 30 for about 7½ miles to a light. Left onto Route 26 South; go 1.3 miles and it's on the right.

Note: After eating, continue along U.S. 30 until you see signs for the Turnpike. Do not backtrack.

McMULLEN'S GENERAL STORE, *Exits 13 & 14, Fort Littleton & Willow Hill*

*And an interesting road from Fannettsburg to Fort Littleton

Good restaurants just aren't to be had in these parts, so we recommend a picnic. You can stock up at McMullen's General Store in Fannettsburg. It's as cluttered and crowded a country store as you can find, where they pump kerosene by hand with cast-iron machinery that rises up through the wooden floor.

Then drive the back road to the Fort Littleton turnpike entrance in search of the perfect spot. You may like Cowan State Park near Burnt Cabins. There's a working mill there that stonegrinds flour, apparently by water power. At any rate, there's a mill race that seems operative, and right by it are many nice picnic spots. The road passes small tumbledown stone houses and wooden ones with massive stone chimneys, Pennsylvania-style.

These houses are old enough and sufficiently unretouched to give you the feel of history, and the fact is that there's plenty of it here. It's hard to think of these eastern hills as the frontier, but it was across them that the first push westward had to go. The road follows the path of a General Forbes, who built Fort Littleton as part of that push and went on, in 1758, to build forts at Bedford and Ligonier. Finally he wrested Pittsburgh (then Fort Duquesne) from the French.

Burnt Cabins got its name, by the way, when some settlers went beyond the temporarily agreed-upon line dividing Europeans from Indians. The Colonial government had the settlers' cabins burned to forestall Indian retaliation, thereby giving the Indians a breathing space, at least till General Forbes arrived on the scene.

HOURS   Mon.–Fri. 9 am–8 pm; Sat. 9 am–6 pm; closed Sun.

DIRECTIONS   You're on your own for this excursion.

A. R. BURKHARDT'S, *Exit 15, Shippensburg*

See page 82 for a very nice local restaurant that offers some fancy cooking and some Pennsylvania specialties. It's 7 miles off the highway, but good restaurants are hard to find west of Carlisle.

DIRECTIONS   From Exit 15 turn left onto Route 997. Follow 997 a bit over a mile to Route 696. Right onto 696 South and go 6 miles to Shippensburg. Left at the first light in town. It's ½ block up, on the left (13 E. King St.).

THE GINGERBREAD MAN, *Exit 16, Carlisle*

The Gingerbread Man is an archetypical brick-plants-and-oak café with a quintessential QSR menu (quiche, spinach salad, and Reuben sandwiches). It's slick, it's trendy, and it's good, distinguished from others of its ilk principally by its woodwork.

BPOs are frequently lodged in old banks, where they simply inherit the craftsmanship of the past. When built from scratch, the results are often handsome, but seldom really impressive. It's hard to believe that the Gingerbread Man's ornate carvings and heavy wooden arches are new. Every square inch is paneled in some sort of dark wood, much of it extravagantly baroque or even medieval. If it weren't for the Tiffany lamps, brass, etched glass, and Pac-Man screen (mercifully off to one corner), you might fancy yourself in Oxford.

The menu offers all kinds of sandwiches ($2.60–$4.50), soups and salads, omelets ($3.60), quiches ($4–$5), and desserts. The Gingerbread Man's bar occupies about half the floor space, and is stocked accordingly.

This kind of light eating is obviously what the Gingerbread Man is best set up to do, and the chili we tasted was spiced just right. But there are a dozen full dinners too, from $5 to $9.60.

Whatever you pick, it's a pretty fair bet, and you're sure to be impressed by the decor.

HOURS   Mon.–Sat. 11 am–midnight; Sun. 1 pm–midnight.

DIRECTIONS   Bear right from Exit 16 onto U.S. 11 South, toward Carlisle. Go 3.1 miles to center of town and turn right at the light onto High St. (Route 74 North). Make the first possible left, just at the courthouse, and you'll bump right into the restaurant in 1 block.

RILLO'S, *Exit 16, Carlisle*

Everyone we spoke to said Rillo's was the best restaurant in town, and since it's a dinner-only place we tried it out that evening. What we found was a posh, quiet, and comfortable suburban place with very good food, fair prices, and attention to detail.

From the outside, it's a low, pseudo-adobe affair with lots of arches. Inside, it's low-keyed and dark, with red tablecloths, candles, a striped awning over the bar, and piped-in Italian music. The basic menu offers the Italian standbys, from $4 to $10, and quite a few American dishes. It's among the many specials that you'll find the more unusual dishes, like the chicken rustica we tried ($8.25)—a lovely mélange of chicken, sausage, broccoli, tomatoes, potatoes, peas, onions, peppers, bacon, and mushrooms, all nicely blended in a buttery sauce—not exquisite, mind

35

you, but with moments of rapture. The house dressing was light but full flavored, and even the anise mints by the door were delicious. We can't say as much for the bread or the MSG buzz that cast a shadow over the experience, but, well, you can't have everything.

Rillo's has been around for 22 years, and even though it's a big operation it still has something of a family-run flavor. And it's not so fancy that you can't get food to take out or sandwiches at dinnertime ($3–$5).

HOURS Sun.–Thu. 5–10 pm; Fri. & Sat. 5–11 pm.

DIRECTIONS Bear right at Exit 16 ramp onto U.S. 11 South. Go 3.1 miles to light at center of town (Route 74, High St.). Left at light, 0.6 mile to a fork and bear right following signs for Route 74. Go another 0.5 mile to sign for restaurant, and then right for 2 blocks.

FORT LOWTHER RESTAURANT, *Exit 16, Carlisle*

For local life, economy, and some pretty decent food, the Fort Lowther is probably your best bet in Carlisle. It's a frowsy old place in a handsomely renewed red-brick neighborhood right by Dickinson College. The sheet-paneled walls and linoleum floor aren't too bad, and the place is renowned for good, cheap breakfasts.

The buttermilk pancakes were light and the big portion of sausage deliciously pungent ($1.49). It used to be that you could get equally inexpensive Dutch cooking at the Fort Lowther, but that's all changed with new ownership. Don't come looking for anything exotic on the lunch menu, but if you'd enjoy sharing the long counter with workers, students, and businessmen, you'll get a good sandwich at a bargain price.

You'll also get the bonus of peering into the Kakolis Bros. Tobacco Shop next door, which is actually a classically seedy pool hall with stained-glass windows, shoeshine chairs, ancient fixtures, the aroma of cheap cigar smoke, and quite an assortment of characters engrossed in racing forms.

HOURS Mon.–Fri. 5 am–2:30 pm; Sat. 6 am–1 pm; closed Sun.

DIRECTIONS   Bear right at Exit 16 onto U.S. 11 South. Go 3.1 miles to light at center of town (Route 74/High St.). Right at the light, 1½ blocks farther, and it's on your right.

THE GINGERBREAD MAN, *Exit 17, Mechanicsburg*

Mechanicsburg has another incarnation of the Gingerbread Man (see page 34), but not much else. This one's not so lavishly handsome as the Carlisle original, but the mood and menu are the same, as are the hours.

DIRECTIONS   Bear right from the Exit 17 ramp onto Route 15 South (signs for Gettysburg). Go 1.2 miles and take exit for Route 114. Right onto 114 and go 3 miles to Main St. Left on Main, ½ block up, on the right.

AU JOUR LE JOUR, *Exit 18, Harrisburg*

Harrisburg's best might not compete with New York or even Philadelphia, and chef David Yocum will be the first to admit it. He has the virtue of a man who knows his limits and does well within them. But his shredded, sautéed zucchini has to be counted a delight by any standards, and if his delicately flavored scallops in butter and wine sauce aren't the equal of the big time, well, they're certainly very good.

Grand pretensions are decidedly "outré" at this small French restaurant that will welcome you even if you're in jeans. Located in a gentrified urban area, amid fine brick buildings on the Susquehanna shore, it's decorated in understated modern taste: framed prints on brick walls, dark ceiling, white tablecloths, bare hardwood floor. It's a relaxing, quiet, and intimate environment that will quickly exorcise all thought of the road.

At Au Jour le Jour the eight lunchtime entrées, such as sausage in puff pastry, scallops in cream sauce, or vegetables in a cheese casserole, run $4–$7.50. Dinners—there are only six of them—are $10.75 to $14.50. All the cooking is French, and all of it is very good.

Au Jour le Jour's owner is a man after our own hearts. He got interested in restaurants during his traveling days, when he made a point of searching out good places and fled fast food like the plague. Eventually this led to his own restaurant, and now other travelers can flee from Holiday Inns and McDonald's to him.

HOURS Mon.–Fri. 11:30 am–1:30 pm and 5:30–9 pm; Sat. 5:30–9 pm; closed Sun.

DIRECTIONS From Exit 18 bear right onto I-83 North. Go about 3.5 miles to the 13th Street Exit and turn right at the light at the end of the ramp. Go 0.2 mile to light and turn left. Then past another light, over a bridge, and follow the road as it bears to the right. Then make the first possible left, which is Washington St. Two blocks to Front St. and left on Front. Bear right at the next light and it'll be on the right in 1 more block (540 Race St.). Not quite as hard as it sounds!

ALVA RESTAURANT, *Exit 18, Harrisburg*

* *Far, but interesting*

It was the chef at Harrisburg's finest restaurant, Au Jour le Jour, who told us he ate at the Alva when he wanted good, cheap food. So we hopped over to this old railroad hotel restaurant to see why it might be worth the 10-minute drive.

The answer came in two parts: a tasty baked chicken dinner for $3.10 and an elderly lady in fur coat and bowler hat looking for a lost cookie pan. It seems the Alva is famous not only for its bargains, but its characters as well. (The governor has been known to drop in, but we didn't learn whether he's counted among the characters.)

The Alva must have had a lot more character itself before it was converted from an earthy downtown eatery to an innocuous family-style restaurant. All the same, it's better looking than most of its type, and the food is a whole lot better tasting.

The Giusti family has been running the Alva for three generations, spicing up the diner-style menu with lots of Italian dishes —eggplant parmigiana ($3.50), pasta ($2.75 up), pizza ($2.50), and antipasto ($2.90). You'll even find an occasional Pennsylvania Dutch special, but whatever you pick, it's sure to be worth the price tag.

The cookie pan was finally located, by the way, though it took several phone calls from one Giusti to another to do it. The woman jammed it half into her shopping bag and marched happily home.

HOURS Mon.–Fri. 6:30 am–11 pm; Sun. 7:30 am–11 pm; closed Sat.

DIRECTIONS Not all that easy, unfortunately. Count on 10 minutes each way. Take Exit 18 onto I-83 North and go about 3.5 miles to the 13th Street Exit. Turn right at the end of the ramp and go 1 block to a light. Straight through the light and two more lights to Derry St. Left on Derry and then left at the fork (marked by a fountain). Go over the long bridge into downtown Harrisburg. The Alva is ½ block beyond the end of the bridge, on the right (19 S. 4th St.). Parking behind the restaurant and at any nearby garage.

ZINN'S DINER
BROWNSTOWN RESTAURANT, *Exit 21,*
Brownstown/Ephrata

Okay, this is *the* exit for Pennsylvania Dutch cooking. And you have a choice—pretty good food, convenience, and kitsch, or authenticity and excellence.

Zinn's is right at the exit, but we first passed it by. Once it really was a diner, but now it's just one cog in a tourist-trap complex that includes a gift shop, candy outlet, and 32-acre "recreational park." We later returned to learn that the prices and the food are actually pretty fair. It's open 24 hours, and you can't miss it since it's got even more signs than it has gimmicks. But if you want the real thing—better, cheaper, and infinitely more interesting—drive the 10 miles to one of the best finds of all our journeys.

From the outside, the Brownstown Restaurant looks exactly like the farmhouse it surely once was, and the dining room looks more like a big country kitchen than anything else. Perhaps it's the wooden chairs at the counter instead of stools, the homey

39

mass of bric-a-brac, the plastic print tablecloths, or the cluttered corner full of general-store merchandise. Or maybe it's the friendly waitresses or the way the picture of Lincoln hangs behind the counter as if he's still an issue. Whatever the reason, the Brownstown is as down-home a place as there is to be found, and the Plain People (as the Mennonites and Amish are called) must think so too, since they make up half the clientele.

Try the lettuce smothered in warm, sweet bacon dressing and the wonderful chicken pie—smooth, thick, and full of noodles ($2.50 on special). You can also get a ham and string bean dinner for $2.40, and pork with sauerkraut or chicken with waffles for about the same. But perhaps you'll splurge and drop $3.45 for the corn pie. These are full-dinner prices, mind you! And from what we sampled, the food will fall somewhere between good and absolutely wonderful.

With dinners so cheap, there's little point in bothering with sandwiches. But they're there if you want them, about 25 of them (70 cents to $2.30). Hearty breakfasts too: two eggs, toast, and coffee for 95 cents; with country bacon, scrapple, or ham, 90 cents more.

We have to confess that we weren't very familiar with Pennsylvania Dutch cooking when we found the Brownstown, and such was our delight that it seemed too good to be true. We had to put the matter to the test. We were prejudiced, and it was with trepidation that we drove back to Zinn's, fearing that the commercial operation might be still better. We're relieved to report that it wasn't. Prices are comparable, with dinners running somewhat higher, and the soups at Zinn's were good. But on dressings, gravies, and vegetables, the Brownstown won hands down.

HOURS   **Brownstown Restaurant:** Mon. & Wed.–Sat. 6:30 am–8 pm; Tue. 6:30 am–2 pm; Sun. 11 am–7 pm.
Zinn's Diner: Always open.

DIRECTIONS   Signs for **Zinn's** begin at Exit 21; you won't miss it (1 mile away). For the **Brownstown,** go straight at end of ramp and just after the bridge turn left onto U.S. 222 South. Go 9.6 quick miles on 222 and turn left onto Route 722 East. Restaurant is ¼ mile up, on the left.

POST OFFICE INN, *Exit 22, Morgantown*

* Far, but excellent

If you get pheasant in puff pastry at the Post Office it will come boned and stuffed with apples, onions, bacon, and rosemary—a rare treat, well worth the 7½ miles you must go to reach this fine restaurant.

Every dish on the large and unusual menu is prepared with care and diligence by a chef who loves her work. Try quail dishes, salmon in puff pastry, venison, trout, or duck in cider sauce. Or how about poached flounder stuffed with crabmeat, shrimp, and clams, served in a wine-cream-and-lemon sauce?

Whatever you choose, you'll surely find a wine to match it. Charles Orlando is especially proud of his wine cellar, which holds over 350 selections. About 85 percent are California, and included are such rarities as Leeward Chardonnay 1980. Only 300 cases of that one were produced, and it'll cost you $50 a bottle.

Since puff pastry seemed to be the house specialty, we tried it around lamb in a wonderful, strong brown sauce made from veal, shallots, and Madeira. The dish was full of character and, we suspect, a good indication of the rich flavors that mark Barbara Orlando's cooking. Unfortunately, these delights can't be had for mere pennies. Dinners are $11–$19 (no lunch is served).

While Barbara does the cooking, Charles takes care of the interior decorating along with the wines. In his capacity as carpenter and antique hunter he's produced a collection of dark, candlelit rooms with white tablecloths, floral wallpaper, and the original wainscotting from this old hotel. Here and there it's a bit rough around the edges, but that just lends an aura of authenticity to the feel of age.

HOURS   Tue.–Thu. 5–10 pm; Fri. & Sat. 5–11 pm; closed Sun. & Mon.

DIRECTIONS   Turn right at the end of the Exit 22 ramp onto Route 10 North. It's 7.3 miles, on the right, and well worth the drive.

TWIN SLOPE FARMERS' MARKET AND FLEA MARKET, *Exit 22, Morgantown*

* Color, not cuisine

If it's Friday or Saturday, you'll find local color galore and numerous cheap, close-to-the-farm eateries in this huge barn of a building. Wander past antique dealers, farm stands, and who-knows-what as you munch a sausage sandwich or a true Pennsylvania pretzel. You may even find the very Windsor chair you've been looking for. If not, try the well-stocked Goodwill next door. (But they don't serve lunch there.)

HOURS   Fri. 11 am–9 pm; Sat. 9 am–3 pm.

DIRECTIONS   Left at end of Exit 22. In 0.3 mile turn right onto Route 10 and go 1 mile to the market, on the left.

99 BEERS–VITTLE HOUSE, *Exit 23, Downingtown*

Sometimes you have to go a long way just to get a decent sandwich, but at least you will get that if you drive the 4½ miles to the Vittle House. The meat will be sliced before your eyes, slapped on decent bread, and handed to you right across the counter.

Inside and out the atmosphere is clean but nondescript. You'll recognize the place by looking for a small white building marked by clumsily cut black letters. And yes, while waiting for the sandwich you can choose from 99 beers, arrayed, of course, on the wall.

HOURS   Mon.–Thu. 10 am–9:30 pm; Fri. & Sat. 9:30 am–10:30 pm; closed Sun.

DIRECTIONS   From Exit 23 take Route 100 South for 4 very fast miles. Then left onto U.S. 30. It's ¼ mile up, on the right.

Entering I-276

MASTER DELI, *Exit 25, Norristown*

There were two slick, trendy-looking ribs places at this exit, but we were quite happy with the Master Deli. We got a good, honest, juicy, tasty pork sandwich here for all of $1.75, and we could have had pizza or any of a number of sandwich combos. The deli is redolent with the aroma of spices, but offers no place for you to sit and enjoy your porker. It's less than elegant too, not much more than a cement-block shack, sort of like the elephant house at the zoo. But the fellow behind the counter was certainly friendly. Addressing us as "youse," he told us he cooked the "porks" and roast beef himself, and we concluded he'd done a pretty good job.

HOURS   Mon.–Sat. 8 am–8 pm; closed Sun.

DIRECTIONS   From Exit 25 bear left on ramp onto U.S. 422 West. Left at first light; it's on the corner.

New Jersey

CAFÉ GALLERY
BURLINGTON DINER, *Exit 6A, Burlington*

See pages 181 and 182 for descriptions of a lovely French restaurant with art gallery, and an earthy but better than average diner.

DIRECTIONS   Eastbound: After crossing Delaware River Bridge keep right, following signs for "Local Traffic" and Exit 6A. Take this exit and then follow signs for U.S. 130. Turn right at the light onto 130. ■ Go 4 miles. The **Burlington Diner** is on the left at junction with Route 541. Turn right on Route 541 for **Café Gallery.** It's the last building before the river, on the right.

Westbound: Exit 6A leads directly to U.S. 130 South. Then as above from ■.

Pennsylvania, New Jersey

Pennsylvania

COZY COTTAGE RESTAURANT, *Exit 1, Fredericksburg*

George Hauser, owner of the Cozy Cottage, has been a poultry man all his life and about 20 years ago decided to do something about the lamentable fact that you couldn't buy a decent chicken dinner in a town whose three poultry-processing plants supply markets from Philadelphia to Chicago.

Every table in the Cozy Cottage has a little card that reads "Fried Chicken on a Bun (no bones)—$1.65." We tried one and we weren't sorry. Not a frozen patty compressed by machines to the consistency of cardboard, this was real chicken, boned and lightly fried. Its juiciness came from the meat itself, not from an impregnation with molten lard.

George and his wife, Ruth, also serve chicken pot pies ($3.25). Or, if you're more traditional in your chicken consumption habits, buy a quarter fryer for $3.25 or half a bird for $3.85 (by far the better buy). Both come with tossed salad and French fries. There are also buckets and tubs to feed chicken-loving armies of all sizes.

It's not all chicken here. Dinner platters (ham steak, veal cutlet, stuffed shrimp, etc.) are around $4. Most of the sandwiches cost less than $1.50; if you want to try something local, order Lebanon bologna—it's made in a neighboring town from spiced smoked pork and beef.

The Cozy Cottage is clean and modern, with cement-block walls, a utility carpet, and a rotating dessert case. In food or charm it's no match for the Shartlesville Hotel, 17 miles up the pike (next entry), but if you just want a bite and the Shartlesville's mammoth spread is more than you can handle, the Cozy Cottage will provide a satisfying taste of Dutch cooking.

HOURS   Sun.–Thu. 9 am–10 pm; Fri. & Sat. 9 am–11 pm. Closed January through mid-March (you might try the 24-hour truck stop across the street).

DIRECTIONS   Eastbound: From Exit 1 enter Route 22 East; it's about ½ mile down, on the right.

Westbound: From Exit 1 enter Route 22 West; it's about 1 mile down, on the left.

SHARTLESVILLE HOTEL, *Exit 8, Shartlesville*

Even before we left for Pennsylvania Dutch country, we had heard about the Shartlesville Hotel. A friend sent us a postcard showing a long table simply blanketed with plates, bowls, casseroles, and platters—30 or more of them, each brimming with a different kind of food. His message was simple: "Don't miss this one."

We didn't, and we were astonished to find that the postcard was no studio scene but an honest shot of the Shartlesville Hotel's daily feast as it appears on every single table in the place.

"We've been serving family-style since 1915 and we're not going to stop now," says a proud Warren Kauffman in his light Swabian accent. Looking around, we see—and hear—that a sizable number of the guests are also genuinely "Dutch."

We attempted—without success—to record everything on our table. There was smoked ham, roast chicken, chicken pot pie, sausage, and ham and chicken croquettes. Vegetables were corn, peas, carrots, turnips, string beans, cucumber salad, and chickpeas. In case anyone wanted "fillers," they could have gone for sweet potatoes, noodles, rice, sweet rice, or that delicious Dutch version of mashed potatoes called potato filling. It consists of boiled potatoes mashed into sautéed onion and celery, with egg, croutons, parsley, and seasonings.

A traditional Pennsylvania Dutch banquet includes seven

"sours"—relishes like pepper cabbage, red beets, pickles, chow-chow, and mustard beans. (There must have been two other sours on the table but we lost track of them.) And to offset the sours are seven sweets, including rhubarb sauce, tapioca pudding, potato doughnuts, shoofly pie, and ice cream.

Everything is fresh and homemade. And not one dish we tasted was less than delicious. To rave about the chicken pot pie's deep, rich flavor would be to slight the sausage's wonderful seasonings, and we haven't the space to rave about everything. But we do want to tell you that the entire spread costs $6.25. That's right, $6.25 for more than you could eat in a month.

We pass along our friend's advice: "Don't miss this place."

HOURS   Every day 11 am–7 pm. Breakfast served 8 am–10 am, May through September only. Closed December 23 through January 15.

DIRECTIONS   From Exit 8 bear right if eastbound, left if westbound, to stop sign at Old Route 22. Turn left onto 22 and you'll see it. Couldn't be much closer.

SKYVIEW RESTAURANT,
PA 737/Krumsville/Kutztown Exit, Krumsville

It's probably a sin not to serve Pennsylvania Dutch food in this part of the world, and the Skyview is no sinner. Even though it looks like any other '50s-style stainless-steel-and-glass diner, its cuisine is far from truck-stop fare. Here, you'll have no trouble satisfying a sudden craving for Schnitz und Knepp mit Schunka Flaish (dried apples, dumplings, and ham), Ponhaus und Brodwurst (pork sausage and scrapple, which is fried cornmeal-and-pork mush), or Sauerkraut und Pork mit Epplesass (you're on your own). All are $4.45, accompanied by apple butter, cottage cheese, and lettuce with bacon dressing.

Another craving you can quench at the Skyview is for corn fritters. Like giant pancakes filled with corn, they are light, smooth, and just a bit surprising—it's hard getting used to whole pieces of corn in your flapjacks ($1.50). Try them with a dollop of apple butter. Although corn fritters are generally taken as a side dish, no one laughed in our faces when we ordered them for breakfast.

The Skyview belongs in the great class of misnamed restaurants. The only view of the sky comes when you walk outside and pull your neck straight back; otherwise, the restaurant's vista is of Interstate 78.

HOURS   Sun.–Thu. 6 am–9 pm; Fri. & Sat. 6 am–10 pm.

DIRECTIONS   From the exit labeled "PA 737/Krumsville/Kutztown," turn left and you'll see it.

CITY-VU RESTAURANT,
Exit for PA 145 North/MacArthur Rd., Allentown

This is one of those modern Greco-glitzy diners that have replaced the barrel-roofed lunch cars of the '30s and '40s. Although they're not usually known for gourmet cuisine, these jazzy diners often have the advantages of long hours, large menus, and low prices.

The City-Vu meets all those standards in spades. In fact, there's a sign outside that broadcasts a rather startling bargain: complete dinners for only $2.49. Although that price applies only to one dinner a night, there are other bargains as well, like beef stew and salad bar for $3.45 or sautéed chicken livers on rice with vegetable and salad bar for $3.95.

Every week, Harold Mickley has to make up 80 gallons of pork and sauerkraut to satisfy the demand. His regular customers love it; they pour in on Monday nights, when he sells it for $3.20 with second helpings free.

Most of the soups are homemade; the City-Vu's most popular is the French onion, and Harold makes no secret of the recipe. It seems that while vacationing in Montreal he came upon a most unusual onion soup made with beer and he brought the idea home. Although you can't taste it, the beer certainly does impart a flavor that's distinctive.

There's an extensive dessert menu featuring home-baked crumb pies, cream pies, cheese pies, shoofly pie, and ice cream.

HOURS   Open 24 hours every day but Christmas.

DIRECTIONS   I-78 disappears for a while and leaves you on U.S. 22 in this part of Pennsylvania. Take the exit labeled "PA 145 North/ MacArthur Rd." It feeds you into Route 145 North and in ½ mile you'll see City-Vu on the right.

New Jersey

ABOUT CLINTON

If New Jersey brings to mind tract housing and oil refineries, a stop in Clinton is a must for your reeducation.

At the foot of Main Street is a butterscotch-colored iron bridge and a sparkling, duck-inhabited mill pond. Not only are all the buildings in town Victorian, but they've been kept in pristine condition. One turreted house (two doors down from the Seasonings Café) has the most diverse selection of windows that one building could get away with.

The **Clinton House,** a grand old porticoed hotel, is the most venerable dining spot in town, but we found that for quality and value you couldn't do much better than the **Seasonings Café,** a delightfully unpretentious gourmet restaurant with remarkably low prices, or the **Lazy Daisy,** a vegetarian eatery.

SEASONINGS CAFÉ, *Exit 15, Clinton*

When she was 20 years old, Debbie Ronquist decided to use her college tuition money to open a restaurant in her hometown. Three years later, after innumerable compliments and suggestions that she write a cookbook, and after having been featured in *Bon Appétit* and *Colonial Homes,* she's finally concluded that she made the right decision. And after our visit to the Seasonings Café, we most heartily concur.

Her soups, for example, have received unending praise, and although customers continually request recipes, Debbie says she has none; she can't even reproduce her own efforts when she wants to. We tried two of her creations, both of them superb—a roundly flavored smoky ham and vegetable soup and a Dutch corned beef chowder with corned beef, apples, cinnamon, celery, and potatoes. Despite their heights of perfection, soups cost only 70 cents for a cup, 90 cents for a regular bowl, and $1.50 for a large bowl that is served with a home-baked muffin.

In all her dishes, Debbie emphasizes visual appearance as much as flavor. An order of crab puffs—her angelically delicate concoction of crabmeat and fluffy baked egg whites featured in *Bon Appétit* and then chosen for its anthology—comes on toast points arranged around three sprigs of parsley sitting in a carrot curl like flowers in a vase ($2.95 as an appetizer, $4.25 as an entrée).

The Seasonings' menu is sensibly limited to a manageable number of items, but it allows Debbie to show off her versatility as a cook. There are eight light appetizers, several home-baked breads and muffins, salads, a small number of interesting sandwiches, burgers, omelets, and a few entrées. Most entrées are $4.50 or less and, in fact, the most expensive item on the regular menu is $5.95! On Friday and Saturday nights, when candles go on the tables, special entrées are served at slightly higher prices.

At lunchtime, you can get a cup of soup and half a sandwich for $2.95; throw in some salad and it's $3.25. Or, at any time of day, four small tea sandwiches, each filled differently, come with a fresh fruit cup for $4.25. An absolutely gorgeous plate of sliced fruit and cottage cheese served on a bed of greens is $3.95.

If you would rail at the thought of such exquisite flavors unaccompanied by fine wine, Debbie invites you to bring your own.

HOURS Sun.–Thu. 11 am–7 pm (possibly later); Fri. & Sat. 11 am–10 pm.

DIRECTIONS See the Lazy Daisy, below.

THE LAZY DAISY, *Exit 15, Clinton*

A strictly vegetarian restaurant, the Lazy Daisy occupies the front of an old music-hall building recently reopened for its original purpose. Café curtains and fresh daisies in hand-thrown vases brighten up the restaurant's two small rooms.

The menu rests on salads ($1.75 to $3.25), sandwiches (most at $1.95), hearty soups ($1 and $1.50) and sautéed vegetable dishes (under $2.50). Owner Debbie Borup's veggie burger ($2.25) is a local favorite. It's made from sautéed carrots, onions, celery, sesame seeds, ground sunflower seeds, and oatmeal, and is served on whole wheat bread with tomato, onions, and sprouts.

Every evening, a different quiche comes with soup or salad and bread for $4.50; at $6, dinner specials like spinach lasagne swirls (whole wheat, of course) are served with soup or salad, bread and dessert. Desserts here are delectable—carrot cake, oatmeal fig bars, apple-raisin pie, and carob cake are typical. There are also fresh-squeezed juices, herbal teas, milk shakes, and various fruity blender concoctions.

It's a cozy little spot, perfect for a refreshing snack or a complete meal—healthfully unsinful on either count.

HOURS Mon. 11 am–3 pm; Tue.–Fri. 11 am–9 pm; Sat. 11 am–5 pm; closed Sun.

DIRECTIONS From Exit 15 bear right, following signs for Clinton. In about ½ mile you'll see the **Lazy Daisy** on the right. Shortly after, turn left at the Clinton House and go 1 block to an iron bridge; turn right over the bridge and directly onto Main St. You'll see **Seasonings Café** on the right, almost at the end of the block.

51

Pennsylvania

WASHINGTON RESTAURANT
SHORTY'S HOT DOG LUNCH,
Exit 4 (I-70 West), Washington

See page 17 for these two rather different small-town restaurants.

DIRECTIONS I-79 and I-70 run together near Washington. Get onto I-70 West and go to Exit 4. Then follow directions on page 18.

EAST AND WEST INTERNATIONAL DINING
HARTNER'S, *Exit 25, Ogle*

See pages 23 and 24 for an unusual restaurant featuring the cuisine of many lands and a good country cookin' sort of place.

DIRECTIONS From Exit 25 turn onto Route 228 West, which will lead you immediately to U.S. 19. Turn right on U.S. 19 North. **Hartner's** is ¼ mile up, on the right. **East and West International Dining** is 1 mile up, also on the right.

IRON BRIDGE INN, *Exit 31, Mercer*

See page 55 for a description of this good brick-plants-and-oak café.

DIRECTIONS From Exit 31 turn onto Route 208 West toward Leesburg. In about 3 miles turn right onto U.S. 19 North. The inn is 1 mile up, on the left.

MERCER DINER, *Exit 33, Mercer*

See page 56 for an inexpensive, down-to-earth diner.

DIRECTIONS From Exit 33 turn onto U.S. 62 West for Mercer. Go about 4 miles to U.S. 19 and turn left. The diner will be on the left in about ½ mile.

SUE'S CAFÉ, *Exit 36A, Meadville*

In Sue's Café, you can look at the outsized wallpaper murals and imagine you're someplace else—the Swiss Alps awash with wildflowers, New England in the fall, the Pacific Northwest. Even the chairs, which have been put together with cedar logs and slabs, are somehow reminiscent of Canada's north woods.

If you can get into the decor, this really is a fun place—attractive in its own way, friendly, and lively. The food, with one exception, is the up-to-date fare of brick-plants-and-oak cafés: big salads with cute names ("Romeo and Julienne Salad" was our favorite), fried potato skins, burgers on kaiser rolls with assorted toppings, and fancy pocket-bread sandwiches. It would be hard to spend more than $3 on any of these, and every day there's a lunch special of soup and sandwich (or salad) for $2 to $2.50. You can also order mild or hot Buffalo-style chicken wings ($2.50), homemade soups (95 cents for a mug that looks like a

53

bowl), or chili ($1.45). These lunch items all stay on the dinner menu, along with such entrées as liver and onions, ham steak, fried shrimp, pasta dishes, veal parmigiana, etc. ($3.95 to $6.95).

Although the cooking is good (not just cheap), Sue's Café seems to have missed one all-important standby of the BPO café: there's no carrot cake for dessert.

Will the word reach these parts before you do? Five fried potato skins says it does.

HOURS   Mon.–Thu. 7 am–8 pm; Fri. 7 am–9 pm; Sat. 7 am–8 pm; Sun. 8 am–3 pm.

DIRECTIONS   From Exit 36A you are fed onto U.S. 6/322 East. After 1.7 miles U.S. 6 bears off to the left but you should go straight (Park Ave.). In 0.7 mile, turn left onto Chestnut St. Sue's Café is on the right (251 Chestnut).

I-80

Pennsylvania, New Jersey

Pennsylvania

IRON BRIDGE INN, *Exit 2, Mercer*

How glad we were to see again the old familiar brick-plants-and-oak café, complete with fried zucchini and potato skin appetizers. We hadn't come across one of these since Stroudsburg, by the New Jersey border. At the Iron Bridge the brick is in the free-standing fireplace, and the plants are in the windows that overlook a lovely little stream. While we were there, about 100 folks turned out to watch the state game department stock the stream with trout. So while we enjoyed a good steak sandwich ($4.95, charbroiled), we watched them watch the fish.

The cole-slaw side dish was fresh and creamy, with a welcome bite. That was enough encouragement for us to succumb to the Texas sheetcake, a wide, low-lying brownie topped with crumbled pecans and vanilla ice cream. Good stuff, all of it, as is often found in restaurants of this kind.

The menu, too, is typical: spinach salad ($3.10), quiche ($3), a host of plain and fancy sandwiches ($2.80–$3.70), steaks ($10–$14), and a changing seafood special for $9.

The Iron Bridge is a good bet; if you're headed east it's about 45 miles to the next oasis.

HOURS Mon.–Sat. 11 am–1 am; Sun. 11 am–10 pm.

DIRECTIONS It's 2.6 miles south of Exit 2 on U.S. 19. On the right.

MERCER DINER, *Exit 2, Mercer*

* *Not great, but cheap and colorful*

Without a doubt the Iron Bridge (above) has better food, but perhaps you'd like to get closer to the nitty-gritty of local life and save a few bucks while you're at it. Consider then the Mercer Diner in the center of town, just a few blocks from the impressive Mercer County Courthouse. It's a medium-sized diner in stainless steel, with a pink countertop and startlingly ladylike, lacy curtains in robin's-egg blue. The food's okay, the coffee's thin, and the clientele is an even mix of rugged and reputable. Breakfast all day.

HOURS Sun.–Thu. 6 am–9 pm; Fri. & Sat. 24 hours.

DIRECTIONS Go 2½ miles north of Exit 2 on U.S. 19. It's on the right.

THE WOLF'S DEN, *Exit 7, Knox*

We were surprised to discover that a place like this could harbor a first-rate restaurant, even though many people had recommended it to us from as far away as Williamsport. It's not only a touristy, reconstructed barn with built-in waterwheel, wishing well, and Muzak, but it's an integral part of a huge miniature golf/water slide/campground complex that awaits its yearly flood of RVs.

But the taste speaks for itself. Here we tried a superb creamy, chunky, spicy Manhattan clam chowder, the memory of which lingered for a good 40 miles; the Den's salad dressings were almost as good. We tried other items from the $4.50 all-you-can-eat buffet (which included pork chops and nicely sauced chicken) and found them quite tasty. But when food sits around for a while in those sumptuous displays, it just can't be as good as what you'd get from the regular menu.

At lunchtime there are plain and fancy sandwiches at prices like $3.50 for a club or $2.25 for an unusual cucumber salad sandwich. A simple hamburger is $2.35—not bad for a fairly posh decor with tablecloths and handsome place settings. But even better, at lunch you have a choice of six casseroles ($3.75), like turkey Devonshire or a mélange of hot Italian sausage, zucchini, tomatoes, and pasta beneath a crust of provolone.

The dinner menu is mostly American fare with special touches like ham in rum-raisin sauce ($6.75) or filet of flounder stuffed with a crabmeat dressing and served with Hollandaise ($8.95). Even the plain, but wonderful, prime rib ($11.95) comes with a bread dressing, and you'll find such other temptations as marinated strip steak, pan-fried in butter, and served with a cognac/mustard sauce ($12.50).

If you can close your eyes to the tourist kitsch and your ears to the Muzak, we think you'll get as good a meal at the Wolf's Den as can be got in this part of the world.

HOURS May–Dec.: every day 11 am–10 pm. Jan.–Apr.: Tue.–Sun. noon–9 pm; closed Mon. The lunchtime $4.50 buffet is noon to 2 pm, every day but Sunday.

DIRECTIONS Just north of Exit 7. There's no way to miss it; signs everywhere.

CLARION RESTAURANT, *Exit 9, Clarion*

The Clarion has been located in its Main Street basement since the last century, famous for its sincere effort to produce good, home-cooked meals and for its murals, which are certainly its most spectacular feature.

These murals are simply wonderful—worth the trip all by themselves. They wrap around two walls and up onto the ceiling, depicting in the deepest and lushest greens the hills of Pennsylvania and the campus of Clarion State College. Primitive to be sure, they nevertheless have an intriguing depth and even a sometimes startling realism, as when in one corner it really seems as if the Allegheny River is going to pour right onto the floor. And the woodsy theme goes on in the whimsically sculptured stairway of painted stones into which miniature goldfish ponds have been built.

There's food here too—breakfast, lunch, and dinner, all of it made from scratch and cooked to order. They're very serious about that last point, and the owner assured us that each dish, even the sauce and gravy, is started when the order reaches the kitchen, not a minute sooner. We were skeptical, but perhaps that explains the extraordinarily long time it took the food to reach our table. When it got there it was good, but nothing to make such a fuss about. We suspect rather that the place was just having some organizational problems that day.

In any case, the prices won't plunge you into debt. Dinners are mostly in the $3–$5 range, with sandwiches from 70 cents for a frankfurter to $2.75 for a club. There are subs, pizzas, and a wide choice of breakfasts (including eggs Benedict!). If what you want isn't on the menu, they'll make it for you anyway.

Despite the hangup, it really is a good place, light enough to be pleasant, even though underground, and dark enough to be relaxing—unpretentious, comfortable, and friendly. And do check out those murals!

HOURS   Every day 6 am–8 pm; in Jan. and Feb., 6 am–2 pm.

DIRECTIONS   From Exit 9 turn right if westbound, left if eastbound, onto Route 68 North. Go 2.1 miles to Main St. Turn right onto Main and it's 1 block to the Clarion, on the corner, on the left.

AMERICAN RESTAURANT, *Exit 13, Brookville*

The American Restaurant is aptly named, for it illustrates beautifully the two stages of life that so many small-town American restaurants go through. There's the Main Street original—unique, folksy, and funky. It's got a ceiling as curved as a Quonset hut's and there's a funny round doorway at the far end of the long, narrow room. The place is so odd—it's almost like being inside a rifle barrel—that you don't mind the fluorescent lighting and unfortunate paint job. Besides, the food is good, solid, home-town stuff, right down to the coffee. The prices are modest, and the American's famous apple pie is really first-rate.

So, deservedly, the restaurant prospered. Then came the new interstate just a mile from town. The restaurant had to move to keep the highway business, and when it did it lost its charm. They built a mammoth, soulless barn of a building right by the interchange, made sure it got cathedral ceilings and an ample quantity of brick, furnished it in Formica, and erected an embalmed deer family right by the door. They even had some splashy "family" restaurant–type menus printed up in shiny red, white, and blue.

But the American Restaurant didn't abandon Main Street in the course of all this. Both American Restaurants exist, and you can take your pick—absolute convenience right at the exit or local color for the trouble of a mile-and-a-half drive. The food will be the same honest cooking either way. The menu, which is typical for this kind of fare, offers burgers at just 90 cents, soup for 70 cents, and dinner between $2.95 and $5.50.

The pie is 80 cents a slice, and in the Main Street original it goes for half-price when it's a day old. We doubt you'll find touches like that out by the highway.

> **HOURS**   At the highway: Mon.–Sat. 6 am–midnight; Sun. 6:30 am–
> 11:30 pm.
> In town: Mon.–Fri. 6 am–9 pm; Sat. 6 am–5 pm; closed
> Sun.

DIRECTIONS   The highway version is ¼ mile south of Exit 13, on the left, on Route 28. For Main St., go ½ mile south on Route 28 to a blinking light and turn left onto Route 36S. Continue 0.8 mile to first light in town. It's 1 block farther, on the right.

SLAGLE'S ICE CREAM, *Exit 13, Brookville*

Not far from Main Street, just over the bridge from the Brookville Locomotive Works (which makes coal-mining equipment) and right by the enormous domed, yellow-brick pantheon of a building that was meant to be a theater but is now the world's most magnificent machine shop, sits Slagle's Ice Cream, where Jim Slagle has been making his own for 25 years.

Tain't fancy—only a soda fountain and display freezers in a large room with no place to sit. Glazed-block walls make it look like a high school gym. But it's clean, and the ice cream is good, all of it made right here from fresh fruit and natural flavorings.

Jim does serve more than just ice cream. He's got doughnuts, homemade soups (85 cents a cup), and although there are no sandwiches on the menu he'll be glad to make one for you. Burgers go for $1.10. If you want to take home a pint of his potato salad, it will also cost $1.10.

HOURS   Summer: every day 7 am–10 pm. Winter: Sat.–Thu. 8 am–8 pm; Fri. 8 am–9 pm.

DIRECTIONS   From Exit 13 go ½ mile south on Route 28 and turn left at the blinking light. Go 1 mile to second light, turn right and go 2 blocks over the bridge. It's on the left.

DIMELING HOTEL COFFEE SHOP, *Exit 19, Clearfield*

Just breakfast and simple lunches of soup, salad, and sandwiches here, but in what is surely the grandest environment ever inhabited by a humble coffee shop. The Dimeling is a magnificently ornamented old hotel, built to be a showpiece back when Vanderbilts and Mellons strode about these hills. Its wide green awning still shades the steps that lead from sidewalk to entryway. Above the soaring first floor rise five more stories whose height is emphasized by vertical ranks of bay windows, their white stone frames projecting grandly from the lacquered brick façade.

The grandeur doesn't end with the exterior. The room now occupied by the coffee shop—if you can call this cavernous space with 30-foot ceilings a mere "room"–was built to be a bank. It boasts high arched windows, magnificent ornamental woodwork, fluted columns, murals, and marble floors. Quite a setting for $1.35 hamburgers and chef's salads at $2.50.

But the bank went bust in the Depression. Now, way down at floor level is a scattering of plain wooden tables and original bentwood chairs, some benches along a wall, and a lovely little circle of wooden booths standing all by itself, out in the middle of everything. Even the counter is special—it's topped with an unusual black, rubberlike substance and trimmed with gold.

The people of Clearfield know what they've got in the Dimeling. It's the best food in town, all fresh, all cooked from scratch by local women who've been doing it for a long, long time. Clearfielders rebelled when there was talk of tearing the place down. They're so attached to the Dimeling they don't want any changes, not even tablecloths. When the owner tried that amenity, the customers complained without mercy. When he tried to replace the benches with booths, the lawyers of Clearfield, who consider the benches their private lunchtime perch, simply refused to go in again until they were returned.

Today's infatuation with antiques has put a gleam in the eye of the Dimeling's owner. There are plans afoot for a complete restoration, and we don't doubt that the hotel's grand dining room, now sadly idle, will soon be serving the fanciest food that Clearfielders will buy. Then the now-funky lobby's fine woodwork will glisten once again, and rooms will cost more than the current $20–$25.

That, we guess, will be all to the good, but like the lawyers, we hope that the coffee shop will remain simply the grandest sandwich spot on earth.

HOURS   Mon.–Sat. 6:30 am–2 pm; closed Sun.

DIRECTIONS   From Exit 19 turn right if eastbound, left if westbound, onto Route 879 West. Go 1.4 miles and turn right onto U.S. 322. Go 1.5 miles on 322 and bear left at the light, toward downtown. Three blocks to the first light, a right, and 1 more block bring you to the Dimeling, on the corner.

SNOW-SHOE RESTAURANT, *Exit 22, Snow Shoe*

* *Not great, but always open*

Ever eager to find support for the follow-the-truck-driver theory of highway eating, we tried the Snow-Shoe but were disillusioned once again. Trucks aplenty, but not even a commendable coconut cream pie!

On the other hand, it is a 24-hour place, it's right at the exit, and it's a long way from here to anything a whole lot better.

HOURS   Always open.

DIRECTIONS   Can't be missed from Exit 22.

THE FAMILY RESTAURANT, *Exit 24, Bellefonte*

Bellefonte struck us as a wonderful old town, currently fallen on hard times, but without that gritty, depressed feeling. Its gorgeous examples of mansard-roofed, turreted architecture in stone and brick are cut right into the surrounding hills, and we fell in love with the Brockerhoff Hotel, a sort of Bavarian fantasy that might have pleased mad King Ludwig with its ornamental slate roof and magnificent Art Nouveau entryway of wrought iron.

Bellefonte isn't the town for fine dining, but we did find decent homemade soup and sandwiches in the Family Restaurant, an authentic small-town eatery in sheet paneling, stainless steel, and lime-green woodwork, with friendly folks behind the counter and a window on Main Street. It's $1 for a burger here, with 20 other inexpensive sandwiches and about seven down-home dinners ($3.25–$3.75).

Bellefonte really does have a font—in a pleasant park about two blocks from Main Street, where a domesticated stream meanders by a copse of pines and an old gazebo. It's a good spot for an after-lunch stroll. Or buy a sub at nearby **Bonfatto's** and munch it in the park.

HOURS   Mon., Tue., Thu. & Fri. 8 am–7 pm; Sat. 8 am–6 pm; Wed. & Sun. 8 am–2 pm.

DIRECTIONS From Exit 24 turn right if eastbound, left if westbound, onto Route 26 South. Go 1.2 miles and turn right onto Route 550. Two more miles will bring you to the first light, in the center of town. Right onto Main St. It's 1 block to the **Family Restaurant,** on the right. Three blocks down, the next left will bring you to the park, and you'll pass **Bonfatto's** on the way.

SUGAR VALLEY INN, *Exit 28, Carroll*

Just an ordinary place. Nothing especially lovely, interesting, or tasty, but decent enough, cheap enough, and a lot more inviting than what's right at the exit. Hold out if you can, but if you gotta have a burger, it'll do.

HOURS Mon.–Thu. 11 am–7 pm; Fri. 10 am–8 pm; Sat. & Sun. 8 am–8 pm.

DIRECTIONS 1.4 miles south of Exit 28 on Route 880.

THE VALIANT TRENCHERMAN, *Exit 30S, Lewisburg*

* *Far, but different*

It's eight miles from exit to eatery here, but since anything even resembling a natural foods restaurant, much less a good one, is a rarity hereabouts, we stretched our rules.

Purists, however, will be disappointed. Once it was the real thing, and it still serves brown rice, tabouli, and a variety of vegetarian dishes. Red meat is conspicuously absent. But the old menu just didn't go over in Lewisburg. Now the Valiant Trencherman is just an all-around good restaurant featuring Indian, Chinese, and continental cooking (and bagels!). Even with such a wide collection of possibilities it takes nearby Bucknell University to keep the place alive.

It's the kind of homey restaurant where the cook may be your waiter and your waiter may be the owner. The three small rooms each have a different feel—ultra-modern, with white walls and a skylight in the rear, old and odds-and-ends antiquey in the front. The middle is, well, just sort of not-quite-finished.

Seafood is the specialty, a choice of 13 entrées from several cuisines. There's curried shrimp, for example, at $8.75, and haddock with dill and sour cream at $6.95. Stir-fried chicken comes in Szechuan, anise, or garlic/ginger sauce for $7.25. Vegetarian entrées, three of them, are about $5.

At lunchtime the Trencherman has eight variations on your basic bagel. Cream cheese and lox is the real thing, of course ($2.95, and very good), but you can also get a cinnamon and raisin number with peanut butter! There are salads to satisfy any taste, good soups, pita pockets, and a variety of full luncheons from the dinner menu ($3–$5.35).

Everything we tried here was good (we passed on the peanut butter bagel), and much of it had a whiff of health food about it, even if billed as French chicken soup with apples, celery, and thyme.

A brief side trip to Lewisburg, by the way, would make for a pleasant diversion. It's a very pretty place and apparently quite unselfconscious. And a trencherman, you may wish to know, is a glutton. The line from *Much Ado About Nothing* reads, "He is a very valiant trencherman; he hath an excellent stomach." You may be tempted to put your own to the test when you see the Trencherman's dessert specialty: fresh fruit cheesecake. In summer they even go out and pick wild berries for it.

HOURS Mon.–Thu. 11:30 am–2 pm and 5–8:30 pm; Fri. 11:30 am –2 pm and 5–9:30 pm; Sat. noon–3 pm and 5–9:30 pm; Sun. 10 am– 2 pm and 5–7:30 pm.

DIRECTIONS Exit 30S puts you on Route 15 South. Go 7 very quick miles to a light at a high school. Make a left and go four lights to Second St. Turn left. It's ½ block up, on the right.

BETSY ROSS TEA ROOM, *Exit 31S, Milton*

If the name conjures up images of Ye Olde American Baloney, you've got it wrong. This is the kind of place we love to find. The Betsy Ross is a village lunchroom that's been the labor of the

Steely family for 40 years, all but unchanged since the '50s. The cooking is done by Mary Steely, just as she was taught at home by her mother. It's cheap, it's good, and it's as local as you can get.

Not elegant, however. The walls are sheet paneling, the woodwork's lime green, and the floor is checkerboard vinyl. But it certainly has a charm of its own, helped along by the lace-curtained windows containing displays of painted plaster figurines.

Mary's mother waitressed here for 25 years before she bought the place. When it came time for Mary to take over the cooking, Mom just pointed to the kitchen and said, "If you can cook at home, you can cook in there."

"Home cooking" is something of a buzz word in the restaurant game, but surely this is the real thing. A huge plate of ham, string beans, and boiled potatoes ($2.40) proved it. The meat was juicy, tender, and delicious, its flavor nicely imparted to the humble spuds. The corn and chicken soup (75 cents) was good and meaty, even if not superb—just like home.

You can get breakfast, lunch, or dinner at the Betsy Ross, but if you don't want any of them, at least give the old-fashioned soda fountain a try. They still make vanilla phosphates here and offer sundaes that even *sound* sinful, like the "midnight dream" or "lover's delight" (only $1). There are 25 inexpensive sandwiches and ten full dinners at around $3. Look for the Pennsylvania country specialties, like the ham and beans we enjoyed, or chicken and waffles.

It's hard to know how much longer the Betsy Ross will go on. Times are bad in Milton and the competition from the chains is rough. Mary's daughter doesn't intend to carry on the tradition, so get there soon.

HOURS   Mon.–Fri. 5 am–7 pm; Sat. 5 am–6 pm; closed Sun.

DIRECTIONS   Exit 31S will put you on Route 147 South. Go a quick 1.7 miles to the exit for Broadway. Turn right at the end of the ramp and continue 1 mile into Milton. It's on the left, just before the road ends in a T. Look sharp, there's not much of a sign.

PINE BARN INN, *Exit 33, Danville*

Danville is a little town on the eastern branch of the Susquehanna and, to judge from its many fine houses, it must have once been a lovely place. But hard times have hit, and the only thriving enterprises we saw were the Geisinger Medical Clinic ("the diagnostic Mayo of the East") and the Pine Barn Inn, which makes a good portion of its living catering to the clinic's visitors.

It's a "nice" place, a handsome one even, carved out of an old barn and with a very strong local reputation. More refined than rustic, from the outside it looks like an up-to-date motel (which it is, in part). And even though the old stone foundation makes up the dining room walls, they're painted so evenly white and the exposed beams are so perfectly straight that it feels more like a new building made to look old.

The menu is basically steak and seafood, about $9–$16 for dinner. Lunchtime offers quite a few burgers and sandwiches for $3–$4, three regular entrées at $7–$8, and three specials that can get as exotic as sesame pork with green peppers over rice ($3.95).

Good food, all of it, though nothing terribly exciting. And even if the salad bar's lettuce was only iceberg, there were deviled eggs and a delicious deep-green sweet-and-sour dressing from a family recipe.

HOURS   Mon.–Fri. 7 am–10 pm (breakfast till 11 am, lunch till 5 pm); Sat. 8 am–10 pm; Sun. 8 am–8 pm.

DIRECTIONS   From Exit 33 bear right onto Route 54. Go 3 miles along the river to a light and turn left, following signs for Geisinger Medical Clinic. Go straight 0.6 mile to sign for Pine Barn Inn, and then left, up the small hill.

MAGEE HOTEL, *Exit 35, Bloomsburg*

Word has it that *the* way to eat when you're on the road in central Pennsylvania is at the old downtown hotels. And sure enough, in every town of any size at all we found a solid old hostelry offering at least a buffet lunch, and often more. The Magee is where this local tradition started, and its three-star success in the Mobil travel guide has inspired others to follow suit.

We heard about the Magee from nearly everyone, and since we have an abiding affection for old hotels, we were eager to make its acquaintance over lunch. What we found was good, but not the equal of its reputation.

The first disappointment was the decor. This is a fine old brick hotel which must have once had a dining room to match. Why, then, did they have to sheath its walls in barnboard and nail up a batch of fake beams? Still, the salad bar was very pretty, with big, lovely fresh mushrooms, pickled eggs, a good, sweet house dressing—and more than just iceberg in the lettuce bin! Next we tried the mushroom soup ($1 a cup), which was only fair, and then a light, tasty quiche Lorraine, distinguished by its ample chunks of bacon ($3.25). The stuffed tomato was the equal of the soup, but the coffee was quite good. A mixed bag, all in all, and one that we would have more happily accepted without the barnboard and Muzak.

Lunchtime at the Magee also offers sandwiches, from $2.45 for a burger to $3.50 for a Monte Cristo. Full luncheons are around $5, and on Fridays there's an all-you-can-eat smorgasbord for $4.

These smorgasbords are good deals. There's another one on Saturday from 4:30 to 9 that features seafood ($7.95); on Sunday from 11 to 2:30, it's roast beef and baked ham at $6.95. Regular dinners, however, are another matter. The menu seems to change monthly, but when we were there dinner began at $11.95 and soared up over $18.

Rooms in the hotel, by the way, go from $24 to $35.

HOURS Mon.–Sat. 7–11 am for breakfast, 1–2:30 pm for lunch, 4:30–10 pm for dinner; Sun. till 8 pm.

DIRECTIONS See Russell's, below.

RUSSELL'S, *Exit 35, Bloomsburg*

There's a new kid on the block in downtown Bloomsburg, and to our minds it's the perfect place for a delightful highway meal. Russell's has excellent food prepared by an owner/chef who really cares, moderate prices, and a menu that goes from sandwiches through a wide variety of soups and salads to chicken Cordon Bleu (the latter at $6.95!). All this is served up in a pleasant, simple, and tasteful decor—light and airy, with friendly yellow tablecloths, candles at night, and local artwork that's really worth looking at.

The story behind this discovery stars Russell Lewis, who for eight years worked at the Magee across the street. There he first learned about cooking. Then he went to college, and when he wasn't bending over the books he was in charge of soups for "the best French chef in central Pennsylvania." Now he's returned home and with his wife, Maria, operates his own establishment.

His is the enthusiasm of a young man dedicated to excellence. He makes sure that the salad forks and plates are kept refrigerated, for example, and prepares 48 different soups a month, entirely from scratch. And he's determined to keep the prices and the pretensions low. Russell wants his place to be for everyone, even if that means calling chicken Kiev "country buttered chicken" and dubbing beef Bourguignonne "country beef stew." So, at lunchtime a fine hamburger costs only $2.45 and a Monte Cristo $2.75. There are ten other sandwiches at similar prices, along with soup du jour for 75 cents a cup/95 cents a bowl and eight modestly priced salads. Try shrimp Louis, described as a mountain of lettuce, piled high with shrimp, tomatoes, cucumbers, peppers, and eggs. A mountain well worth the climbing at $3.95.

There's a large selection at dinnertime too: ten fine seafood entrées from $6 to $9 and 13 others, from spaghetti and meatballs in Russell's own sauce ($3.95, with salad!) to veal scaloppine ($9.95). In between are the likes of beef Rolande and roast beef stuffed with a mushroom/scallion mixture and topped with a special sauce. All come with salad, potato, vegetable, and rolls.

Russell's is evidence that good eating is catching on in America. The small towns of New England are already rich with this sort of restaurant, and we're happy to see one in the mountains of central Pennsylvania.

HOURS   Mon.–Thu. 10 am–midnight; Fri. & Sat. 10 am–2 am; Sun. 8 am–2 am. Breakfast till noon. Only light meals served after 10 pm.

DIRECTIONS   From Exit 35 turn left if eastbound, right if west-bound, onto Route 487 South. Go 2.3 miles to a light and turn right onto Main St. It's 0.2 mile on Main to the **Magee Hotel,** on the left, and 0.3 mile to **Russell's,** on the right.

THE FAMILY DINER, *Exit 40, White Haven*

Sometimes we tell you about diners because the fare is at least decent, which makes them ten steps ahead of the fast-food joints. But here's one that's really good.

In the humble little Family Diner we tasted a minestrone with sausage that was just terrific—full flavored, rich, and better than we've had in some fancy Italian places where the price tag was a lot higher than 65 cents a cup.

The soup alone would have won our plaudits, but then we tasted a full half-pound hamburger that overlapped its regula-tion-sized bun by a good inch and a half all around—thick, juicy, delicious, and a mere $1.40!

What explanation had these simple splendors? we asked the owner on our way out. We learned that he'd just acquired the place and was making every effort to establish his reputation. "Is *everything* here that good?" we asked innocently, and with a non-chalance that made believers of us, he said it was.

You mustn't think the Family Diner is one of those "family restaurants" that litter the roadside. Even though it has sprouted a bricked-over entryway and a few coach lamps, the Family Diner is a real one, in stainless steel and red candy stripes even on its metal awnings. We expect that more "improvements" are in the cards, but if that's the price for good food, so be it.

HOURS   Every day 6 am–8 pm.

DIRECTIONS   From Exit 40 turn left if eastbound, right if west-bound. Then make the first possible right just beyond the interchange. Go 2 blocks, follow the road through a left turn, and then go 3 more blocks to a stop sign. Turn right and go to next stop sign (Main St.). Left on Main, and it's 2 blocks to the diner, on the left.

POCONO HERSHEY RESORT, *Exit 42, Lake Harmony*

More for the fun of it than the food, you might want to check out this glorified motel/ski resort with pool, sauna, an enormous lounge, two restaurants and, perhaps, a heart-shaped hot tub somewhere off one of those long corridors.

Downstairs, there's "Molly Maguire's Copper Kettle," which serves sandwiches, salads, soups, and omelets, at decent prices, but in an atmosphere that synthesizes a college dining hall with a family restaurant. Upstairs it's classier, with white tablecloths, carpeting, high ceilings, and a nice view of the mountains, but dinner is fixed-price at $16.95—a lot to pay for deep-fried scallops or broiled filet of halibut, even if the halibut is "wine tender" and the appetizer is included. But Molly does serve an elegant break-fast at only a bit over diner prices. Two eggs, home fries, and toast are just $1.55. For $2.65 you get juice, a short stack of pancakes, one egg, bacon, home fries, and coffee. No charge for the table linen.

HOURS   Upstairs: every day 7:30–10 am for breakfast, 6:30–8:30 pm for dinner. Downstairs: Sun.–Thu. noon–8 pm; Fri. & Sat. noon–10 pm.

DIRECTIONS   Just north of the road, right at Exit 42. Can't miss it.

FLOOD'S, *Exit 50, Stroudsburg*

Stroudsburg is a very pretty little town, and although it's a center of Pocono tourism, it seems quite happily unselfconscious. Flood's was the only sign of the trendy we saw, and we were happy to find it, since unselfconscious mountain towns aren't noted for their food.

Flood's is a very handsome, light, up-to-date sort of place in natural oak, with plants aplenty and booths painted a strong, deep-summer green. (The owner is an Irishman, as proud of the green as he is of the 25 beers on tap and the 150 bottled varieties.)

The food is equally up to date: fancy sandwiches, salads, quiche, and crêpes at lunchtime, along with good homemade soups. The prices are good too. Quiche Lorraine is only $1.25; a burger is $1.75; and deli-style sandwiches, with salad, go for around $2.50. Soup and salad are $2.50 too, but if you're feeling adventuresome you might want to go to the top of the menu and drop $3.25 for schinken fondue, a baked sandwich of French bread dipped in white wine and loaded with Gruyère, ham, and tomato.

One touch we especially appreciated was Flood's offering of cheese plates with crackers and fresh fruit. These run from $2.50 for one cheese to $6.50 for five—Jarlsberg, Brie, garlic and herb, Vermont cheddar, and the like.

At dinner the lunch menu is augmented by about ten full meals in the $7–$9 range, mostly steak and seafood, except for a vegetarian platter and duck in orange sauce.

HOURS Mon.–Sat. 11 am–2 pm and 6–11 pm. Closed Sundays and the second week in March.

DIRECTIONS Eastbound: From Exit 50 bear left, cross the river, and go 2 blocks farther to Main St. Turn left on Main. Flood's is on the right in ½ block.

Westbound: From Exit 50 bear right and go 1 block to light at Main St. Left on Main. Go 0.2 mile to Flood's, on the right.

COLONIAL DINER, *Exit 50, Stroudsburg*

Hidden behind an add-on stone front and a would-be mansard roof in fast-food red is an honest stainless-steel diner with a

71

properly arched ceiling of gray and pink plastic. It's sparkling clean, and the food is decent, if not gourmet. Since the owner is Greek, the usual dinner fare is augmented by souvlaki on pita with garlic and cucumber sauce ($1.80) and baklava at 80 cents a slice.

There's more here yet. It seems they've gone and added a full-blooded Greek restaurant to the back of this place and called it "Athens by Night." It must be a bit more than Stroudsburg can handle, since it's open only on Thursday to Saturday nights from 4 to 10 P.M. We couldn't find out much about it, but it does offer half a dozen full Greek dinners—moussaka, for example, at $6.95 and skewered, marinated lamb on rice pilaf for $8.95.

HOURS　Every day 6 am–10 pm.

DIRECTIONS　Follow directions for Flood's, above. It's right across the street.

GREEN LANTERN COFFEE SHOP,
Exit 53, Delaware Water Gap

Delaware Water Gap was once a thriving resort community, studded with gingerbread hotels and frequented by the likes of Teddy Roosevelt. Now, though, it would make Atlantic-City-before-gambling look like a boom town.

We liked this frowzy, sleepy place, and the Green Lantern Coffee Shop captures its spirit perfectly. Way off to one side of the 40-foot square room, beneath fluorescent lights and an entirely unnoticed tin ceiling, is a simple Woolworth-type lunch counter. The rest of the space is occupied by a hodgepodge of old wooden counters, store fixtures, and tables that form a large square and offer for sale an odd assortment of trinkets and antiques.

Mr. and Mrs. Samuel Kosmerl bought the Green Lantern for their retirement. If you meet Mrs. Kosmerl you'll find a smile and a trusting simplicity of heart that would disarm the archest villain. Making special things for special people is her pleasure, especially for the hikers who are always stopping by off the Appalachian Trail. There's now a special Hiker's Salad, featuring an abundance of hard-boiled eggs amidst the usual greenery "because they seem to like that sort of thing so much."

Sam Kosmerl was once the chef at the prestigious Shawnee Inn. Now he supervises the Green Lantern's humbler fare: steak sandwiches at $1.25, for instance, or hoagies at $1.45. But even at these low prices the soups are made from scratch and the home fries are never frozen.

Clearly the Green Lantern is not the place for everyone, but if this kind of experience appeals to you, don't miss it. And be prepared for a game of Ping-Pong. Sam likes to challenge his customers, and usually he wins.

HOURS Summer: every day 9 am–9 pm. Winter: every day 9:30 am–8 pm.

DIRECTIONS Take Exit 53 for Route 611 South and follow signs for Delaware Water Gap to a light 0.3 mile from the exit. Left at the light and go 0.2 mile up the hill. It's on the left.

DEER HEAD INN, *Exit 53, Delaware Water Gap*

* Color, not cuisine

We half wish we could tell you about an energetic young couple who lovingly restored this fine old Victorian inn; who fell in love with the decayed dining room surrounded by walls of French doors; who decided that only a fine restaurant could do justice to such a setting.

But the blinds remain leaden with dust, even though the barroom comes to life on summer weekends when John Coates, Jr., plays his jazz piano, as he has done here every weekend for ten years (Saturday nights only in winter). Then, the place is crowded. But during the regular lunch hour it's just a wonderfully funky, huge old room. In its center is a large square glass-block bar, and a faded mural of what appears to be a colonial deer hunt runs all around the room just above the dark, weathered paneling.

Lunchtime is just a service to the local people—hamburgers and steak sandwiches at prices that aren't going to send you to the poorhouse. If you've a hankering for faded glory, come take a look. It can't be long before that young couple shows up.

HOURS Lunch: Mon.–Sat. noon–1:30 pm. Bar: Mon.–Sat. 6 pm– 2 am. Closed Sundays.

DIRECTIONS Follow directions for Green Lantern Coffee Shop, above. The Deer Head is right across the street.

New Jersey

BLACK FOREST INN, *Exits 25 & 25N, Stanhope*

It's called the Black Forest, and on the outside it's a handsome, more-or-less Bavarian-looking inn in stucco and timber. The menu is studded with items like Jaeger schnitzel in wine and cream sauce, kalbsteak, smoked eel on pumpernickel, and goulash with spaetzle. All the same, when you ask owner/chef Heinz Aichen about his reputation for German cooking with a light touch, he gets just a bit indignant and declares that his is not a German restaurant, but simply one with good, all-around continental cuisine.

Well, we won't start splitting culinary hairs. The fact is that there are French dishes on the menu too, and it was in France that Heinz learned his trade. Perhaps that explains the "light touch" and his reluctance to being pigeonholed.

Whatever the case, he's put together a fine restaurant, and for leisurely dining, you're not likely to do better in this part of New Jersey.

There are 12 lunch entrées, from $4.50 for a mushroom and cheese omelet to $7.50 for a small filet mignon with Béarnaise sauce. In between are schnitzel, sauerbraten, and goulash, with a few sandwiches at around $3.75, cucumber salad at just $1, and a chef's salad for $4.75. Onion and potato leek soups are always available for $1. You can finish off your meal with the likes of kirschtorte, peach melba, apple strudel, chocolate mousse cake, or Black Forest sundae for a surprising $1.50–$1.70.

Dinners are in the same vein, but the prices run from $10.50

for sautéed breast of capon to about $15. Let yourself go, with appetizers like headcheese in vinaigrette and Black Forest ham. We have to say that the Black Forest's decor didn't seem quite up to its menu, what with a low tile ceiling, innocuous paintings, and imitation wood grain paneling all around. But it's still a pleasant place. Real flowers, white tablecloths, and pewter plates help a lot.

HOURS Mon. & Wed.–Fri. 11:30 am–2 pm and 5–10 pm; Sat. 5–10 pm; Sun. 1–9 pm; closed Tue.

DIRECTIONS Eastbound: From Exit 25 follow signs for U.S. 206 North. It's less than a mile, on the right.

Westbound: Same as above, but take Exit 25N for U.S. 206 North.

CARMINE'S PIZZERIA
RINALDI'S BAKERY
ROMA ITALIAN DELI
NETCONG SWEET SHOP RESTAURANT,
Exit 27, Netcong

Sometimes the best way to learn something about the towns by the road is to walk down Main Street and buy a bit of lunch from each store you pass (a tactic that isn't bad for the digestion either, considering that you've been bouncing around in the car for a couple of hours). Netcong has nothing so well defined as a Main Street, but it is set at the foot of a lake and smack in its center is a miniature Little Italy, perfect for ambulatory eating.

These four little places are right next to one another in an isolated block of buildings. **Carmine's** displays tempting calzone and good Sicilian pizza, but **Rinaldi's** is still more alluring with its lovely 4-by-12-inch strips of pastry stuffed with apples or cherries (a mere $1.50). There are even bigger and more tempting stuffed horns for $2.95, each a meal in itself, not to mention good, crusty Italian bread, bagels, rolls, cookies, and lots more. (Yes, bagels! Okay, so it isn't ethnically pure.)

Buy the bread at Rinaldi's and then walk four doors to the

Roma for lunch meats and cheese. The selection is not enormous, but it's the real Italian stuff and there are cannoli for dessert.

When it's time to sit down over coffee, head for the **Netcong Sweet Shop,** but don't expect anything unusual. It's just an ordinary lunchroom—long, narrow, and plastic, with a fountain behind the counter.

While you're in Netcong, check out the shopping in some of the other stores that share the block. You won't find local crafts, imported woolens, or even an antique shop. But you will find an odd-looking grocery and the tiniest dime store we've ever seen.

> **HOURS**   **Carmine's:** Mon. & Wed.–Sat. 11 am–midnight; Sun. 2:30 pm–midnight; closed Tue.
> **Rinaldi's:** Tue.–Sat. 6 am–6 pm; Sun. 6 am–2 pm; closed Mon.
> **Roma:** Mon.–Sat. 6 am–6:30 pm; Sun. 11 am–2:30 pm.
> **Sweet Shop:** Mon.–Fri. 5 am–5 pm; Sat. 5 am–3 pm; closed Sun.

DIRECTIONS   From Exit 27 turn left if eastbound, right if westbound, onto U.S. 206 North. Go about 0.8 mile and turn left following signs for Netcong Center. Town is just beyond the turn.

NORTH AMERICAN LOBSTER CO.,
Exits 45 & 47, Parsippany

Loud, bright, and fast, but also beautiful to look at, wonderful to smell, a treat to the palate and a relief to the purse—that's the only way to describe this best-yet version of fast food. So even though it's a chain, we've included it (it's a small, local chain, anyway!).

Half the place is a long, narrow gourmet shop and fish store, with at least 50 species gorgeously arrayed on ice. But the wonderful aroma of fried seafood overwhelms you the second you enter, and you know there's got to be more to it than just what you see. If you follow your nose past a room divider, you'll find an equally long and narrow fast-food setup, and although it's unapologetically plasticky, the colors are decent and there's even some real wood in sight.

But come for the clams, not the decor. They're wonderful,

mostly because the frying is light and quick, leaving them tender and delicious. They were so good, in fact, that we utterly rejected a trial of the sauces that came with them.

You really don't need much more than truly fresh fish and a light touch with hot oil to produce great fried seafood. That's what they do best here, drawing a large crowd of pleasant-looking suburban folks. Soup, however, is another matter. The Manhattan clam chowder, though chunky and flavorful, tasted too much like spaghetti sauce. Stick to what they're set up to do well, and you'll do just fine.

And you won't go broke: those juicy clam strips, with chips, were just $2.50. Fish filets and oysters are about the same, with shrimp and scallops at $3.69 and $3.99. There's lots else, including a raw bar, seven linguine dishes, half a steamed lobster ($4.50), and even a soft-shell crab sandwich at $3.49.

HOURS   Mon.–Sat. 11 am–9 pm; closed Sun.

DIRECTIONS   See Par-Troy, below.

PAR-TROY DINER, *Exits 45 & 47, Parsippany*

If the North American Lobster Co. doesn't suit you or the hours are wrong, you can get a decent meal at the Par-Troy, a Greco-glitzy diner in brick with at least a dozen arches in its façade and the customary display of gorgeous pies and strawberry-bedecked cakes. It's on the dark side within, and the menu is large. Burgers are $1.90, soup 85 cents a bowl, and pastrami on rye, $3.50. A slew of dinners go from $6 to $12.

HOURS   Always open.

DIRECTIONS   Eastbound: From Exit 45 turn left and go 0.1 mile to the light. Left at the light and then it's ½ mile to the **Par-Troy,** on the left. Half a mile later is a small shopping center on the left, just after a light. **North American Lobster Co.** is in there.

Westbound: From Exit 47 turn onto U.S. 46 West. Go 1.2 miles to the **Par-Troy,** on the left. Half a mile later is a small shopping center on the left, just after a light. **North American Lobster Co.** is in there.

PANTANO'S, *Exit 61, Paterson*

Pantano's is one of those nearly windowless Italian restaurants that leave you unsure of whether it's a legitimate eatery or a nightclub. But Pantano's most decidedly is a restaurant, and rather a good one, drawing a well-off lunchtime clientele to its industrial part of town.

Here they find a much better than average menu in an atmosphere that hints, ever so faintly, of the sinister. It's dark inside —deep red carpeting, dusky paneling, with only a sprinkling of tiny tavern lights for illumination. It's posh and comfortable too, with white tablecloths and soft black leatherette chairs—a bit like a closely draped bedroom at midday, a great place for a secret tryst or the discussion of a slightly shady deal.

You get all this theater for $4.50–$6 at lunchtime. Chicken française is typical at $5.50, and while this isn't really the place for a hamburger, they're available, along with a few sandwiches, for $3–$4. Pasta dinners start at $4.25 and run up to $7 for tortellini carbonara. Others go to $12, with no less than a dozen veal dishes.

HOURS   Mon.–Thu. 11:30 am–10:30 pm; Fri. & Sat. 11:30 am–11:30 pm; Sun. 11:30 am–10 pm.

DIRECTIONS Eastbound: From Exit 61 turn left at end of ramp onto River St. Go 0.3 mile to Pantano's, on the right.

Westbound: From Exit 61 turn right at end of ramp. It's on the right in 0.2 mile.

PETE'S LUNCHEONETTE, *Exit 66, Hackensack*

With a name like "Hackensack," this town had to have its funky eateries. We felt obligated to search them out even if it has its fine restaurants too. When we came upon three diners, each with a distinct personality, all lined up in a row along the surprisingly pleasant Hackensack River, we knew we'd made the right decision.

Pete's was certainly the friendliest place. He and Maria Lepera have run it for most of its 45-year existence, and the warmth of their personalities more than compensates for the plastic furnishings and pale-green colors. Absolutely everybody says "good morning" here, and they mean it.

And absolutely everything's homemade, from the tomato sauce, which is always allowed to ripen, right down to the salad dressings. But Pete is especially proud of his soups ($1 a bowl) and stews ($2.75), all made from scratch. Your burger will arrive on a hard roll, and you'll get two eggs and toast for $1.25.

Don't be put off by the frumpy, squarish stucco building, with its sign painted right on the wall. Pretend you're in Italy, which is even easier on Friday when some of that tomato sauce winds up in a lasagne special for $2.75.

HOURS Mon.–Fri. 6 am–6 pm; closed Sat. & Sun.

DIRECTIONS See directions for White Manna Diner, page 81.

HERITAGE DINER, *Exit 66, Hackensack*

The Heritage has the least charm of the Hackensack trio, but the best hours. It's a 24-hour-a-day, Greco-glitzy diner behind a brick façade (with a canopied entryway, no less). Inside, gold brocade draperies harmonize oddly with the phoniest-looking hand-hewn beams we've ever seen.

Despite all this, the Heritage is somehow pleasant. Perhaps it's the gorgeous and prominent display of baked goods. It might have been fairer to test the cheesecake or luscious-looking Black Forest cake, but the incongruity of apricot hummentashen (Jewish holiday cookies) in a Greek diner was irresistible. Well, they weren't patisserie quality, but they were good enough, even if the crust was nearly half an inch thick in places.

Customers here are solidly middle class—a "safe" place with moderate prices: $1.50 for a burger and $4.50–$10 for dinner.

HOURS   Always open.

DIRECTIONS   See directions for White Manna Diner, page 81.

WHITE MANNA DINER, *Exit 66, Hackensack*

* *Color, not cuisine*

You can't beat the White Manna for character. It looks like an old Wurlitzer jukebox, and it's not much bigger. There's not a right angle in the building. Everything's curved, à la moderne, with bulbous ornamentation here and there, glass block in the rounded corners, and a horseshoe-shaped counter.

Everything, from cooking to dishwashing to cashiering, goes on within the few square feet of work space, all of it orchestrated by a waitress who moves like lightning even when she's standing still. You'd better move quickly too—if you hesitate over your order she may just let you know what she thinks of such wasteful indecision.

Hamburgers are only 60 cents here—tiny things that begin life as meatballs and meet their fate on the grill beneath a single blow from a heavy spatula. Soup is 55 cents, and there are five or six sandwiches at about $1. If you go for the two eggs with toast (80 cents), the jelly will be plunked down before you in an undisguised generic jar.

The original manna came from God—a gift to the Jews during the Exodus from Egypt. Dining-car magnate Jerry O'Mahonney, however, built the White Manna to dispense hamburgers to the New York World's Fair. That was in 1937. But now this little Art Deco jewel seems entirely at home on the shores of the Hackensack.

HOURS　Mon.–Fri. 6 am–6 pm; Sat. 6 am–4:30 pm; closed Sun.

DIRECTIONS　Eastbound: From Exit 66 turn left at end of ramp onto Vreeland Ave. Go 1 block to a light and turn left onto Hudson. Go under bridge and 1 more block to light at Kennedy and turn right. Go 1 block on Kennedy and then left onto River. Then as below from ■.

Westbound: From Exit 66 turn right onto Kennedy. Go two lights to River St. and turn left. ■ **Pete's Luncheonette** is 0.4 mile up, on the left. It's 0.9 mile to the **Heritage Diner,** on the right, and the **White Manna** is 1.6 miles, also on the right.

Pennsylvania, New York

Pennsylvania

A. R. BURKHARDT'S, *Exits 9 & 10, Shippensburg*

Today Burkhardt's calls itself "a unique eatery," which should be a tip-off to its brick-plants-and-oak decor. But this is no trendy newcomer. In fact, it's been here since 1920, now in its third generation of Burkhardt owners. Only recently was it transformed from a down-to-earth village restaurant/hotel, and the menu is still studded with local specialties.

There's a wonderful pork pudding, for example, that sometimes comes with breakfast. This is delicious but unencouraging in appearance, a gray-brown mound of meat made from Lord only knows what parts of the pig, boiled down and flavored to perfection. It's a rich, spicy, juicy treat that will delight anyone who loves good sausage. Unfortunately, pork pudding is available only from November to March, the butchering season, but you'll know it's homemade, and you'll know it's local.

You can get veal française here ($7.50), pork tenderloin in wine ($6.50), cheesy vegetable casserole ($4.50), and quiche ($2.95). And you can get BBQ chicken or ribs ($5.25–$6), any of nine salads, soup du jour (60 cents–$1), and sandwiches for as little as $1. But if you look carefully for the specials (or ask for them), you'll find that Burkhardt's always takes advantage of what's locally available, which tends to come out with a Pennsylvania Dutch accent—scrapple, slippery pot pie, sweet-and-sour hot slaw, wilted spinach, and even dandelion greens.

HOURS   Mon.–Thu. 6 am–9:30 pm; Fri. & Sat. 6 am–10 pm; Sun. 6 am–3 pm.

DIRECTIONS   Use Exit 9 if northbound, Exit 10 if southbound. In either case, follow signs to Shippensburg (about 1½ miles). Burkhardt's is at 13 E. King St., in the center of this small town.

ALVA RESTAURANT, *Exit 23, Harrisburg*

It's about 2½ miles out of your way to this downtown hotel, a Harrisburg institution where local charm comes as a side order with every dish. Good food and low, low prices. See page 38 for full description.

DIRECTIONS   From Exit 23, head south (sign says U.S. 22 East, but it's actually south). In 1 mile, U.S. 22 turns off to the east, but you should continue straight on Route 230 East, which becomes Cameron St. In 1½ miles, turn right onto Market St. Go 0.3 mile to corner of S. 4th St. The Alva is on your left (19 S. 4th St.). About 10 minutes.

SHENANIGAN'S, *Exit 40, Hazleton*

Except for a few dormant spells, there has been a restaurant on this spot since 1914, when the United Hotel took over the former Lehigh Valley railroad station. What we liked about Shenanigan's is that its pressed-tin ceiling, stained-glass windows, ceiling fans, and old brick walls don't sparkle with pristine perfection, but wear a patina that comes from service in an era when turn-of-the-century decor was natural. Unfortunately, the plethora of advertising mirrors, Tiffany-style lamps, and etched glass isn't quite so authentic.

In keeping with other restaurants of its ilk, Shenanigan's serves eight different hamburgers, each with a sassy sobriquet. In this case, the nicknames derive from local banks, possibly because their employees make up much of the lunch crowd. Thus, the First Valley Burger is topped with Canadian bacon and cheddar cheese, while the Hazleton National Burger has ham and Swiss with sautéed onions. All burgers are $2.25; we tried

83

one with sautéed mushrooms and green peppers. Though the meat was moist and the roll good, we were disappointed to find canned mushrooms and mushy peppers between the two.

Soups are all homemade here; sandwiches—surprisingly—include kosher pastrami and corned beef along with American standbys like roast beef, ham and Swiss, turkey, BLT, etc. They are reasonably priced from $1.70 to $2.10; triple-decker clubs are only $2.50. Greek and chef's salads run up to $2.95.

At dinnertime, much of the lunch menu remains, and to it are added continental selections like chicken Kiev, veal française, fettucini Alfredo, and coquilles St. Jacques (most, $6.95 to $8.75). The salad bar, with soup and bread, comes free with dinner, or for $2.50 as an entrée. Consider it if you're on a tight budget, along with the occasional all-you-can-eat specials for $2.99 and the children's portions that come with a bottomless ice cream bowl.

HOURS Mon.–Sat. 11 am–11 pm; Sun. noon–10 pm.

DIRECTIONS From Exit 40 turn right if northbound, left if southbound, onto Route 924 North. In about 2 miles bear right onto Route 93 South (West Broad St.). Go 0.8 mile to Wyoming St. (First Valley Bank on corner). Right on Wyoming and 1 short block to Shenanigan's, just before the tracks on left (awning says United Hotel).

ALBERDEEN INN, *Exit 43, Mountain Top*

For 101 years the Alberdeen Inn has been one of this area's choice spots for leisurely country dining. Now, the 4-mile drive from interstate to inn takes you through subdivision housing tracts that underscore the Alberdeen's value to northeastern Pennsylvania as a reminder of a more gracious past.

The cuisine is continental, and seafood dishes like shrimp stuffed with crabmeat ($9.75) are the most popular. (The preference for seafood, we have found, has nothing to do with proximity to the sea.) But owners Ed and Lenore McCabe are most proud of what they can do with spinach. As an entrée, spinach-stuffed veal is their own favorite ($9.75). But it's a side dish that is their true love, and everyone else's too—spinach casserole.

Don't come begging for the recipe; you won't be the first, and Ed and Lenore would sooner give away the inn.

The Alberdeen draws its clientele from a wide chunk of Pennsylvania's coal country. Reservations are strongly urged on Saturday nights; phone (717) 868-9283.

HOURS   Tue.–Sat. 5–9 pm; closed Sun. and Mon.

DIRECTIONS   Northbound: From Exit 43 turn right. ■ In 2½ miles bear left after stop sign and, in about ¼ mile, at another stop sign, turn right onto Main Road South. In 0.9 mile bear right onto Alberdeen Rd. and go 0.8 mile to the inn, on your left.

Southbound: From Exit 43 turn left at stop sign and go 0.3 mile to another stop sign. Turn left, then as above from ■.

DUNMORE CANDY KITCHEN, *Exits 54 & 55, Dunmore*

For a potpourri of restaurants and a charming little candy factory/soda fountain, see page 93.

DIRECTIONS   Northbound: From Exit 54 turn right for **Yantorn's Italian American Cuisine,** which will be on your right in ½ mile. For all other restaurants, including **Candy Kitchen,** turn left from Exit 54 onto East Drinker St. In 0.9 mile bear left at fork by the veterinary hospital. The restaurants follow shortly, on both sides of the street.

Southbound: Shortly after Exit 55 leave I-81 and enter I-84 East. Take Exit 1 on I-84, then follow directions given at the top of page 94.

New York

WHOLE IN THE WALL, *Exit 4S, Binghamton*

Whole in the Wall caters to a wide range of natural foods tastes—from the miso soup and macrobiotics crowd to those who would be content with chicken soup so long as it had whole wheat matzoh balls. Even some arrow-straight Binghamtonians have found meals they could wholly enjoy.

There are a dozen sandwiches, including almond butter and jelly on home-baked bread (whole wheat, of course), tempeh burgers in pita pockets, grilled cheese and scallions on bagel, falafel, and pita pizza. Most are less than $2.

A large chef's salad (made by a vegetarian chef) costs $3, and a bowl of tofu chili is $2.75. We tried the chili. It was quite good, and rather spicy (as requested), but we couldn't help searching among the kidney beans for hunks of meat. No luck. There are also quiches, Mexican specialties, and a variety of stir-fries including shrimp and veggies ($5.50 top). The dinner menu drops nothing from lunch but adds whole wheat pizza (try it with a tofu or broccoli topping) and tempura. À la carte prices are generally $2.95 to $5.25; add $1.50 or so for full dinners.

All this naturally good eating takes place in friendly company, to the accompaniment of light jazz or classical music in a century-old storefront, transformed over three years by owners who—while working full-time jobs—scraped three layers of tile off the wooden floor, pulled old wainscoting off the walls, turned it around, and added intricate door casings that they rescued from a local mansion just one day before its appointment with the wrecker's ball. The result of their labor is a light, airy, very woody place, not highly finished but quite acceptable, made even more so by the good food.

HOURS Tue.–Fri. 11:30 am–2 pm and 5–9 pm; Sat. 11:30 am–9 pm; closed Sun. and Mon. Usually closed for vacation the first week of July.

DIRECTIONS See Number 5, below.

NUMBER 5, *Exit 4S, Binghamton*

Take a fire engine company and move it out of its red-brick station house. Enter an entrepreneur. What do you get? Nine times out of ten, a restaurant with ladders hanging from the ceiling, fireman photos on the walls, and the original pole between the floors.

Even though the clichés of firehouse dining can be found at Number 5, they won't burn your sense of good design. The downstairs lounge is actually quite beautiful, one of the better examples of the brick-plants-and-oak decor so common in renovated buildings converted to restaurants. Oval marble-topped café tables are arranged throughout the room, and scattered among them are a few chess and backgammon tables. Upstairs, the dining room is darker, softer, stodgier, a little overdecorated with firefighters in fancy gilt frames and dusty old books in wall-length shelves.

The menu is a somewhat overwritten compendium of steak and seafood dishes. Filet mignon (à la carte, $10.95/complete dinner, $13.95) is embellished with a bacon wrapping; Greek tenderloin ($11.55/$14.95) is broiled in lemon butter and seasoned with oregano and garlic. In the same price range are a dozen poultry and veal dishes and about 20 seafood dishes, from charbroiled swordfish ($9.95) to coquilles St. Jacques ($11.95) and filet of sole Oscar ($12.95). Our appetite wasn't up to any of this, but we were quite satisfied with Number 5's "Cobb Salad," a cornucopic chef's salad with avocado, watercress, chicken breast, and crisp bacon in addition to the usual. As an entrée, it's just $3.95. Looking around somewhat guiltily, we saw that we weren't the only ones to make a meal of salad and Number 5's unusual but tasty onion soup laced with apple brandy.

HOURS   Mon.–Thu. 5–10 pm, until 11 on Fri. & Sat.; Sun. 5–9 pm.

DIRECTIONS   Exit 4S (off I-81 and Route 17) feeds you onto Route 363 South. Drive 1.7 easy highway miles on 363 until it ends. Bear sharply right onto Route 434 West (signs for Vestal), which puts you onto one loop of a cloverleaf and then a bridge across the Susquehanna River. Turn left at the first traffic light after the bridge (South Washington St.). **Number 5** is on the corner, on your left, and a few doors down is **Whole in the Wall.** Much easier than it sounds, and returning to the highway is equally simple.

TRUFFLES, *Exit for Route 17 West, Binghamton*

See page 201 for a description of this superb gourmet shop–restaurant, only a few quick miles out of your way.

DIRECTIONS   From I-81 enter Route 17 West to Exit 70N in Johnson City. Then, as on page 202.

THREE BEAR INN, *Exit 9, Marathon*

The Three Bear Inn was founded by the second settler to park his canoe in the Marathon area. One hundred eighty-three years later, it's a cozy old place with good steaks ($6.45–$9.45), good sandwiches ($1.50–$2.50, available at dinnertime), and some excellent desserts. The walls are covered with vinyl and studded with brass so as to suggest leather padding, and the gleaming oak tables are set with candles. Old photos of the inn share the wall space with a mammoth-sized bear trap.

The inn offers fried chicken and a few seafood dishes too, but it's a long way from the sea. Better stick to the steaks and the delicious homemade cheesecake and walnut pie ($1.35).

The name, by the way, comes not from the fairy tale but from the three bearskin rugs that once hung on the inn's front wall. So, there's no porridge on the menu. But we did hear nice things about the bean soup, made according to a recipe from the U.S. Senate restaurant.

HOURS   Every day 7 am–2 pm and 5–9 pm.

DIRECTIONS   From Exit 9 take Route 221 West to the only traffic light in Marathon. Left at the light and you're there. Inn is on the left, flanked by the Bear Dairy and Three Bear Motel.

ELM STREET BAKERY, *Exit 11, Cortland*

The Elm Street Bakery is indeed a bakery, but it's also a natural foods store, a deli, and a restaurant. It's the labor of love of Paul Voiland, a midwesterner who left his lucrative position with a major natural foods distributor to bring his career down to a more human scale. What pleases him most is offering alternatives for regular folks who would otherwise buy their food at the A & P or McDonald's.

When they come here instead, they are first faced with

shelves of gleaming glass jars and clear Lucite tubs filled with whole grains and beans, dried fruit, granola, teas and spices. Fresh local produce sits in baskets on the wooden floor. Paul points out that this is the way groceries used to be sold before the supermarkets took over.

At one side is a small cluster of café tables arranged around a potbellied stove. While you're thinking about what to order, follow the warm, yeasty smells to the open bakery at the rear. You'll see the great mixing bowls and beaters and, best of all, the monumental hearth oven.

It's a 125-ton, wood-fired beauty, 19 feet long, 18 feet wide, and twice the height of a man. Patterned after Viennese ovens, it allows breads to bake "on the hearth"—directly on hot bricks. Two hundred loaves at a time: whole wheat, pumpernickel, sourdough, and raisin breads. Italian bread and croissants too, and carob cakes, apple turnovers, and honey-sweetened cookies. There's even pizza, including a "Reuben pizza" with rye crust, corned beef, sauerkraut, Swiss cheese, and Russian dressing.

On the way back to your seat, select a baked goodie to eat with your lunch. You can help yourself to coffee, tea, or the soup of the day from a crockpot. Although it would be easy to make a meal of snacks here, you might prefer to get down to business with spinach and mushroom salad, a filled pita pocket, or one of several melted-cheese combinations. For dessert, if the bakery won't do you, order a delicious strawberry compote or Häagen Dazs ice cream.

Prices at the Elm Street Bakery are most reasonable: 75 cents for soup; $1.35 to $2.99 for sandwiches.

On your way out, you can buy a pound of cheese (20 or so to choose from) and a loaf of bread. With your next meal in hand, you're ready to hit the road.

HOURS   Tue.–Sat. 10 am–6 pm; closed Sun. & Mon.

DIRECTIONS   From Exit 11, turn left if northbound, right if southbound. At second light (Elm St.), turn left, and in 2 blocks you'll see the bakery on the left (138 Elm).

THE GREAT WALL, *Exit 11, Cortland*

Despite its Occidental surroundings on Main Street, Cortland's only Chinese restaurant is the real thing. No chop suey here, but your choice of Szechuan, Hunan, and Mandarin specialties in three degrees of spiciness. Be warned: "Hot" really does mean hot! Hot or cool, the Great Wall's cooking is excellent, if our dinner of beef and baby corn with broccoli was a true test. At lunchtime, an entrée, soup, and tea go for $2.99. Amply portioned dinners are $5–$8; if the spices prove too much, employ Chinese beer to cool your palate.

The affable young manager, Mr. Yeung, learned to cook in Hong Kong but recently got himself an engineering degree from Cornell. He circulates among the diners in a Cornell T-shirt, one of a thousand that he bought, we were told. If it's not busy, he'll sit and talk with you or cook up a special request. And he'll remember you if you stop in again on the way back. "Ah!" we heard him say to one customer, "you were here last winter."

Except for the subdued tone and photos of the Great Wall, this restaurant looks much like the hamburger shop it once was. Cheap table settings belie the quality of the food.

HOURS   Mon.–Sat. 11:30 am–9 pm; closed Sun.

DIRECTIONS   From Exit 11, turn left if northbound, right if southbound. At the first light turn right onto Clinton St. Go 2 blocks to Main St. Left on Main, and it's on the right (14 Main St.).

RESTAURANTS ON MARSHALL STREET, *Exit 18, Syracuse*

Not surprisingly, restaurants with good, quick, cheap food crop up like wildflowers in the shadows of large universities. The richest turf around Syracuse University is Marshall Street, or "M Street," as it's called by the SU crowd. Almost a dozen eateries are packed into one short block here, and all of them have to be hits or they couldn't pay the rent.

The students will probably tell you first about the **King David Restaurant,** an inexpensive Middle Eastern place that has been serving falafel and pita since the days when people thought pita was misspelled pizza.

The **Coney Island** makes New York City students feel at home with its low-priced hot dogs, steak sandwiches, homemade chicken soup, and zeppoli (New York–style pizza fritters). **Cosmo Pizzeria** serves breakfasts and sandwiches as well as the expected, and is open almost any time you'd be interested in eating anything with tomato sauce.

We hunted a little farther for something that offered more leisurely dining, and we came up with **Faegan's Pub, Ltd.** Just across from the foot of Marshall, on South Crouse Avenue, Faegan's is a spiffy brick-plants-and-oak café. Parquet floor, café curtains, bentwood chairs. Good pub sandwiches, homemade soups, salads, quiche, carrot cake. Get the picture?

DIRECTIONS Northbound: From Exit 18 turn right on Adams St.; go about ¼ mile to University Ave. Right on University for 1 short block and you'll be at the head of Marshall St. The restaurants are to your right.

Southbound: From Exit 18 follow signs for Adams St. Left on Adams, to the third light, then right onto University Ave. It's 1 short block to the head of Marshall St.; the restaurants are to your right.

MARIO'S DINER, *Exit 28, North Syracuse*

The house specialty at Mario's is frittata. "Frittata" sounds like a mixture of fritos and a tostada, and well it might be since the word translates as "all mixed together." But what Mario Biasi mixes together are home fries, onions, eggs, broccoli, ham, and pepperoni. If you like, he'll throw in some sweet Italian sausage, bacon, or cheese.

Watching him make this concoction is restaurant theater at its best, and his quick, jerky motions make it all look like a silent film played at double speed. When he's finished, the jumbled mass of piping-hot food is turned onto a plate, overflowing it in all directions. We asked if it always comes that big and Mario exclaimed, "Big? That's a small one." He often asks people if they are especially hungry, and if they answer in the affirmative he doubles or triples the potatoes (without upping the price). We wondered what size plate he uses then! For $2.85, it's a tremendous bargain, even for our "mini-frittata." Somehow, the motley collection of ingredients works well, and we thoroughly enjoyed our meal (even though we could not finish it).

This is an old stainless-steel Silk City diner. It's not in pristine condition, and its bright-green bamboo curtains add a certain *je ne sais quoi.* But it's certainly a respectable enough place to pass an hour, and Mario's gentle, sincere personality makes up for any shortcomings in decor.

He also serves sandwiches (80 cents to $1.90), omelets ($1.20–$2), liver and onions or breaded veal ($2.25), and other diner regulars. Two eggs with home fries and toast is $1.35; add sausage, bacon, or ham and it's $1.95. The most expensive item you can buy is a steak sandwich for $3.15.

Since we visited Mario's, by the way, we've seen frittata served at two other restaurants in widely separate locations. One of them had a "frittata du jour." We're hereby going on record as predicting that frittata will someday be a restaurant staple. Remember when you didn't know how to pronounce "quiche"?

HOURS Mon.–Fri. 5:30 am–2 pm; Sat. 5:30 am–1 pm; closed Sun.

DIRECTIONS From Exit 28, follow sign for North Syracuse, turning onto Taft Rd. Go about 1 mile, through three lights. Just past the third light (the junction with N.Y. 11), pull into the first driveway on the right (after barbershop) and you'll see Mario's about 100 yards in front of you.

Pennsylvania,
New York

Pennsylvania

RESTAURANTS IN DUNMORE, *Exit 1, Dunmore*

* *Color, not cuisine*

This is coal country, and driving down the hill into Dunmore is like entering a mine—it doesn't get any prettier as you get farther in. If hunger strikes, you'll find something open almost any time of day, but nothing you'd want to visit with a big date.

First in line is **Yantorn's Italian American Cuisine;** at the time, we weren't in the mood for tomato sauce, so we continued down the street. Half a mile later is the **Big M Restaurant,** a few pizza joints, and the Dunmore Dog and Cat Hospital (where you can drop off your doggie bag). In another half-mile comes **Pompey's Diner** (looks like a Vesuvius survivor) and finally, the **Tiffany Restaurant** (hardly a jewel).

Actually, the sweetest thing we saw in town was the **Dunmore Candy Kitchen,** and it was sweet by any standards. We happened to be there in late March when they were stocking up for the Easter rush. Every conceivable inch of wall space was festooned with chocolate bunnies, lambs, crosses, birds, and eggs, as well as battleships, baseball bats, and astronauts, all aglitter in their cellophane wrappers and tinsel bows. This floor-to-ceiling candy cornucopia completely obliterated the soda fountain, which actually shuts down at this time of year. But at any other time, you can wash down the first course of sucrose with another—ice cream, floats, shakes, or sundaes. Truly a heaven for sugar junkies.

HOURS Every day 11 am–5 pm and 7:30–9:30 pm. Closed Sundays in summer. Easter season: 11 am–10 pm.

DIRECTIONS From Exit 1 turn right and go the short distance to a stop sign at a T junction. Turn right here onto Drinker St. and in 0.3 mile you'll begin to see the restaurants described above. The Candy Kitchen is about 1½ miles down, on the left.

New York

EL BANDIDO, *Exit 4E, Middletown*

See page 212 for a description of this Mexican restaurant. It's only 2 miles out of your way.

DIRECTIONS From Exit 4E enter Route 17 East. Go 1 mile to Exit 122 on Route 17. Turn left onto Middletown Rd. (County Road 67); go 1.1 miles and you'll see it on the right.

THE BACK COURT, *Exit 13, Fishkill*

We've eaten at restaurants with views of harbors, cities, rivers, valleys, and mountains, but this is the first to overlook a racquetball court. Lest unhappy visions of bowling-alley food float into memory, rest assured that the Back Court purveys modern American cuisine—fancy salads, big sandwiches, dressed-up hamburgers, and carrot cake desserts. To these at dinner are added veal and chicken specialties and other continental dishes.

To find the Back Court, one enters the All-Sports Fitness and Racquetball Club and walks down a plushly carpeted corridor past glass-enclosed racquetball courts, swimming pool, and sports shop. The short journey may prove a minor adventure in itself; we took a wrong turn and found ourselves elbowing our way through the teen boys' karate class.

The gorgeous carpet runs right into the tastefully decorated restaurant. Whether you've been taking a beating behind the wheel or on the court, you'll melt right into the cushy chairs.

The Back Court's salads are colorful, crisp, and luxuriant. We had a very nice spinach salad with a lively vinaigrette, and an equally good cheese steak—top round with grilled onions and provolone on hard roll ($3.95). Each day there are several home-made soups; half a sandwich (Reuben, tuna melt, etc.) and a cup of soup goes for $2.95.

When we visited, the Back Court's dinner menu was in a state of flux. The new menu will offer all the lunch items at slightly higher prices, but will retain the old menu's continental accent by offering chicken and veal dishes ($7.50–$10), seafood specials ($8.50–$12), and surf-turf combinations (about $13).

If you've got an extra $7 and the time for athletic indulgence after lunch, you can purchase a day pass to the pool, sauna, whirlpool, and courts, where you can try to work off all the weight you've just put on.

HOURS   Mon.–Sat. 11 am–3 pm and 5–10 pm. Closed on Sunday.

DIRECTIONS   From Exit 13 turn left if eastbound, right if west-bound, onto Route 9 North. Go 0.8 mile and turn right shortly before the traffic light. One hundred yards puts you in front of the fitness center. Parking lot and entrance are on the left side of the building.

BOB'S DINER
VILLAGE LUNCHEONETTE, *Exits 20 & 20N, Brewster*

* *Color, not cuisine*

The attractive town of Brewster is relatively unadulterated by such amenities as fast-food chains and highway strips to put them on. There are local restaurants here, though none proved a real discovery. (Check out the entries for nearby Danbury, Con-necticut, in the New England *Interstate Gourmet* for some genuine "discoveries.")

Bob's Diner is a cute little building that looks like a pint-sized train depot. (Two doors away, in fact, is its big daddy, the Tudor-style Amtrak station.) Behind Bob's café curtains, its cuisine holds no surprises—reasonably priced American diner fare all the way, but nothing to write books about. The absence of even a homemade soup, and the surprised look when we inquired, sent us scooting down the street to see what else we might find.

What we found was a lesson in regionalisms. At the Village Luncheonette, we learned that those long sandwiches variously known as grinders, hoagies, heros, and submarines are in this part of the world called "wedges." But a grinder of any other name tastes no more sweet, and although the Italian sausage wedge we sampled was acceptable, it inspired no poetry.

The real specialty at the Village Luncheonette is fried egg sandwiches—on English muffin or hard roll, with cheese, bacon, ham, or sausage ($1.25 to $2.25). Not bad.

If hunger strikes in Brewster, you'll be able to put it down, but it probably won't melt away without a fight. For some real dining, press on to Danbury.

> **HOURS** **Bob's:** Always open.
> **Village Luncheonette:** Mon.–Sat. 6 am–9:30 pm; Sun. 7 am–2 pm.

DIRECTIONS   If eastbound, take Exit 20N; if westbound, take Exit 20. On ramp, follow signs for N.Y. 22. This feeds you into I-684 North. Almost immediately, take Exit 10, following signs for Brewster. Turn right onto N.Y. 22 and go 0.8 mile to junction with N.Y. 6. Turn right and in 0.6 mile you'll be in the center of Brewster. The **Village Luncheonette** is on your right, and 0.1 mile farther, **Bob's Diner** is on your left.

New York State Thruway, Adirondack Northway

New York State Thruway

VENUTI'S DELI, *Exit 7A, Elmsford*

If a quick and delicious roast beef sandwich for car-seat consumption is all you need, check out Venuti's Deli, page 215.

DIRECTIONS At Exit 7A enter Saw Mill River Parkway North. Go about 1 mile on Saw Mill and take exit for N.Y. 119 East/Elmsford. Bear right onto N.Y. 119 East. Go through one traffic light, then 1½ short blocks. It's on the left, at 23 Main St.

PLAZA DINER RESTAURANT, *Exit 14, Nanuet*

In a section where roadside food is hard to come by, this was the best we could do. It's a glitzy diner with tilework everywhere, ludicrous little Formica canopies over every table, shiny red pincushion booths, and plastic plants. Don't come for the decor—come because it never closes.

As with many diners of this genus, the menu is extensive. You can order chicken Marsala, ziti parmigiana or sautéed bluefish; borscht, vegetable soup, or beef stew; hamburgers, clubs, or a tongue platter. Prices aren't great but they aren't horrendous either—$5 to $6.50 for dinner specials à la carte; $4.25 to $6 for salad platters; $2 to $3.25 for sandwiches. The best buy appears to be a nice-looking salad bar of which you may avail yourself (evenings only) for $2 if you purchase a sandwich as well.

If you don't mind a stand-up dessert, we recommend you mosey over to **Joseph's Italian American Pastry Shop** in the same shopping center.

HOURS   Always open.

DIRECTIONS   From Exit 14 turn left onto Route 59 East. In less than a mile, you'll see it on your left, in a small shopping center across from the gargantuan Nanuet Mall.

RAMAPO VALLEY CENTER, *Exit 15, Sloatsburg*

The Ramapo Valley Center sells more than just food; it's a New Age bookstore and workshop center as well as a totally vegetarian grocery and restaurant. Practically in the dooryard of Harriman State Park, it's also a convenient stop for hikers seeking dried fruit and nuts, cheeses, natural juices, honey-sweetened sodas, and other pick-ups before they climb Bear Mountain.

Because a large part of RVC's business is take-out, most prices are by weight or volume. When you order a lunch of curried vegetables, for instance, they weigh what you want and charge you $2.50 a pound. Soups are sold by the quart ($1.95), and there are always two or three to choose from—miso, squash, and a mixed bean/vegetable soup when we were there. Chili is $1.95 a pound. Soyburgers and sandwiches ($1.75 each) are served on pocket bread. You can also get vegetarian egg rolls and an unusual vegetarian knish filled with broccoli, bok choy, carrots, and celery ($1).

Every morning owner Tom Adamoyurka (the name is Russian) fires up the ovens and pops in a potpourri of eggless, sugarless, animal-product-less baked goods, including breads, cakes, cookies, pies, and whole wheat calzone.

In good weather, there are tables outside, but at other times everyone is served at a single large table in the center of the store. Be prepared to find yourself engaged in talk of herbology, midwifery, or Tibetan Buddhism.

HOURS   Winter: every day 10 am–6 pm. Summer: Mon.–Thu. 10 am–6 pm; Fri.–Sun. 10 am–9 pm.

DIRECTIONS From Exit 15 follow signs for Route 17 North, through extensive twisting ramps that eventually end at Route 17. You'll shortly come to a light; go straight through it and you're on Route 17 North. Take 17 North for 3½ miles and you'll see Ramapo Valley Center on your right, across from a church in the village of Sloatsburg.

GASHO OF JAPAN, *Exit 16, Central Valley*

In case you haven't noticed, there's a Japanese import sweeping the restaurant business the way Toyotas blew into the auto industry a decade ago. It's called the Japanese steakhouse. If you haven't been to one, it's worth one visit to watch the show: You're seated around a hibachi table on which an agile chef cooks your meal between dexterous bouts of salt shaker juggling, spatula flipping, and knife tapping. But like everything that catches on, these restaurants have become commonplace, usually clones of one another. Gasho of Japan, however, is different.

Owned by Shiro Aoki, son of Yonosuki Aoki who invented this style of tableside cooking (it's no more traditional in Japan than McDonald's) and founded the Benihana restaurant chain, Gasho has retained the tableside performances of Benihana and its many imitators, but has found a much more inspiring theater in which to present the show.

The building itself—set in an extensive landscaped complex with motels, tennis courts, swimming pool, fish pond, Japanese gardens, meditation area, and a large map to help you find your way around—is an authentic 12th-century Samurai farmhouse of the type called *gasho*. These come from the Hida Mountains ("the Japanese Alps"), where they were made of keyaki wood lashed with rice rope and fastened by wooden pegs. In the late 1960s

Mr. Aoki supervised a crew that in three years dismantled a gasho, transported it to America, and rebuilt it, board by board, peg by peg, in the authentic fashion.

The decor is deliberately sparse, so as to show off the gasho's beautiful geometries and the soaring triangular roof.

The food here is all fresh and of high quality; you *know* it's prepared to order! Shrimp, steaks, and chicken are the basic fare, all sautéed with vegetables and sesame seeds and served with ginger or mustard sauce. Lunches run $3.50 to $5.25; the same dishes in somewhat greater portions are $8 to $12 at dinner. (Children's dinners are $4 to $5.) Although the food is wholesome and tasty, it's the cooking, not the eating, that's meant to be noticed.

Mr. Aoki, by the way, has transplanted three other gashos and converted them to restaurants. But the buildings are difficult to obtain, and take years to relocate, so the Gasho restaurant empire is not likely to explode.

HOURS   Lunch: Mon.–Sat. noon–3 pm. Dinner: Mon.–Thu. 5:30–10 pm; Fri. 5:30–11 pm; Sat. 5–11 pm; Sun. noon–10 pm.

DIRECTIONS   From Exit 16 follow signs for N.Y. 32/Harriman. Turn right onto N.Y. 32, go 1.6 miles through the town of Central Valley, and you'll find Gasho on your left.

ABOUT NEW PALTZ

We didn't see any railroad in New Paltz, but it certainly has an "other side of the tracks." Most of the action happens at the crusty, gutsy downtown area, but there's also a celebrated historical district where pre-1700 stone houses are still occupied by descendants of the families that built them. New Paltz is also home to a state college and, on the outskirts of town, the Shawangunk Mountains are a paradise for rock climbers who affectionately call them "the Gunks."

Such diversity of influence makes for good eating, and New Paltz has some choice spots. We visited two—the **Gay Nineties Bistro,** a wonderful place for omelets or ice cream, and the **North Light,** a purveyor of modern American cuisine with continental accents. Two other downtown restaurants come highly recommended—**Bacchus,** a gourmet Mexican restaurant, and **Wild Flour Café,** a homey, natural foods kind of place.

All four of these restaurants have well-deserved reputations for quality food, but none are sights to behold. If you are in search of atmosphere, we suggest you venture a little farther from the highway, to Huguenot Street—America's oldest— where you will find the **Locust Tree Inn,** a charming Colonial hostelry in a gorgeous sylvan setting.

GAY NINETIES BISTRO, *Exit 18, New Paltz*

For a funky, pine-paneled, slat-boothed eatery on New Paltz's sloppy Main Street, the Gay Nineties sure surprised us with its food. This is *the* place for eggs at any time of day, we were told, and once inside we saw that everyone in town—from the well-dressed to the dungareed—knew it.

We enjoyed an excellent spinach omelet, served with crisp home fries and whole wheat toast for just $1.80. But that's just the beginning of the Gay Nineties eggstravaganza. Other omelets include, in addition to the expected, such exotic fillers as avocado and zucchini, cream cheese and ricotta, broccoli and sprouts; some are topped with herb sauce or Mornay. They come in all kinds of interesting combinations, with prices ranging from $1.80 to $3.25. You can also order poached eggs Florentine, Benedict, Mornay, Diane, or what they call Frittato Mexicano (with chili peppers).

But there's more here than huevos. Although hardly anything noses over $4 (and many items are under $3), there is also a complete line of full-meal salads, sandwiches, burgers, and Tex-Mex specialties. Each weekday there's a lunch special for $2.50— ours was a broccoli–mushroom–cream cheese crêpe served in a cheese sauce with toothy homemade bread. It would have been a bargain at a much higher price.

And then there's the parade of sweets. It starts out modestly with some very nice cookies, brownies, pastries, and fresh fruit muffins, picks up speed with egg creams, malteds, smoothies, and milk shakes, and roars to its finale in an orgy of ice cream delights. "Foops," the most extreme, is said to consist of bananas, peaches, pineapples, and strawberries, five scoops of ice cream, chocolate syrup, whipped cream, and nuts. It comes with a warning: "Adjust your sucrose abilities as you would any challenge."

HOURS Mon. 7:30 am–5 pm; Wed.–Sun. 7:30 am–9:30 pm; closed Tue.

DIRECTIONS See directions for New Paltz entries, below.

THE NORTH LIGHT, *Exit 18, New Paltz*

* Untried, but a local favorite

Funky chic, the North Light reserves its elegance for what's on the plate, not on the walls. College professors, local businessmen, skiers, and climbers who care less about rough surroundings than smooth dishes give it rave reviews. We have to take their word on faith, since the restaurant was closed when we stopped by.

Lunch offerings are typical of brick-plants-and-oak cafés: homemade soups (gazpacho, cream of cauliflower); sandwiches (Reuben, pastrami, avocado/tomato/Swiss, most between $2.30 and $3); chili, quiche, and other entrées ($4–$7).

Every three weeks the dinner menu changes, but the North Light's loyal clientele maintains that its quality does not. Some examples of what you are likely to find are vegetable crepes Mornay ($6.95), broiled halibut with salsa verde ($8.95), and veal piccata ($9.25).

We were sorry to have missed a chance to eat in this one. Let us know how you find it.

HOURS Tue.–Thu. noon–9 pm; Fri. & Sat. noon–4:30 pm and 6–10 pm. Sunday brunch, noon–3 pm; dinner, 4–9 pm. Closed Mon.

DIRECTIONS FOR NEW PALTZ RESTAURANTS
From Exit 18 follow signs for New Paltz, turning left onto Route 299 West. One and a half miles takes you to the downtown area. The **Gay Nineties** is on your right, shortly before the intersection with Routes 32 and 208. Just past this intersection, on the left, is the **North Light.**

SCHNELLER'S RESTAURANT, *Exit 19, Kingston*

Schneller's calls itself "The Wurst Place in Town," and that it has been since 1956. Originally a butcher shop–grocery, it later expanded to include an upstairs restaurant. But even if your goal is a sit-down meal, the market is worth a visit. It's a carnival of meats and cheeses, all hanging from the ceiling and walls like organ pipes. The shelves are festooned with imported foods, fruits and fresh vegetables, freshly baked breads, strudel, and tortes. If you need to pick up a house gift, you'll have trouble only deciding what to bring.

The festive atmosphere follows you up the stairs. Colorful primitive murals of Old World scenes lead you to the dining area, two pleasant rooms that are sweetly but simply decorated. (A balcony is used in summer.) The amiable waitresses talk about the restaurant with such affection that you might think they owned it (they don't).

Schneller's cuisine ranges from Eastern European peasant to fine continental. The same prized wursts and baked goods sold downstairs appear on the restaurant tables. Stocks for sauces are all homemade from beef, veal, turkey, and goose (yes, goose). Potatoes are fried in lard that's rendered right here, and there's not a preservative, tenderizer, or taste enhancer in the house. As the menu bluntly states, "This is not a fast-food restaurant. We do not use microwaves or buy prefrozen, prepared, institutional, computerized foods. Our kitchen is where it is at."

Indeed it is. From this kitchen emanates some of the most exuberant German food we've come upon. Although sausages are often the repositories of otherwise useless meat byproducts, the homemade bratwurst ($4) we had for lunch at Schneller's seemed to have been made from the finest cuts of pork. It was served with very good bread and tangy German potato salad. Although we weren't at all sorry to have ordered the bratwurst, we looked longingly at our neighbor's sauerbraten, served with red cabbage and spaetzle ($4.80).

If your taste is more American than this, you can get salads, burgers, steaks, and generous sandwiches, all of them quite affordable. There are also platters of wurst, salami, headcheese, and just plain cheese, and, for those who like their meat raw, steak tartare.

The dinner menu is more of the same (most items $7.50–$8.50), introduced by a complimentary Boursin-liverwurst appetizer. As we write, reviewing the alluring list of schnitzels (ten), wursts (eight), and goulashes (three), we find ourselves scheming another trip through Kingston. If you're lucky enough to be there right now, don't miss Schneller's Restaurant. It's the best wurst place we know.

HOURS   Mon. & Tue. 11:30 am–4 pm; Wed. & Thu. 11:30 am–9 pm; Fri. & Sat. 11:30 am–10 pm; closed Sun.

DIRECTIONS   From Exit 19 you enter a traffic circle. Follow signs for Washington Ave. Go ½ mile on Washington to the third traffic light and turn left onto North Front St. Go 2 blocks on North Front and then turn right onto Crown. It's 1 short block to a stop sign and a left turn onto John St. You'll see Schneller's, on the left, as you make the turn. Complicated to read; simple to drive.

COLONIAL DINER
HUB DELICATESSEN, *Exit 19, Kingston*

* *Not great, but quick and cheap*

Both of these are inexpensive, in-and-out sorts of places, which is the main reason to visit either of them instead of Schneller's (above). The diner is a shiny stainless-steel Silk City of '40s vintage; inside, the color turquoise reigns supreme. Lively but not gaudy, the color scheme is refreshing after so many diners upholstered in Day-Glo orange.

A cup of soup here (50 cents) would be considered a bowl almost anywhere else, and a bowl (just 60 cents) is almost beyond measure. We tried the chicken noodle, which was said to be homemade but didn't taste it. Later, we learned that Manhattan clam chowder is their forte. Still, we hardly recommend you go out of your way for the food here unless your love for old diners blinds you to the reality of their cooking.

The Hub is a kosher deli owned by an Italian. Though it's an unlikely marriage, Anthony Paduano happily slices the Hebrew National while whistling *La Bohème*. At the counter up front, you can order your sandwich—corned beef, roast beef, pastrami, chopped liver, etc. ($2.50–$3)—then take it to one of a dozen little tables in the back of the store. There are also knishes, derma (Jewish haggis), bagels with Nova Scotia lox, whitefish, and a creamy rice pudding.

HOURS   **Colonial Diner:** Always open.
           Hub Deli: Mon.–Fri. 8 am–6:30 pm; Sat. 9 am–5 pm; closed Sun.

DIRECTIONS   From Exit 19 follow signs for Kingston. In 1.2 miles you come to a light. Cross intersection in center lane (signs for Route 32 South/Broadway). Bear gently left onto Broadway. You'll see the **Hub Deli** within the first block, on left, then shortly thereafter, on right, the **Colonial Diner.**

ABOUT CATSKILL

Although it's some 2½ miles from the Thruway, Catskill is worth the detour. Packed within a few short blocks on Main Street are a Japanese restaurant, a gourmet shop, a natural foods place, a modern greenhouse café on the river, a tavern serving pub lunches, and the most outstanding example we've seen of an uncelebrated restaurant genus—the village luncheonette.

MAYFLOWER LUNCHEONETTE, *Exit 21, Catskill*

The food is simple: no cooked breakfasts at all—just, as they say around here, "coffee and"; for lunch, standard American sandwiches, neither exciting nor expensive. The soda fountain goes as far as it can in combining ice cream and syrup with various liquids and toppings to make ice cream sodas, floats, sundaes, shakes, malteds, frosts, and frosted malteds. The man behind the counter will happily orient you to soda-jerk lingo and its regional variations across the country.

But what's really special is the place in which this limited menu is served. We consider it the queen of American luncheonettes, a candidate for piece-by-piece transplanting to the Smithsonian Institution someday.

Up front is the old soda fountain, its black marble counter as gleaming, and its hardware as glistening, as the day they were born. The plaster walls are cream-colored with white trim, their moldings delicately detailed at every turn. The rear half of the room is divided by booths, each back-to-back unit carefully cut in an elegant profile from a single hardwood slab.

This American grandeur is not the product of a far-ranging antiques search. Emanuel Cominos, whose family has been scooping, fizzing, and whipping up sweet snacks here since 1933, was never in on the craze for old things. He just liked the shop the way he found it, and did nothing to change it. Nor did he make a big deal of it, proclaiming with a grandiose plaque that it was now to be called "The Sweet Shoppe" or "Ice Cream Parlour." All that he has to show for his taste and restraint is the restaurant's unselfconscious beauty.

Old diners have had their share of celebration in recent years; if their cousins, the small-town lunchrooms and soda fountains, ever get their due, paintings of the Mayflower will probably appear in galleries, books, and on Christmas cards. You might want to get there first.

HOURS   Mon.–Sat. 6 am–9 pm; closed Sun.

DIRECTIONS   See Harbor Lights, below.

HARBOR LIGHTS, *Exit 21, Catskill*

* *Untried, but likely*

It's a sunny winter day. We're at a window table in the Harbor Lights restaurant, where no seat is far from the view of Catskill Creek. We are trying, fruitlessly, to imagine a spot more lovely than this one. A redwood and cedar building with clean lines and sharp angles. But soft touches too—plants, woolly wall hangings, watercolors. Different dining levels, each with south-facing windows looking out onto the creek. Two outdoor dining decks perched above a 65-boat dock.

We doubt we'll ever find a dreamier setting for a meal, but we can only dream about how it will taste. We're visiting in February when the restaurant, alas, is closed for vacation, and although we sit by the window and chat with the manager, there isn't a thing to eat.

So we can tell you what Harbor Lights serves but not how it tastes. The lunch menu is brick-plants-and-oak café fare all the way: in-vogue sandwiches, embellished burgers, fancy salads, quiche, etc. ($3.50–$5). At dinnertime, the menu changes hats, donning the attire of a steak and seafood house. Sirloin, filet mignon, fried scallops, veal Cordon Bleu, coquilles St. Jacques, king crab (most, $9–$12). Also, their own steak Cagney (tender-loin stuffed with crabmeat in Newburg and topped with Hollandaise, $13.25).

We can only assure you that it almost doesn't matter how the food is. The setting is four-star.

HOURS Mon.–Sat. 11:30 am–2 pm and 5–10 pm; Sun. 1–8 pm. No Saturday lunch in winter. Closed mid-January to early March.

DIRECTIONS From Exit 21 turn left, following sign for Catskill. It's 2½ miles along a curvy road, but if you stay on the main thoroughfare you eventually find yourself on Main St. in the center of town. The **Mayflower Luncheonette** is on your right. For the **Harbor Lights,** pass the Mayflower, go through the light, and take the second right (Green St.). Driveway is on the left.

RED'S RESTAURANT, *Exit 21B, West Coxsackie*

Restaurants that assault you with a battery of billboards aren't usually our type. Aside from blighting the countryside, they tend to serve food blighted by mass production and mechanical preparation. Signs crowing about Red's Restaurant line the Thruway for 20 miles, but we went in anyway. We're glad we did.

This is the original Red's, much imitated elsewhere. It's large, all right, but oh, what charm. A low-lying building with awnings and window boxes running its considerable length, the place looks and feels like an overgrown bungalow. Inside, it's pretty as an old Worcester car in its own way: gleaming knotty-pine paneling, red leather-backed chairs, and varnished oak floor.

When they opened Red's 40 years ago, the Barber family wanted to break the old axiom, "Don't eat steak in a seafood house or seafood in a steakhouse." They pride themselves on doing both well, but we especially appreciated the small touches that make this family restaurant special.

Like its famous "pink sauce," an accompaniment to all fish dishes. It's made from mayonnaise, chili, and other spices. With a taste all its own, it can best be described as a cross between tartar sauce and Thousand Island dressing. But not quite. Or Red's blue cheese salad dressing: the blue cheese, sour cream, garlic, and spices are whipped with air to a super-creamy consistency.

Red's makes all its own soup stocks, and you can taste their goodness in the goulash. Excellent. The Manhattan clam chowder is also good, full of chunky clam pieces. And Red's always tries to do something interesting with vegetables. If you order spinach, for example, you'll find a robust preparation of spinach, onions, olive oil, and garlic. Carrots are glazed with honey or maple syrup.

If you aren't stuck on steaks or seafood, try the liver here. It's sliced to order, thick and juicy, and served with bacon and onions. Raves.

Most dinner entrées run $7.50 to $9, served with rolls, salad, potato, and vegetable or cole slaw (homemade, of course). Whole-meal salads are about $4.50, except for the chunky lobster salad that features 8 ounces of cold lobster meat for $12.90. Sandwiches, available at any time, are $3 to $4. Low-priced half portions are offered to juniors, seniors, or anyone else with a skimpy appetite.

Whatever you eat at Red's, leave room for the rice pudding. If it can be found creamier, we'd like to know where.

HOURS Sun. & Tue.–Fri. 11:30 am–9:30 pm; Sat. 11:30 am–10:30 pm. Closed Mondays except in July and August.

DIRECTIONS   From Exit 21B turn left onto U.S. 9W South, following sign for Coxsackie. Go 1.8 miles, and it's on your right.

JACK'S OYSTER HOUSE, *Exit 23, Albany*

When New York City's mayor Ed Koch declared that the city of Albany had nothing to offer but a certain downtown restaurant, he left upstaters with little doubt on two accounts: who they didn't want as their next governor, and which restaurant he meant.

Jack's has been in Albany longer than just about anybody except Jack Rosenstein, 88, who started the business when he was 20. It's where everybody who's anybody gets taken to dinner when visiting New York's capital city. Despite all this prestige, there's nothing stodgy about the place. It's still the salty, downtown seafood house that it's always been, with lots of varnished old wood, a checkerboard floor, white tablecloths, leather-backed chairs, and a pervading spirit of crusty savoir-faire. But what really clinches the restaurant's character are the waiters, all of them with black ties, white aprons, gruff voices, and big bellies. They seem as much a part of the decor as the woodwork.

Except for three Jewish holidays a year, Jack himself is in the kitchen shucking oysters and clams. His underlings are the cooks who have been making chowder and stew to the same recipe for 40 years. A few are rank neophytes with only 25 years on the job.

For all that has been said about Jack's seafood, it is ironic that what we found most outstanding was the Roquefort dressing. Truly *great* it was—the best we've had anywhere. But we don't dispute any claims for Jack's fine seafood. The Manhattan clam chowder was very, very good—not so tomatoey as to overpower the fresh vegetables and clams. A tasty shrimp Newburg sauce covered the moist and tender filet of sole. And a basket of fresh breads was a welcome accompaniment.

Each day a full page of specials is printed to reflect the market. Visiting in winter, we found broiled scallops with clams Genovese, filet of haddock, swordfish, and butterfly shrimp as well as a number of meat dishes. Every spring, beginning about a month too soon, Jack's phones ring incessantly with inquiries about Maryland soft-shell crabs. Shad and shad roe are also early season hits.

Dinner entrées, with vegetable, salad, and potato or rice, run roughly $8.25 to $12.25. At lunch, $4.50 to $6.95. Hot or cold sandwiches and omelets are also available at lunchtime ($3.25–$4.25), and at any time of day you'll find clam or oyster stew ($4.75), chowder ($1.35), or borscht ($1.20).

HOURS   Every day 11:30 am–10 pm.

DIRECTIONS   From Exit 23 go straight (signs for I-787/Downtown). Stay on the long network of ramps, following signs for U.S. 20 West. On street level, immediately turn left and pass under elevated highway, then turn right onto Broadway North (signs are clear). Go 3 short blocks to light just after enormous SUNY building. Left here (State St., but no apparent sign) and you'll see Jack's on your left. Quite easy, really; it takes just 5 minutes to get here.

GEMINI RESTAURANT JAZZ CAFÉ, *Exit 23, Albany*

It sounds like a nightclub but it isn't. It's a charming, funky hole in the wall with no more than a dozen small calico-covered tables. Prominently positioned in the large bay window is a grand piano that is gustily played by Fats Jefferson, but at no time does the music prohibit conversation or concentration on the excellent food.

A mushroom Stroganoff crepe, for instance—mushrooms simmered in Burgundy, sour cream, and spices, wrapped in a light crêpe shell—was richly flavored yet delicate. For $3.95, it came with wonderful unpeeled, not-too-greasy home fries. We felt like gorging on mushrooms that day, so we also tried Gemini's beer-battered fried mushrooms, served with an unusual strawberry rum dip ($2.75). Our cream of vegetable soup held big chunks of obviously fresh vegetables, boldly seasoned with red pepper.

We didn't try them, but the Argentine turnovers called "empanadas"—chicken, beef, and cheese—were highly recommended ($3.50). Other Gemini specialties include chicken dishes (honey walnut chicken, curried chicken, others, all $6.50), crab-meat-stuffed rainbow trout ($7.50), and pork chops à l'orange ($7.50). There are also 6-ounce hamburgers ($3.25 and up), all kinds of crêpes, and 3-egg omelets ($3 and up). For drinks, you might like hot spiced cider or any of a dozen coffees flavored with orange peel, anise, cinnamon, nutmeg, and the like.

Fats Jefferson is a bald and buoyant black man true to his name. In the 75-plus years he's been tickling the ivories, he has picked up just about every style of music that's hit the charts— ragtime, '30s-style cabaret, boogie-woogie, big-band swing, hot jazz, cool jazz, modern pop. He's a one-man show worth going out of the way for, and he's free with your meal. But there's a $2.50 per person minimum to pay his way ($4 on Friday and weekends).

HOURS   Every day 4 pm–1 or 2 am.

DIRECTIONS   From Exit 23 go straight, following signs for I-787/ Downtown. Stay on the long network of ramps, following signs for U.S. 20 West. In town, U.S. 20 West is called Madison Ave. (signs are clear). Take Madison up the hill through the Empire State Plaza and 0.9 mile from the bottom of the hill you'll see Gemini on your right, at the corner of Madison and Dove. It's actually very easy to get here, and it takes between 5 and 10 minutes, depending on traffic (which is surprisingly light in the evening).

NOTE: At this point the New York State Thruway becomes I-90. Travelers continuing on the Thruway toward Buffalo should skip to page 129.

Adirondack Northway

ABOUT SARATOGA SPRINGS

It's a grand old town, haunted by the ghosts of Diamond Jim Brady, Lillian Russell, and several Victorian hotels. Lovely houses line the street from Exit 14 to downtown, and once there you'll find memorable food in all price ranges. And don't forget **Sam's Place** at Exit 13S, the diner with Pavarotti. We passed up two excellent places, **Chez Sophie** and **Charles,** judging them too expensive for a traveler's meal. But if you've the time and the purse, do check them out.

SAM'S PLACE, *Exit 13S, Saratoga Springs*

* Untested, but unique; a local favorite

How about a streamlined stainless-steel diner with great Northern Italian cooking and Pavarotti on the stereo? Even at $10 a meal it sounded like our sort of place, and we rushed over to check it out. Dinner only, alas, and we were there for lunch. But it's too intriguing a possibility to drop. So we pass on to you what we heard and urge you to let us know what you find.

HOURS   Summer: every day from 4:30 pm–10 pm or later, depending on the traffic. Fall, winter, & spring: Thu.–Sun. 4:30 pm–10 pm or later; closed Mon., Tue., Wed.

DIRECTIONS   Exit 13S puts you on U.S. 9 South. Go ½ mile and you'll see Sam's Place on the left, in blue accents, beneath a big "DINER" sign.

C'EST CHEESE, *Exit 14, Saratoga Springs*

Frank Lasky wanted it to be just a gourmet deli, the Zabar's of Saratoga Springs. But so tempting was the smoked turkey on bagel twist that the number of tables just kept growing. Now there are 16 of them (little ones, with just enough room for two plates, salt and pepper), and people seem never to tire of his infinite variations on the bagel-cheese-meat-and-garnish theme. They like the spanakopita too, and the fish, the salads, the fresh-squeezed juices, and the desserts. He hasn't gotten any complaints about the prices, either—$2.99 for bread, cheese, soup, and fruit; quiche for $2.09, sandwiches for $2.95, and a cheese platter (there are 70 kinds in the store) for $3.50.

C'est Cheese is a busy, happy place, full of delicious aromas and ideal for a quick meal. It's located right on Broadway. Nearby, old hotels lend a sense of faded grandeur to the scene, but when you stop into Frank's shop the step is lively and the food delicious.

Half of it is what Frank intended it to be, a gourmet shop—light, bright, and pleasant, with $20-a-pound chocolates imported directly from Belgium and picked up by Frank at the Albany airport. From the deli counter you carry your order to a table by the window. It's hard to choose from the tempting array, and the profusion of signs doesn't help much, but you'll probably like whatever you end up with.

HOURS July and Aug.: Mon.–Sat. 10 am–8 pm; Sun. 10 am–3 pm. Sept.–June: Mon.–Sat. 10 am–6 pm; closed Sun. Closed first two weeks of January.

DIRECTIONS See end of Exit 14 entries, page 115.

MRS. LONDON'S BAKE SHOP,
Exit 14, Saratoga Springs

Pretty, pink, pricey, and delicious is the only way to describe Mrs. London's. Not only are the tables pink marble and the wallpaper pink flowered, but the flowers are pink too, along with the waitresses' uniforms, the curtains, and the menus. It's charming, and even if you're no pinkophile, come for the unforgettably rich and wonderful whiskey cake.

This dark, buttery, not-overly-sweet gem abounds with the deep, rich flavor of two kinds of chocolate, subtly laced with whiskey flavor. Best of all, every other bite simply explodes with a little burst of fresh fruit flavor. You won't soon forget it—or its $3.50 price tag.

There's a lot more in this vein—tarts, cheesecakes, puffs, Napoleons, croissants, and brioches—but you can also get a memorable breakfast or lunch here. Poached eggs ensconced in a pair of brioches and served with Hollandaise ought to prove a welcome change from "two over light," but they'll cost you $5.50. So will Brussels waffles or French toast (from brioche bread) with Black Forest ham and real maple syrup.

Lentil soup ($3.50), quiche ($5.50), smoked chicken salad ($5.75), fettucini with broccoli ($7.25), and lamb curry ($8.50) make up the lunch menu, along with crêpes and salads.

We're not sure Mrs. London cooks as well as she bakes, but if she even comes close, it'll be worth the money.

HOURS   Wed.–Sun. 8 am–3 or 4 pm, with desserts till 5 pm; closed Mon. & Tue.

DIRECTIONS   See end of Exit 14 entries, page 115.

LILLIAN'S, *Exit 14, Saratoga Springs*

Lillian's is a brash and bold brick-plants-and-oak café. There's plenty of ersatz Tiffany and imported barn beams, as well as poster-sized portraits of Diamond Jim Brady and actress Lillian

Russell, both of whom lived in town and were rumored to have held secret rendezvous in a tunnel dug between their mansions. The hint of mischief and the loud jazz set the tone at Lillian's. Diamond Jim, who had a stomach as big as his bankroll, probably wouldn't tunnel into this place just because it took his lover's name, but Lillian's has his kind of menu: good steaks and sandwiches, at prices lower than he was accustomed to—$2.35 for a simple burger, less than $10 for most dinners.

HOURS Mon.–Thu. 11:30 am–4 pm and 5 pm–midnight (lunch menu only after 10 pm); Fri. & Sat. 11:30 am–4 pm and 5 pm–1 am (lunch menu only after 11 pm). Closed Sundays, except in July and August; then, same hours as on Friday and Saturday.

DIRECTIONS FOR EXIT 14 RESTAURANTS

From Exit 14 bear right from the ramp onto Route 9P North (Union St.). Go 1.6 miles to stop sign at end of Union. Turn right, go 1 block to the light, and turn left onto Spring St. Go 3 blocks on Spring to light at Broadway. Right on Broadway and through one light. For **Mrs. London's** take the next right onto Phila St. Go 1 block; it's on the left. For **C'est Cheese** and **Lillian's,** continue straight on Broadway. C'est Cheese is on the right at the next light; Lillian's is a few doors farther down.

BOSTON CANDY KITCHEN, *Exit 18, Glens Falls*

How about lunch in a true candy store/soda fountain, complete with checkerboard linoleum floor, marble countertop, a round mirror etched with Art Deco ice cream cones, and fluorescent lighting? It's a noisy, happy place where everyone knows everyone, but if you don't, it won't matter much.

Hamburgers are all of 90 cents; turkey sandwiches, $2.50; and clubs, $3.25. You can get decent soups with chunky fresh vegetables, and the shrimp sandwich, if not so chunky, had nevertheless a quite lively flavor.

Get dessert from the old-fashioned fountain or succumb to the menagerie of chocolate bunnies, birds, and bears that adorn a large percentage of the store. The Boston Candy Kitchen really is just that. In the back room (not much bigger than your kitchen) the chocolate gets poured into the innumerable molds and out come the bunnies, brown ones and white ones, up to 3 feet tall.

If you're interested, show it and they'll give you a tour before you can ask.

The Ferris family has been doing it this way since 1929, and from the looks of things they'll keep right at it for another 50 years. People who enjoy their work this much just don't give it up.

HOURS Mon.–Sat. 7 am–4 pm; closed Sun.

DIRECTIONS From Exit 18 turn right if northbound, left if southbound, and go 1.3 miles to a fork at the second light. Bear right onto Hudson Ave. (unmarked) and go 0.6 mile to Elm. Left on Elm, ½ block, on the right.

BRANDYWINE'S, *Exit 18, Glens Falls*

It's not all that hard to find good restaurants that make everything from scratch, but we haven't come across many in small towns that make each and every sauce to order for each and every dish. But that's how chef Sue Prescott wants it, and thus does she infuse everything with her delicate touch.

Brandywine's is a very handsome restaurant in which dark wood, antique fixtures, and white tablecloths set a relaxed but dignified tone. The lounge is Victorian pubby, featuring a stately bar and glorious brass chandelier rescued from an Odd Fellows hall. The dining room is lighter, and if you choose it for lunch ($3–$4.50 for a good selection of sandwiches, omelets, quiche, salads, and soups) you can watch midday life in Glens Falls through the large front windows.

Dinners are $8–$14, all of them continental. Chicken comes à la Russe, Marengo, Kiev, Citron, or Brandywine (less than $9 each), the latter being a breaded breast wrapped around a hard-boiled egg, deep fried and served with Hollandaise. Six veal dishes, three steaks, and a fish du jour complete the menu, except for a dozen sandwiches, which, luckily for the traveler, are still available during dinner at near the midday prices.

And do try a dessert. Sue is especially proud of them.

HOURS Mon.–Fri. 11:30 am–9 pm; Sat. 5–9 pm; closed Sun.

DIRECTIONS From Exit 18 turn right if northbound, left if southbound, and go 1.3 miles to a fork at the second light. Bear right onto Hudson Ave. (unmarked). Go 0.7 mile to a large, five-corner intersection. Take sharpest possible left onto Glen St. Brandywine's is ½ block down, on the left, dressed in green.

PROSPECT MOUNTAIN DINER AND RICKSHAW

COFFEE AND . . . , *Exit 22, Lake George*

* *Untried, but famous*

Lake George is the Atlantic City of the Adirondacks, only smaller, nicer, and minus the gambling. But it does have almost as many touristy restaurants. If you pass these by, you'll find at the other end of town a much-written-about diner and Chinese restaurant, which give you the choice of Oriental tranquillity or Edward Hopper Americana. It's two restaurants side by side, bound to each other by a narrow corridor. You can have your wonton soup amidst stainless steel or bamboo, but diner fare is served in the diner only. Closed, alas, in winter.

Back on the strip is Coffee And . . . , a pleasant little lunchroom open all year round. It specializes in large, thin, light pancakes with syrups of fresh-ground coconut, lingonberry, and more familiar flavors. Three pancakes go for $2.25, and they were really quite nice. We also enjoyed the shiny robin's-egg-blue walls, which made us think of spring. Whatever the season, they have soup and sandwiches here too, all at reasonable prices.

> **HOURS** **Prospect Mountain Diner and Rickshaw:** Summer (mid-June–Labor Day): always open. Fall (Labor Day–late Oct.): open at all times except Tue. 10 pm–Wed. 10 pm. Winter (late Oct.–early May): closed for season. Spring (early May–mid-June): same as for fall.
> **Coffee And . . . :** Summer: every day 6:30 am–2:30 pm. Winter: same as summer but closed on Sundays.

DIRECTIONS From Exit 22 turn right if northbound, left if southbound. Almost immediately you'll see signs for U.S. 9 and Lake George. Right onto U.S. 9 and go 0.8 mile to **Coffee And** . . . , on the right. Another 0.8 mile brings you to the **Prospect Mountain Diner and Rickshaw,** also on the right.

THE PILLARS RESTAURANT AND MOTEL,
Exit 23, Warrensburg

There's not much beyond steaks and seafood on the menu, but Ray Wassel has a way of making a prime rib more than just a great chunk of meat. We couldn't believe the size of it. "Doggy bags are our specialty," said Ray in a proud, gravelly voice. But nothing could induce him to reveal the special touch he imparted to the natural juices. Whatever, it was light and wonderful, turning a merely great rib into a memorable event. Guests at neighboring tables overheard our raves, and a lively discussion ensued across the room about the enormous portions and how good absolutely everything was.

It's that kind of place—a small and friendly combination inn/motel/restaurant. The dining room is a warm but unpretentious collection of ten Early American tables, a few couches before a fireplace, and a small bar off to one corner. Guests lounge about before and after meals, chatting with each other or with Ray, who drives them to the ski slopes, hiking trails, and train station. He's been doing it for five years now, ever since he retired from the Americana Hotels to start his own more intimate operation. And his customers love it.

They don't mind the prices either, which are moderate considering the quality of the food. Dinners are $8–$12; any of a dozen sandwiches at lunchtime run from $2.25 to $2.95. For breakfast you can get two eggs, toast, sausage, potatoes, juice, and coffee for $2.45! Rooms are $30–$40 for a double. But if you want to be in the area for a while, call Ray to ask about his package deals with the ski areas (518) 623-5361. A young couple from Rochester said it cost so little they were embarrassed to eat the food—$26 a day for lodging, breakfast, dinner, cocktail, lift tickets, and transportation to the slopes!

HOURS   Breakfast: every day 7–10 am. Lunch: summer and fall only, every day 11:30 am–1:30 pm. (NOTE: Across the street is Potter's Diner. They'll have lunch if you miss it at the Pillars.) Dinner: every day 5–9:30 pm. Closed for two weeks in early spring and two weeks in late fall.

DIRECTIONS   From Exit 23 turn left if northbound, right if southbound, and go 0.1 mile to Route 9. Turn right onto Route 9 North and go 0.9 mile; it's on the left.

DRAKE'S RESTAURANT, *Exit 28, Schroon Lake*

* *Slim pickin's*

It's 30 miles from Schroon Lake to anything we could find to write about, and though the roads are full of tourist eateries in summer, even those are hard to come by once the snow flies. Drake's, a year-round place with a local clientele, doesn't serve lunch in winter, but it does put up some pretty good sandwiches in summer—Reubens, burgers, turkey, and the like at $3.50–$4. Dinners are simple Italian and American affairs ($5–$8, a lot less for kids). The decor is very plain, despite an abundance of pine paneling, but there's a most welcoming wood stove in the front room.

HOURS   June 30–Labor Day: every day 7 am–10 pm. Labor Day–June 30: Thu.–Mon. 5–9 pm; closed Tue. & Wed.

DIRECTIONS   From Exit 28 turn left if southbound, right if northbound. Go 100 yards to blinking light. Turn right onto Route 9 South and go 1½ miles to Drake's; it's on the right.

CORNER DRUG STORE, *Exit 31, Westport*

* *Color, not cuisine*

Its pink walls bear a picture of local celebrities Dan and Brenda Kirsher, and for $2 you can get their hot single, "Chattanooga Shoe Shine Boy," with "I Don't Want to Cry" on the flip side. You can also get sandwiches here, in an environment all but unchanged since 1957—and not because anyone tried to preserve it.

The people behind the counter are more than just friendly. They'll tell you all about ice fishing on Lake Champlain—how and when to get your shack out and why you shouldn't do it with your Bronco, no matter how thick the ice. They'll also lament that these days almost no one's even heard of a cherry Coke.

Whether you've heard of it or not, you can get one here.

HOURS   Mon.–Sat. 7 am–5 pm; closed Sun.

DIRECTIONS   See Inn on the Library Lawn, below.

THE INN ON THE LIBRARY LAWN, *Exit 31, Westport*

If moderately priced meals with a continental touch and the warm, friendly feel of a country inn appeal to you, then by all means drive the 4½ miles to the Inn on the Library Lawn. Whether you're after a pita burger with sherried mushrooms ($2.75) or chicken breast stuffed with bacon, artichokes, capers, and thyme ($7.95), you're sure to enjoy what's served in the tastefully modernized dining room. And you're sure to get your money's worth.

Handsomely set tables, new woodwork, a wall of books, and large bay windows that overlook Lake Champlain set a clean, light, and comfortable tone. The inn has been around since 1900, but had stood vacant five years when Joan and Walter Hawley revived its ten rooms and restaurant. Now they're doing their best to combine city taste and country cordiality, producing even such rarities as roast quail (from a nearby farm) in juniper berry sauce ($9.95).

Lunch at the inn can cost as little as $2.25 for a turkey sandwich with chips and pickle. Or go for broke and try medallions of beef served with egg Benedict and broiled tomato ($4.50).

An unusual touch to the dinner menu is a different egg dish every night ($5). There's a spinach pasta dish with ricotta and ham for just 50 cents more. About ten other entrées complete the menu, $12.25 tops. Affordable elegance and a most pleasant break from the long haul to Montreal.

HOURS May 15–Oct. 15: every day, noon–2 pm and 5–9 pm. Oct. 16–May 14: Sun.–Wed., dinner only, by reservation; Thu.–Sat. noon–2 pm and 5–9 pm.

DIRECTIONS From Exit 31 turn right if northbound, left if southbound, onto Route 9N South. Go 4½ easy miles straight through tiny Westport. The Inn is on the right, at Washington St., and the **Corner Drug Store** is across the street.

NORTH COUNTRY CLUB RESTAURANT, *Exit 34, Keesville*

A good place for a quick sandwich is this Ethan Alleny, family sort of restaurant with Muzak. The sandwiches are big, there are a lot of them, and the prices are good ($1.50–$2.45 for garden varieties, $3.95 for a triple-decker club). Furthermore, the people are friendly and the clientele mostly local. For full dinners you can spend up to $16.50 for surf 'n turf, or as little as $4–$6 for Italian dishes, but we think you'll be happiest with the burger at $1.75.

HOURS Mon.–Fri. 11:30 am–10 pm; Sat. & Sun. noon–1 am.

DIRECTIONS From Exit 34 turn right onto Route 9N North. Go 1.3 miles to Route 9 and turn left. It's on the left, just after the turn.

McINTOSH'S APPLE BARREL, *Exit 35, Peru*

According to owner Brett Heiss, this part of New York is the largest McIntosh apple growing area in the world. So when this Manhattan cabbie with a taste for fine food turned restaurateur, he decided to take advantage of the local specialty. Right next to duckling à l'orange ($12.50) you'll find duckling with apples and brandy. There's veal McIntosh too, in which he sautés the meat with a touch of apple brandy and then adds slices of the fruit to sour cream to make the sauce.

The veal McIntosh was quite good, but don't get the wrong picture. While the ample menu has many continental-style dishes, its foundation is steaks and seafood ($8.50–$17). We suspect more apples end up in the pie than in the chicken breast with apple dressing ($8.75). Still, if the skill brought to the veal carries over into the more common dishes, the prime rib here has just got to be far better than average.

Many plants and an antique store's worth of old tools make up the decor of this dinner-only restaurant, along with heavy pine furnishings and exposed beams (it really was an apple barn once, built in 1830). The total effect is light and pleasantly cluttered, except in the more intimate upstairs loft.

HOURS   Mon.–Thu. 5–10 pm; Fri. & Sat. 5–11 pm; Sun. 1–9 pm.

DIRECTIONS   From Exit 35 turn left if northbound, right if southbound. It's the first building on the right, an apple core's toss from the Northway.

ANTHONY'S CLASSIC CUISINE, *Exit 37, Plattsburgh*

Anthony's would like to be a full continental restaurant, but local tastes this far upstate just don't allow for that. Good news for the traveler, actually, since it allows a choice of familiar and unusual dishes, all of them prepared with care, in an environment that is tasteful and relaxing.

Of the four continental dishes, veal Honfleuroise is the house specialty—thinly sliced veal topped with shrimp, crabmeat, and scallops in a cognac-laced cream sauce ($12.95). But if that sort of thing doesn't suit your mood, you'll find an ample choice of steak and seafood dishes ($9–$15), prepared, we suspect, with a little extra touch here and there. Sandwiches with soup or salad ($3.95) are available in the pub.

The decor at Anthony's shows an obvious concern for quality. A converted farmhouse has been done over in light woods, brick, and plants to produce an intimate environment of nooks and crannies. White tablecloths provide a touch of elegance to the otherwise informal tone. An odd feature of the place is the sunken dining room just two tables wide, which had been an indoor swimming pool in the old farmhouse.

The lounge is more on the earthy side, but not so casual as to exclude Victorian sofas and a piano bar—quiet jazz or mellow oldies on weekend nights.

HOURS   Lunch (Apr.–Oct. only): Mon.–Fri. 11:30 am–2 pm. Dinner: Sun.–Fri. 5–9 pm; Sat. 5–10 pm.

DIRECTIONS   From Exit 37 turn left at light onto Route 3 West. It's on the right, immediately at the exit.

CARBUR'S, *Exit 37, Plattsburgh*

Carbur's in Plattsburgh is a branch office of the Burlington, Vermont, original. Carbur's specializes in great sandwiches and soups in an atmosphere of barnboard, beams, and Packard ads. It's comfortably subdued and quite pleasant, especially in the Rib-It dining room, where the varnished stone walls are the original foundation. And the food *is* good, from the tasty, chunky beef and mushroom soup to the hefty sandwiches.

These come with names like "Lady Chatterley's Liver," "Burger Man of Alcatraz," and "Ausable Spasm" ("what happens if you overgorge yourself"), which is roast beef with Swiss, tomato, and garlic mayonnaise.

While waiting for your "Sanitary Landfill," which may dispose of you forever, you can read all about the world according to Carbur in a monster menu of 25 pages. In addition to sections on salads, beverages, and vegetarian dishes, it even has some spicy parts: one sandwich is called the Bellows Falls, which you are asked not to mispronounce lest you embarrass the waitress. It consists of "slices from the erogenous zone of turkey, corny [*sic*] beef, provolone cheese, lettuce, tomato and chili mayo in a club sandwich." Prices for most sandwiches run a bit over $3, usually some oddball figure like $3.17. Anything for a chuckle.

Full dinners are less playful—mostly steaks and seafood ($6–$14) called by their mundane names, though the menu writers couldn't resist a few rib ticklers in the Rib-It Room.

HOURS   Mon.–Thu. 11:30 am–9 pm; Fri. & Sat. 11:30 am–11 pm; Sun. noon–9 pm.

DIRECTIONS   See end of Plattsburgh entries, page 125.

PHOENICIA, *Exit 37, Plattsburgh*

In the '70s it was quiche. In the '80s it may be falafel that steals America's culinary heart. If you haven't had a chance to try it, stop in at Phoenicia.

This is a small and uninspired lunchroom converted to a Lebanese restaurant by Bahia and Ibrahim Dergham, a mother-and-son team who fled their country's civil war in 1975. All they brought were each other and the cooking ability that Bahia had used in feeding a family of six.

To make falafel, she soaks five different kinds of beans overnight and each morning grinds them with onion, parsley, cumin, and other spices. When a sandwich is ordered, she forms the falafel paste into ovals, fries them, and envelops the lightly browned nuggets in two halves of pita. We quite enjoyed our falafel sandwich ($1.45), which was large and nicely flavored with a light tahini sauce.

For appetizers, Phoenicia also serves stuffed grape leaves, hummus, and baba ganoush (all $1.25). We tried the ganoush and appreciated its sweet eggplant flavor; it certainly wasn't wanting for garlic. There are also three kinds of kebab—the familiar shish kebab with chunks of top round; kefta kebab with ground beef, parsley, and onion; and kibbe kebab, in which ground beef and barley are stuffed with onion and pine nuts (all around $2).

You can also get American-style breakfasts, hamburgers, and meat pies here. But do dip into the exotic at least enough to try one of Bahia's baklavas for dessert; she makes them with cashews, almonds, and walnuts. Take your pick.

HOURS   Mon.–Wed. 7 am–midnight; Thu.–Sat. open 24 hours; closed Sun.

DIRECTIONS   See end of Plattsburgh entries, page 125.

THE STEAKMAN, *Exit 37, Plattsburgh*

It's not the finest food or the most handsome decor this side of Lake Champlain, but it is a 24-hour-a-day Tad's Steakhouse sort of place that offers two (count 'em, two) 6-ounce rib steaks, two baked potatoes, and double portions of soup, salad, and garlic bread—all for just $6.90. It may not be so cheap when you get there, but we weren't about to pass up such a bargain. It was certainly worth the price.

There are also fish dinners at $2.69, and hefty cheeseburgers with fries for $1.99. You walk your tray past the stack of baked potatoes by the grill and carry it off to a dark, fairly cozy corner. Not bad, but nothing to inspire poetry either—unless you rave about the money you save.

HOURS   Always open.

DIRECTIONS FOR PLATTSBURGH RESTAURANTS
From Exit 37 turn right onto Route 3 East, following signs for Plattsburgh. Go 1.1 miles through the fast-food forest, then bear left at the

fork onto Cornelia St. Go 1.2 miles on Cornelia to Route 9 (Margaret Pl.). Turn right. **Carbur's** is immediately on your left. For the **Steakman,** continue along Margaret and you'll see it on the right at Clinton St. For **Phoenicia,** turn left onto Court St. just past Carbur's. At the end of Court you'll be at City Hall Place; Phoenicia is across the street (sign says B & J).

I-90

New York, Pennsylvania

New York State Thruway

CHIEF TAGHKANIC DINER, *Exit B2, East Chatham*

It'll take you only a minute to reach this spotlessly clean diner; see page 224.

DIRECTIONS   From Exit B2 enter Taconic State Parkway South. In about 1 mile, take the first exit (N.Y. 295). Turn left, pass under the highway, and you'll see it on your left.

JACKSON'S OLD CHATHAM HOUSE, *Exit B2, Old Chatham*

* *Far, but the best around*

There's no sign claiming "Washington Slept Here," but at Jackson's they'll tell you that Theodore Roosevelt's great-grand-father once had a store on this very spot. It burned down in the early 1800s. The building that replaced it looks something like a cross between a lodge and a country inn; it serves sandwiches, steaks, and other American specialties in an atmosphere of deer trophies and rifles. Teddy would have liked it.

We chatted with manager Michael Diem as he brought in armloads of firewood to feed the two potbellied stoves. "This is a well-behaved, fun place," he explained, and credited that spirit to the mix of classes and ages that frequent the restaurant. To encourage families with children, any item on the menu is available to them at half price.

Although food is served in the old lounge, the main dining

127

area is a new addition. Furnished in Ethan Allen Colonial, it's not as authentic or charming as the front room, but neither is it overbearingly tacky.

For our lunch, we enjoyed the day's special, a fresh spinach soufflé with ground beef. For $3.25, it was an excellent bargain, served with peas (frozen but decent) and huge "ranch fries." These were potatoes that had been quartered lengthwise, partially baked, and then fried. Delicious. Other lunch items include cold meat and seafood platters ($5–$6), hamburgers ($2.50), grilled cheese variations ($2 and up), deli sandwiches ($4), and omelets ($3 and up).

All except the platters are served during the dinner hour, when a large selection of beef, poultry, seafood, and veal dishes (most, $10–$13) is added to the menu. A five-rib rack of lamb (with or without garlic) is the house specialty, and from what we could see, it should feed two heartily, although the menu specifies "serves one" ($15.95). In fact, all the portions looked prodigious, a house policy that Michael attributes to the country-inn ethic of abundance. His advice to guests on their way to Jackson's is, "Save your appetite."

The Shaker Museum is just a mile and a half from Jackson's. Stroll around it if you feel the need to walk off your meal.

HOURS Lunch: Wed.–Sun. noon–2 pm. Dinner: Tue.–Sun. 4–10 pm. Closed Mon.

DIRECTIONS From Exit B2 bear right (sign: "Commercial Traffic") and then turn left, following signs for N.Y. 295. After 1.3 miles turn left at a T onto N.Y. 295 East. Go 0.7 mile and turn left at sign for Old Chatham. It's 3.2 miles down a winding road through beautiful Shaker country. On your right.

NOTE: At this point, the New York State Thruway becomes I-87 for travelers headed in the direction of New York City. Please turn to page 110; it will be necessary to work backward because restaurants are listed in this book from south to north.

JACK'S OYSTER HOUSE, *I-687 Interchange, Albany*

See page 109 for a description of this excellent seafood house where everyone who's anyone dines in Albany.

DIRECTIONS   From exit labeled "I-687" (no number) follow signs for Albany/Rensselaer. In about ¾ mile take Clinton Avenue exit. At first light (end of ramp), turn left onto Broadway. Turn right at the third traffic light (not counting blinking light) onto State St. Jack's is on your left; a parking lot is 1 block past it.

RUBY'S DINER, *Exits 25 & 26, Schenectady*

* *Color, not cuisine*

One of the most common myths about diners is that they are made from retired railroad cars. During the heyday of dinerdom —the '20s through '40s—diners actually were made to look like railroad cars because railroads represented the ultimate in traveling luxury, an imaginary trip to some faraway place. But in fact, the closest most diners got to riding the rails was atop the flatcar that hauled them from the factory to their resting place.

Ruby's Diner is the rare—perhaps the only—exception. It really *is* a converted railroad car but, ironically, it doesn't look like one. That's because the old car was split lengthwise and widthwide. Each of the quarters was then spread out and the big space in the middle filled up with tables and chairs. New walls and a roof were built to connect the various segments. You have to look hard to see the remnants of Ruby's origin, but they're there: thumb-latch windows, mahogany booths, and tiny rectangular clerestory windows behind the counter.

It's not exactly shining or spotless, but that doesn't bother the men who work at the GE plant across the street. This is the most local of workingman's diners, and it's a good opportunity for travelers to peek in on the industrialized side of upstate New York. What we saw we liked, especially the middle-aged waitresses who clucked over their customers—and with each other. We witnessed two of them enthusiastically discussing the day's racing form. "How do you pick 'em?" "You don't want to know how *I* pick 'em!"

And Ruby's is cheap. The most expensive item on the menu is $3.85. Burgers are 90 cents, a meatloaf sandwich, $1.90. We tried the homemade Manhattan clam chowder—not the best, but quite respectable, with chunks of corn, potatoes, peas, and clams. A big bowl of it was just 85 cents. One surprise was a peach omelet at $2.50. We passed but later regretted it, for we've not seen another anywhere, let alone in a diner.

HOURS Mon.–Wed. & Fri. 5:30 am–6 pm; Thu. 5:30 am–7 pm; Sat. 5:30 am–3 pm; closed Sun.

DIRECTIONS If eastbound, take Exit 26; if westbound, take Exit 25. Both will put you on I-890, a fast loop through Schenectady. Take Exit 4B and follow signs for Erie Blvd. Drive ½ mile on Erie and you'll see Ruby's on the left. Rejoin Thruway by continuing along I-890; no need to retrace your steps.

MIKE'S ITALIAN RESTAURANT, *Exit 28, Fonda*

Here's a workingman's town loaded with workingman's bars but few restaurants. When we found Mike's, its Formica, vinyl, and fluorescent decor didn't lead us to expect much, but we discovered that Mike is a pretty hard worker himself. Born on a farm in Italy, he never knew what it meant to hire help or work a mere 40-hour week.

Now he's in the States, running his own little restaurant assisted only by his daughters, and he's at it from 7 A.M. to midnight six days a week. He makes all his own pasta (some of it is sold uncooked in plastic bags), grinder rolls (also sold for home consumption), and, in the summer, pastry. Tomatoes come from a nearby cannery, and Mike sets the sauce a-simmering every morning. By the time you eat it, the flavors are nicely mellowed.

Mike has pizza in four sizes (from $4.95; 50 cents a slice), grinders ($1.65–$2.25), and typical Italian dinners ($2.75–$3.75).

It's a simple menu, as befits the unpretentious kind of place it's served in. But for what it is, everything Mike serves is well prepared, tasty, and definitely a good value.

HOURS Sun., Mon., Wed. & Thu. 11 am–11 pm; Fri. & Sat. 11 am–midnight; closed Tue.

DIRECTIONS From Exit 28 turn left. In ½ mile you'll come to a T.

Turn right onto Route 30 North; go 0.3 mile to another T. Right again, onto Route 5 East, and you'll see it, almost immediately, on the right.

BILL'S LUNCHEONETTE
GARI'S PLACE, *Exit 29, Canajoharie*

Bill and Barbara McCloud are just about the sweetest, most sincere restaurant owners you could ever meet. Their warm manner and gentle humor will make their humble luncheonette feel like your favorite aunt's kitchen. When we requested a glass of milk, Barbara lit up and gently teased, "My goodness, won't your mother be proud of you!"

Proud or not, Mom would like Barbara's brownies as much as we did—they're the thickest, fudgiest ones we've ever had, and she guarantees that they'll last you until Syracuse.

But Bill does most of the cooking. He's locally famous for omelets, even though he has no idea what makes them so special. Perhaps, he suggests, it's the well-seasoned grill they're cooked on (thereby cutting down on grease). We think the secret is in the eggs: Bill picks them up daily from a nearby farm, so they couldn't be any fresher unless you cooked them in the coop.

He also cooks his own roast beef and turkey, and makes his gravy the right way, from real pan drippings. Here you can get a plate of sliced ham, potato or macaroni salad, rolls, lettuce and tomato for just $2.75. A hamburger is $1.10, and the costliest dinner is just $4.75; sandwiches, of course, are much less. On the day we visited, the special was homemade lasagne with tossed salad and Italian bread for $2.50.

With its old decorative moldings behind the counter, Bill's was a splendid example of luncheonette design, but Barbara told us that the restaurant was about to move around the corner. We don't know what it will look like then, but we're sure that Bill and Barbara will make it feel like home.

If Bill's is closed when you arrive in Canajoharie or if you prefer Italian food, you might give Gari's Place a try. It's a simple corner pizza and sub shop, a little more comfortable and subdued than most. In addition to pizza with ten toppings and eight or so subs, Gari serves pasta dishes ranging in price from $2.75 (spaghetti with tomato sauce) to $3.50 (manicotti or stuffed shells). In addition, there are calzone, antipastos, and that great non-Italian upstate treat, "wings"—which is to say chicken wings in a bucket, served with medium or hot (and we mean *hot*) sauce.

> **HOURS**   **Bill's:** Mon.–Fri. 6 am–7 pm; Sat. 7 am–2 pm; closed Sun.
>   **Gari's:** Mon. 11 am–8 pm; Tue.–Thu. 11 am–11 pm; Fri. 10 am–midnight; Sat. 4 pm–midnight; Sun. 5–10 pm.

DIRECTIONS   From Exit 29 turn right at stop sign, onto Route 5S West. In 0.3 mile you'll come to a traffic light. For **Bill's,** go straight through the light; its new location is in the second building on your right. For **Gari's,** turn right at the light and go 1 block; it's on the corner, on your left.

EMPIRE DINER, *Exit 30, Herkimer*

* *Not great but cheap, and almost always open*

This is a sleek stainless-steel De Raffele diner, pink and gray inside, pleasant and cheerful throughout. Before you even leave your car, you know all about the bargains. Carnival signs in the windows broadcast them loud and clear: ALL YOU CAN EAT— MONDAY, FRIED CHICKEN, $3.99; TUESDAY, SPAGHETTI AND MEAT BALLS OR SAUSAGE, $3.50; WEDNESDAY, PANCAKES AND EGGS, $2.79. Another sign shouts, BREAKFAST SPECIAL—2 EGGS, TOAST, COFFEE, $1.09; PANCAKES AND COFFEE, $1.09.

We were there on a weekend, when the all-you-can-eat deals are off. So we opted for an Empire Burger, a half-pound of beef on a hard roll, with your choice of cheese and mushrooms, bacon, chili, onions, or peppers and, on the side, French fries *and* onion rings. That Brobdingnagian portion came at the Lilliputian price of $2.95. It was worth it. And so, we suspect, are the many other bargains.

HOURS   Sun.–Wed. 6 am–10 pm; Thu.–Sat. open 24 hours.

DIRECTIONS   From Exit 30 turn right onto N.Y. 28 North. In

¼ mile turn left with Route 28 (at blinking light), go 0.2 mile to light, and turn right onto State St. In 0.3 mile you'll see the diner on your left, just before the third light.

MOHAWK STATION, *Exit 30, Mohawk*

The celebrated age of golden spikes and iron men competes with old-time firehouses for honors as the most overused motif in the restaurant business. How many places have lugged in an old caboose, tacked up a semaphore or two, and designated the waiters' station as "Loading Dock" or the dining area as "Station Room?"

Though Mohawk Station has its share of clichés, it's still a pleasant place to dine. In fact, we think it would be even nicer if they eliminated the railroad gimmickry and let the good points shine in their own light. The greenhouse dining area, for instance, is a choice spot with a light, airy feel and plush velvety chairs. The main dining room too is tastefully decorated, with hardwood wainscotting, a soft carpet, and bentwood chairs. Frilly cotton napkins peer out of wine goblets on each table like so many pink carnations.

Lunch here is mostly sandwiches, burgers, and specials— chicken Bordeaux, for instance, which is stuffed with mushrooms, rice, and broccoli, and served in tomato sauce ($4.25). Or quiche Florentine (spinach, bacon, and mushrooms), also $4.25. Sandwiches start at $2.75 (ham and Swiss) and run up to $6.25 for an open-faced steak sandwich. A favorite, in addition to the popular charbroiled hamburger, is London broil on hard roll au jus ($3.25). There is also broiled fish each day, with rice and broccoli, for $3.95.

Another possibility is the colorful salad bar (which here is called the salad cart because it's set out on a baggage wagon). We were happy to see that it was well endowed with greens: endive and Romaine as well as salad-bar standbys. It's $3.95 all by itself at lunch, $4.95 at dinner.

Dinner here is typical steak-and-seafood-house fare, running from $7.95 for broiled pork chops or London broil to $17.95 for lobster tail. And, of course, the salad bar comes with your dinner.

If you just want something quick and light, you might simply visit Mohawk Station's bar (sorry, "Club Car"), where giant rounds of Swiss, cheddar, and blue cheese, along with a variety of crackers, are set out for free. You must imbibe to partake, but you can do it with Coke or coffee if you're not up to beer or booze.

HOURS   Mon.–Sat. 11 am–10 pm; Sun. noon–9 pm.

DIRECTIONS   From Exit 30 turn left onto Route 28 South. The road quickly takes you over two iron bridges (one for the Mohawk River and the next for the barge canal), then curves sharply to the right. Restaurant is on your right, just around the curve, hardly ¼ mile from the Thruway.

VENTURA'S RESTAURANT, *Exit 31, Utica*

Not fancy, but not exactly funky either, Ventura's has the kind of charm that comes only with age. Utica and Ventura's have grown together for 40 years now. It's the kind of place that just about everyone goes to, even those who are put off by plastic plants and dropped ceilings when found elsewhere. At Ventura's, the tone is warm and subdued and, like the restaurant itself, the vested waiters wear the grace of age. They lend an air of class as they tend their customers with charm and efficiency.

The Italian food served here is not quite as impressive as the service, but nearly so. And the prices are astoundingly reasonable. We spent $5.75 for a full dinner that began with an excellent veal-based minestrone and moved on to linguini with sweet Italian sausage in a nicely seasoned tomato sauce. (The linguini, like all the pasta here, is literally homemade—made at home by a friend of the Ventura family.) Salad and fresh-baked bread (both fair) came with the dinner, as did a complimentary glass of wine and coffee. All this was from a special "Italian festival" menu full of many such bargains; we were assured that the festival goes on every night.

There is also a regular menu, with veal dishes, seafood (including frogs' legs, $6.95), and pizza. Nothing was over $10, and on Wednesday and Saturday nights a king-sized prime rib with clams casino, soup, vegetable, spaghetti, and coffee is only $8.95. We'll have to come back to try it, but it'll be tough to choose between that and the zuppa di pesce ($9.50), a fish soup thick with whitefish, clams, escargots, mussels, lobster, crab claws, shrimp, and scallops over fettucini.

HOURS Every day 11 am–11 pm.

DIRECTIONS From Exit 31 go straight, heading for Route 5 West and picking up signs for Downtown. This requires bearing left on the curving ramp. At stop sign, bear right onto Route 5 West and look for signs for Broad St. Left on Broad and go 0.9 mile to Kossuth Ave. Right on Kossuth, and in 0.4 mile you'll see Ventura's on your right, 1 block past St. Agnes Church.

LILY LANGTRY'S, *Exit 31, Utica*

The F. X. Matt Brewing Company, producers of Matt's Premium Beer and Utica Club, is the focal point of Utica's downtown renovation. In the summer, tours begin every five minutes and end up in the brewery's Victorian tavern, where a mug of beer is on the house. Once you've downed it, step outside, walk two short blocks, and have a light meal at another Victorian-styled establishment, Lily Langtry's.

Named for the beautiful socialite who caused an uproar in Victorian society when she launched a stage career, Lily Langtry's is a brick-plants-and-oak café. It's the labor of love of young Brian Raehm, a musician, PR specialist, and entrepreneur on the Utica scene. When he bought the building, he became a renovator as well. The hardwood floors and wainscotting were rescued from old Utica buildings that were about to meet the wrecker's ball. The booths are transplanted church pews. But Brian's pride and joy is the stained-glass skylight he painstakingly installed.

Like most of the Northeast's BPO cafés, the menu at Lily's leans toward big salads, sandwiches, and quiche, but unlike many such restaurants, no full meals are offered here. Hefty sandwiches come on a wide choice of breads, at prices that hover around $3. Full-meal salads (spinach, artichoke heart, and chef's salads) run $2.25 to $2.95. For dessert, it's the ever popular carrot cake ($1.25), but also a choice of puddings—butterscotch, vanilla, chocolate, or lemon.

HOURS Mon.–Fri. 11 am–7 pm (snacks, drinks, and music until 2 am). No food served Saturday or Sunday.

DIRECTIONS From Exit 31 continue straight ahead, following signs for N.Y. 12S, through a series of ramps. At stop sign, bear right onto N.Y. 12S. In 1.3 miles turn right onto Court St. Go through one light and take the next right onto Varick (brewery is on the corner). Go 2 short blocks; it's on your left. Look for the flags.

EMMI'S LUNCHEONETTE, *Exit 34, Canastota*

* *Color and low prices, not cuisine*

To us, the most striking feature of Canastota, or "Canal Town" as it is locally called, isn't any restaurant, but a canal— the Erie Canal, that is. Known as "The Big Ditch," the famous man-made waterway once ran right through town, but it has since been filled in and paved over because it was no longer wide or deep enough to be useful. You can still see where it entered and exited the town; the stretch in between now serves as Canastota's Main Street. If it's summertime when you're there, stop by the Canastota Canal Town Museum and douse yourself in canal lore.

No one will build a museum for Canastota's restaurants, however. There are a few mom-and-pop places, but nothing to go out of your way for. Emmi's, around the corner from the museum, seemed the best bet—a soda fountain/luncheonette with large, unattractive, salmon-colored booths, fluorescent lights, Formica tables, lively local ladies and glum local men. Emmi herself is warm and friendly, in a gentle way. If you don't see what you want posted on the board above the coffee machine, ask and she'll try to make it for you.

Here you can get a hamburger for just 85 cents, a fried fish sandwich for $1.10, or a club for $1.95. The usual sorts of breakfast items are also available at low prices (with good, even if greasy, home fries), and some standard American dinners (fried chicken, Virginia ham, shrimp, or scallops) are as low as $2.65.

HOURS Mon.–Fri. 8:30 am–9 pm; Sat. 8:30 am–5 pm; Sun. 8:30 am–1:30 pm.

DIRECTIONS From Exit 34 turn left onto N.Y. 13 South. Go 0.6 mile, through the light, and you'll see it on your right.

CAFÉ DE PARIS, *Exits 34A & 39, Syracuse*

Imagine a Fire Island bungalow painted an indescribably horrible shade of electric purply-pink with vivid chartreuse trim. Place it at the back of a used-car lot on a major utility road in Syracuse. Then picture it as a French restaurant. Hard to imagine, *n'est-ce pas?*

One's impression on walking inside isn't much better. The place feels a little like a trailer, and you almost expect it to tilt if two people walk to one side. But it's campy good fun, from the faded Toulouse-Lautrec wallpaper right up to the dropped checkerboard ceiling—squares of solid red alternating with others covered with metallic floral wallpaper. Peach napkins stand up at each place setting. Soft French cabaret music is playing. A single waiter, primped up in tux and bow tie, glides gracefully between the candlelit tables.

When they opened Syracuse's first French restaurant, Paul and Ginette Rothman had a difficult time convincing the city's epicures that they meant business, but they've succeeded. Since they obviously didn't do it with their façade, it must have been the food.

Our dinner was excellent, starting with a richly flavored onion soup thick with cheese. A whiff of cinnamon gave it a mysterious quality. Salad, while disappointingly reliant on iceberg, was nicely tossed with vinaigrette. The day's specialty was chicken Alsacienne ($11.95), a gorgeous roulade, presented beautifully with potatoes Lyonnaise, green beans, and carrots, with a pitcher of Bordelaise on the side. The roulade itself consisted of boneless chicken breast stuffed with prosciutto, layered with béchamel sauce, Swiss cheese, and duxelle sauce, and wrapped in an angelically light pastry shell. Even the green beans were excellent, lightly seasoned with garlic; the carrots were slightly candied. Both were obviously fresh.

At Café de Paris, there is a different special each night (sole Bretone, boeuf Wellington, others) and a handful of regular items (veal Française, steak au poivre, duck à l'orange, coquilles St. Jacques). Prices go from $7.95 for coq au vin or beef Bourguignonne to $12.95 for the Wellington. Pastries ($1.50) are also served, made right here by Paul.

We don't argue with excellent food no matter where it's found, and we especially loved it here, in an atmosphere that is the very marriage of camp and elegance.

HOURS   Mon.–Thu. 6–10 pm; Fri. & Sat. 6–11 pm; closed Sun.

DIRECTIONS   Eastbound: From Exit 39 enter I-690 East. Take Exit 9 (Midler Ave.) and turn right. Go ¼ mile to light and turn right onto Route 5 West. Half a mile takes you to the used-car lot on the right at corner of Pearl St. Restaurant is on the lot (1977 Erie Blvd. East).

Westbound: From Exit 34A enter I-481 South and then, soon, enter I-690 West. Take Exit 9 (Midler Ave.). Turn left at the stop sign, then left again at the light onto Midler Ave. Go about ½ mile and turn right onto Route 5 West. Half a mile takes you to the used-car lot on the right at corner of Pearl St. Restaurant is on the lot (1977 Erie Blvd. East).

RESTAURANTS ON MARSHALL STREET, *Exits 36 & 39, Syracuse*

See page 91 for a rundown of restaurants on the periphery of Syracuse University.

DIRECTIONS Eastbound: From Exit 39 enter I-690 East to I-81 South. On I-81, take Exit 18. ■ Follow signs for Adams St. Left on Adams, to the third light, then right onto University Ave. Go 1 short block and you'll be at the head of Marshall Street's restaurant alley, to your right.

Westbound: From Exit 36 enter I-81 South to Exit 18. Then as above from ■.

MARIO'S DINER, *Exit 36, North Syracuse*

This is an old stainless-steel diner where for $2.85 you can feast on Mario Biasi's fabulous frittata. Fabulous what? See page 91 for further details.

DIRECTIONS From Exit 36 enter I-81 North and drive about 3 miles to Exit 28 (North Syracuse). From there, follow directions given on page 92.

TIMOTHY FARMS, *Exit 41, Magee*

* Color, not cuisine

You're in one of New York's major apple-growing regions now. If it's autumn and you have time to "pick your own," you'll be able to fill your trunk with Cortlands, Romes, Delicious, Jonathans, or Macs. But if you just want to grab an apple or two and a burger or hot dog, Timothy Farms allows you the pleasure.

There's nothing fancy or put-on about it. It's just a large open building with tables built out of apple barrels (more for economy than for effect, we suspect) and walls painted with orchard scenes in primitive local fashion. Groceries are sold here, but most of the space is given over to the dining area.

There are more varieties of apples in the grocery section than dishes on the menu. You can have eggs with toast and coffee ($1.10), a hamburger ($1.10), a hot dog ($1 for a large German hot), and not too much else. Do try some cider, by the gallon or the glass; it's pressed right out back, and is as fresh as can be got. But if you want to dine, drive on.

HOURS   Every day 6 am–6 pm.

DIRECTIONS   From Exit 41 turn right onto Route 44 South. It's just past the first light, on the left.

ABOUT ROCHESTER AND HENRIETTA

For a city in the provinces, Rochester is one with considerable culture, civic pride, and thriving high-tech industry. Undoubtedly it has many good restaurants, but the city proper is a good 15 miles from the Thruway—too far for this book.

Just five minutes out of the way, the suburb of Henrietta is more suitable. As you leave the highway in Henrietta, official road signs point the way to a dozen or more steakhouses, chain restaurants, and others that look like chains. It's criminal, but none of the signs say anything about the smaller, owner-operated places with charm, local color, and good, interesting food. There ought to be a law. . . .

There isn't a law, but we've done our part by coming up with three Henrietta restaurants that aren't on any sign. Each is excellent in its own way, one Chinese, one a diner, and the last an unusual brick-plants-and-oak café.

SHANGHAI RESTAURANT, *Exit 46, Henrietta*

We'd heard about the Shanghai long before we got there—first, in the Adirondacks, from skiers who told us about its marvelous Chinese breakfasts on Sundays; then, from a friend of a friend who is not only Chinese and a Rochester resident, but an epicure and professional dietitian to boot. She said that the Shanghai was unquestionably the best Chinese restaurant in the Rochester area. So, when we found that it was also close to the Thruway, we knew we were on to something good.

From the outside, the Shanghai looks like a cheap motel. The interior is Twentieth Century Steakhouse, with a few Buddhas and Chinese vases scattered about. But no one promised beautiful decor. We moved on to address the cuisine.

What we discovered was wonderfully prepared Szechuan and Cantonese dishes, very large portions, and fast service. Most popular are sweet-and-sour items and the dozen or so shrimp dishes.

We covered two bases at once by ordering a dinner of sweet-and-sour shrimp. How they could offer so many of the tasty crustaceans for $6.50 we'll never know. The dish's appearance was bold and bright, and its flavors proved strong and clear.

If you're not in a sweet-and-sour mood, you can also get your shrimp hot and spicy, with snow peas, or with garlic sauce or cashew nuts. There is also the customary assortment of beef, chicken, pork, duck, and fish dishes, as well as some vegetarian specialties. Dinner prices run $4 to $7 for most items. No matter what you order, you'll be offered a complimentary glass of plum wine to sip as you contemplate the meal just consumed.

Lunch combinations (soup, egg roll, fried rice, and a main course) are $3.65. For timid tongues, there are also American dishes.

About that Chinese breakfast: On Sundays between 11 A.M. and 3 P.M., the cuisine changes to that of northern China, near the Korean border. From this area come Chinese crullers (foot-long fried pastry eaten with soy milk), pancakes stuffed with ground pork and scallions, steamed or fried pork buns, pan-fried wonton-like dumplings, stewed duck, and . . . for something really different . . . jellyfish salad.

HOURS Lunch: Mon.–Sat. 11:30 am–3 pm. Dinner: Mon.–Fri. 3–11 pm; Sat. till midnight. Sun.: breakfast, 11 am–3 pm; dinner, 3–11 pm.

DIRECTIONS See end of Henrietta entries, page 143.

JAY'S DINER, *Exit 46, Henrietta*

Jay's is a modern-style diner with ersatz stone, ersatz hand-hewn beams, ersatz brick, ersatz wagon-wheel chandeliers, and fantastic clam chowder—meaty chunks of clam in a rich, tasty broth. Yankees might object to the broth being thickened, but it sure tasted good ($1 a bowl). And wonderful creamy cheesecake too ($1.45).

In between those two courses, upon which Jay's strong reputation stands, you can get any of the standard diner sandwiches, entrées, or salads. Prices aren't bargain basement, but not high-flying either—a hot turkey or roast beef sandwich is $2.95; half a barbecued chicken with soup and potato or vegetable is $4.95.

When we stopped in, the dinner special was a quite passable casserole of fresh spinach, ground beef, and rice; served with soup, bread, and a side dish, it wasn't a bad buy at $4.05.

In addition to its clam chowder and cheesecake, Jay's is known for date-nut bread, which is served by the loaf with dinner. We arrived just as the day's last loaf went out, but the regular dinner rolls weren't bad either.

HOURS   Always open.

DIRECTIONS   See end of Henrietta entries, page 143.

RED CREEK, *Exit 46, Henrietta*

It's a nightclub, it's a brick-plants-and-oak café, it's a pastry shop. Red Creek is all of these, and a video arcade as well. Purists in any of these realms will not be enthralled, but for those seeking a place with distinctive (and diversified) character, Red Creek makes an interesting roadside stop.

For the purposes of this book, we concentrate on the greenhouse dining room. Earthy, not elegant, it is a BPO rich in plants and rough pine, low on brick and oak. The extensive menu is true to type—a plethora of salads, burgers, quiches, nouveau sandwiches, and cutesy commentary about each.

The "P.D.Q." lunch menu promises you your pastrami sandwich promptly (about $3). A bowl of chili is $1.75; gargantuan medleys of garden greens run $3.35–$3.65. There are also Tex-Mex hits from $2.65 ("mucho macho nacho") to $4.65 (burritos, enchiladas, and the like). Bivalves have also found their way to this inland oasis: for $6.95, you get a dinner of steamed mussels with soup, garlic bread, salad, and rice. In case the selection isn't wide enough for you, they throw in knishes covered with sour cream and piccapeppa sauce ($2.25). At dinnertime, the lunch menu stays in place but to it are added such specials as spanakopita or chicken Normandie ($6.50 and up, with soup, salad, and garlic bread).

Soups are Red Creek's pride. Each day has its own inspiration, but there's always New England clam chowder and a very good homemade cream of mushroom with sherry. In the summer, you'll likely find vichyssoise and gazpacho. A free cup of soup comes with every sandwich served before 8 P.M. on "Souper Wednesday."

HOURS Sun. & Tue.–Thu. 11 am–midnight; Fri. & Sat. 11 am–1:30 am; closed Mon.

DIRECTIONS FOR HENRIETTA RESTAURANTS
From Exit 46 follow signs for I-390 North, and then bear right, following signs for Route 15. At first light, turn left and in ½ mile turn right onto Route 15 North. In 2.2 miles you'll come to Jefferson Rd. For **Red Creek,** turn left onto Jefferson and drive 0.7 mile; it's on the right. For **Shanghai** and **Jay's Diner,** do not turn onto Jefferson but continue straight on Route 15 North. In about ½ mile the Shanghai will be on your right; Jay's is ½ mile farther, also on the right.

The total distance to any of these is about 4 miles, and it will take just 5 minutes. Not difficult, even if it sounds that way.

ENGINE HOUSE #1, *Exit 48, Batavia*

The Thruway doesn't go into Buffalo proper, so in nearby Batavia we give you a chance to sample the Buffalo area's two contributions to the culinary world: wings (chicken wings, that is) and beef on weck (that's Kümmelweck, a kind of hard roll).

One of Batavia's prominent landmarks, Engine House #1 is a grand Romanesque affair, flanked by two more recent towers;

curiously, one is round and the other square. The sand-blasted brick has a lovely ocher glow that is accentuated by the orange-painted trim.

Once you know the name, it'll come as no surprise to learn that this was once Batavia's firehouse. Jim and Sandy Dennis had to battle city hall to save it from demolition, a rescue that took a city-wide referendum to achieve. Even though they won wide public support, they also won the sideways glances of neighbors who could not imagine that the dilapidated edifice might ever be a restaurant.

Now it's been reborn and the doubters proved wrong. Even if firehouse restaurant decor isn't the most original in the world, Jim and Sandy have put together a most attractive environment. The greenhouse dining room is especially fetching; extensive glass, brick, plants, rough-sawn pine, forest green carpet, and red tablecloths create a cheerful, appetizing setting for a plate of Buffalo-style wings.

Now, about those wings: Invented at the Anchor Bar in downtown Buffalo, they are the regional method of searing nasal passageways. Chicken wings are fried, then seasoned with Tabasco, red pepper, and Worcestershire sauce. Given the choice of medium, hot, or extra hot (described by the menu as "smoldering," "scorching," and "suicidal"), we went for "hot." Even now we inhale through clenched teeth when we recall the experience. Mercifully, wings are always served with celery sticks and blue cheese dip, presumably to put out the fire (quite in keeping with this restaurant's theme). Still, the tingly feeling lasted us

almost to Fredonia. (Wings are $2.45 for a single order; $4.25 for a double.)

Beef on weck ($2.75) is roast beef served on a hard roll dotted with large salt crystals and caraway seeds. Before you get it, the meat's juices (the "au juice," as it's called in upstate French) have been allowed to soak into the roll. This makes for sloppy, but tasty, eating, and a dollop of horseradish adds some white heat just in case the chicken wings weren't enough.

If neither of these local favorites appeals to you, there are also homemade soups, salads, omelets, inventive sandwiches, and up-to-date burger variations ($2.50–$3.50). At dinner, continental preparations of chicken, veal, beef, and seafood make an appearance ($6–$9, with some higher).

For a sweet ending to all this, you might like to stop in at **Oliver's Candy Factory,** just down the street; it's open 9 to 9, daily.

HOURS Mon.–Thu. 11 am–10 pm; Fri. & Sat. 11 am–11 pm; Sun. 10 am–2 pm and 3–9 pm.

DIRECTIONS From Exit 48 turn left onto Route 98 South (signs for Batavia). Go 1.1 miles and turn left onto Route 5 East (Main St.). **Oliver's Candy Factory** is on your right. Continue for ¼ mile and you'll see **Engine House #1** on your right.

DEE'S FAMILY DINER, *Exit 48A, Pembroke*

* *Slim pickin's*

With its orange sheet-metal façade that is much brighter than the glum faces of the truckers inside, there's little attractive about Dee's. Except perhaps its proximity to the Thruway, its friendly counterwoman, and its low, low prices. A sign over the cash register reads, "Due to constant price rises, we must raise the price of coffee to 25 cents a cup, including tax."

Homemade soups are only 15 cents more than the coffee. We tried Italian chicken noodle and found it quite passable, even nice, but heavy on the parmesan. Other standbys include chili (60 cents a cup/$1.10 a bowl), hamburgers ($1.10), beef on weck

($2.25), and fried chicken/Salisbury steak–type dinners ($2.89 to $3.95 with potatoes, vegetable, and bread). Daily specials are scrawled on colored construction paper and stuck up on the milk cooler with magnets, e.g., "Hamburger pie with bread and butter —$2.25."

It's a quick stop and the food is decent. If you want atmosphere, you're going to starve here. But you'll do much better at the Asa Ransom House to the west, or at Engine House #1, a few miles east of here.

HOURS   Mon.–Thu. & Sat. 6 am–8 pm; Fri. 6 am–9 pm; Sun. 6 am–7 pm.

DIRECTIONS   From Exit 48A turn right onto Route 77 South. Go ¾ mile and it's on the left at the junction with Route 5.

ASA RANSOM HOUSE, *Exits 48A & 49, Clarence*

Around the beginning of the 19th century, the Holland Land Company offered for $2 an acre (with long-term, interest-free loans) large tracts of land in western New York to "any proper man who would build and operate a tavern upon it." A young fur trader named Asa Ransom quickly took up the offer, and so began an innkeeping tradition that still offers comfortable lodgings to the weary and satisfying meals to the hungry.

Just a bit precious, the Asa Ransom House today is not the kind of place that you'd want to tramp through with mud on your boots, as old Asa surely did. But it is handsome and restful in every respect. A new Colonial-style wing is skillfully integrated with the original building, and the charming dining room successfully mixes antiques with period reproductions. Bob and Judy Lenz oversee all aspects of the inn as if its visitors were family guests. Like concerned parents, they scrutinize every dish to assure its quality. In planning the menu, nutrition is king: salads are heavy on spinach, alfalfa sprouts, and sunflower seeds; vegetables are fresh and meats untreated. Honey is the sweetener of choice. Whenever possible, local products—including wine and cheese—are used.

But don't confuse this with a natural foods granolary. While healthful awareness is upheld, so are the preferences of a conventional American palate. Here, a steak-and-potatoes zealot can happily coexist with an Adelle Davis devotee. The Early American cuisine features two favorites considered delectable by any standard: salmon pond pie (a deep dish of fresh salmon and vegetables in a cheese pastry shell) and smoked corned beef with apple-raisin sauce. Both sell for $7.75. Filling out the menu are the likes of steak and kidney pie, sole in parchment, lamb chops with mushroom and sherry sauce, steaks, and a few vegetarian selections.

Curiously, this restaurant is open for lunch only one day a week. ("We like serving lunch," explains Bob Lenz, "but we like having our mornings free even better.") We were not lucky enough to pass by on a Wednesday afternoon, but had we done so we would have tried the "pineapple hollow"—half a pineapple filled with tuna salad and garnished with wedges of hard-boiled eggs, pineapple, grapefruit, and tomatoes ($4.95). You might prefer a country BLT—grilled, thick-slabbed Canadian bacon with tomato and Swiss on fresh-baked whole wheat bread —for $3.50, or perhaps a vegetarian patty made from wheat germ, walnuts, vegetables, and melted caraway cheese ($2.95).

Should your passage through these parts occur late in the evening, you might want to put up for the night in one of the inn's antique-furnished rooms ($35 single, $50 double). If (and only if) you do so, you will have the privilege of waking up to fresh fruit and "breakfast pie," a pastry-enclosed mélange of smoked corned beef, potatoes, cheese, and egg. What a way to start the day!

HOURS   Lunch: Wed. only, 11:30 am–2:30 pm. Dinner: Mon.–Thu. 4:30–9 pm; Sun. 12:30–8 pm. Closed Fri. & Sat. During summer, reservations are strongly recommended for dining between 6 and 8 pm. Phone (716) 759-2315.

DIRECTIONS   NOTE: This is not as far out of your way as it may seem. Rejoin Thruway by continuing along Route 5 in the same direction as you were traveling; do not retrace your route.

Eastbound: From Exit 49 turn left at light, following signs to Route 5. In 1¼ miles turn right onto Route 5 East. Go 5.4 miles; it's on your right.

Westbound: From Exit 48A turn right onto Route 77 South. Go 0.7 mile and turn right onto Route 5 West. In 10.1 miles, it's on your left.

HELEN'S KITCHEN, *Exit 49, Williamsville*

Don't be fooled by its looks. This little shopping plaza lunchroom has a few surprises in store for you.

First off, you'll notice the two Buffalo-area earmarks: hot-spiced chicken wings (served with celery sticks and blue cheese dip for relief) and beef on weck (that's Kümmelweck, a kind of hard roll). Then, you might observe that souvlaki is available in some form or other at any time of day. At noon we enjoyed a juicy souvlaki sandwich—half a dozen pieces of tenderloin with feta cheese in a pocket of pita bread—for only $2.25. But you can also get a souvlaki dinner with French fries, Greek salad, and pita for $3.95. It even comes with eggs and home fries at breakfast time ($3.25).

Here the surprises end. Aside from these exotics, Helen serves only standard American chowhouse fare—liver and onions, roast beef, meatloaf dinners ($3–$4, with bread, potato, and soup or salad). For breakfast, two eggs, bacon, toast, home fries, and coffee cost $2.25. If it's all as good as the souvlaki, you'll probably be happy you found Helen's.

HOURS   Mon.–Sat. 7 am–10 pm; Sun. 8 am–2 pm.

DIRECTIONS   From Exit 49 turn left onto N.Y. 324 (Transit Rd.). Go 1.2 miles to Transitown Plaza on right. Helen's is in there.

PAUL'S PLACE, *Exit 57, Hamburg*

* Untried, but likely

Here, in a residential section at the edge of blue-collar Buffalo, is workingman's leisurely dining. To its regular customers, Paul's Place is a second home; their reverence is so great, in fact, that we wondered if it isn't their church too. "I've never had a bad meal here, and I come twice a week," said one fellow with a Scottish accent. "You can't finish it, the portions are so large," piped in another. Since the kitchen had closed just before we walked in, we had to take their word for it.

It's certainly homey. With subdued lighting, home-style furnishings, tea towels and other bric-a-brac on the walls, it feels like somebody's living room, which it obviously was before the owners moved upstairs. Eating here is also like coming home after a day's work because you're never sure what'll be served. All meals, even sandwiches, come on a fully garnished plate with an unpredictable combination of side dishes. Macaroni or potato salad, cole slaw, vegetable sticks, and fruit compote are among the possibilities. There's also a large tray that is circulated at random—it is likely to include French fries, chicken wings, pudding, and God knows what else. With dinners, surprise side orders appear without warning, frequently after the plate has been served. The night we were there, it had been deep-fried cinnamon-spiced apple rings.

The main dishes at Paul's Place—the ones you can count on —include seafood (mostly fried), chicken in a basket, grilled pork chops, steaks, sautéed chicken livers, veal cutlet, and roast beef (just $4–$6 for most, with the fixin's). For $3, a chef's salad comes with your choice of Republican, Democratic, or Japanese Government dressings (no explanation offered despite our pleas). Most sandwiches run $1.50 to $3; clubs, omelets, and steak sandwiches are $3.50–$4.

Before you leave Paul's Place, step into the bar and take a gander ceilingward. If what you discover isn't the largest assortment of hats you've ever seen, you must have been born into the millinery trade. Owner/bartender Terry Washburn, "The Man With a Thousand Hats," has appeared on local television more than once. A part of his collection will undoubtedly be on his head when you visit.

HOURS   Mon.–Thu. 11:30 am–8:30 pm; Fri. & Sat. 11:30 am–10 pm. Closed Sundays and for a week in mid-August.

DIRECTIONS   From Exit 57 follow signs for Route 75 South/Hamburg. Go 2.2 miles along Route 75 to light at Main St. Here, Route 75 turns right and you do too. Just after turning, though, the main road bears left, but you continue straight, onto Evans St. Paul's Place is on your right in 0.1 mile (39 Evans St.).

WHITE INN, *Exit 59, Fredonia*

In compiling this series of roadside dining guides, we have often heard references to the old Duncan Hines books that were once culinary bibles for travelers. Thus it was with considerable delight that we came upon the White Inn, a charter member of the Duncan Hines family of famous restaurants.

Since the '30s and '40s, when Hines was scouting out eateries in much the same manner as we do now, the White Inn had fallen into disrepair. Outside, a lurid, flashing sign broadcast ELEVATOR, and inside, the walls were covered with canary-painted plywood.

But in 1980 two philosophy professors at the nearby SUNY college, David Bryant and David Palmer, purchased the inn and threw their hearts—and their hammers—into refinishing every surface and restoring the building's former vitality. Today's White Inn is precisely the kind of small, in-town hotel that we always seek and seldom find. Unlike so many country inns, it doesn't simmer with planned arrogance, and it hasn't a hint of self-righteousness. It was comfortable, relaxing, and fun, and everyone was superbly friendly. We think you'll like it whether you spend a lunch hour or a weekend.

Actually, if you are there for lunch, you won't have to spend even an hour, unless you want to. The White Inn's "Luncheon Express" enables you to get your meal the moment you arrive. There's a steam table with a daily hot dish—chicken à la king, beef Stroganoff, or some other sauced thing—and two soups (minestrone and the day's special). There's also a cold buffet with sliced meats, cheeses, breads, and salad bar. Unlimited access to all this is only $3.25. And if that's too much (or your appetite is limited), $1.95 buys a cup of soup and finger sandwiches (four quarter-sandwiches, each different). There is also a regular lunch menu with salads, sandwiches, and hot dishes.

At dinner, the menu goes continental, with a few American steaks and seafood dishes thrown in, but prices remain quite reasonable ($6–$10 for most entrées, including salad bar and potato or rice pilaf). Sandwiches (Reubens, Monte Cristo, etc.) are also available at dinner ($3.75). We enjoyed the tenderloin tips chasseur (beef tenderloin sautéed with onions and mushrooms, and served with wine sauce over pilaf) but found the veal parmigiana somewhat ordinary. The biggest dinnertime seller is prime rib, available in three sizes ($6.50, $10.95, and $13.95).

If you visit on a Sunday, you can partake of a recently revived White Inn tradition that ran strong through the '30s and '40s:

chicken dinners in seven variations. (The chickens once came out of the poultry barn that still stands behind the parking lot.) For $5.95, you can choose between chicken pot pie, parmigiana, barbecue, paprikash, stew, roast, and Hawaiian.
Rooms at the White Inn start at $20.

HOURS   Lunch: Mon.–Sat. 11:30 am–2 pm. Dinner: Mon.–Thu. 5–9 pm; Fri. & Sat. 5–10 pm (open one hour later in summer). Sun. 8–11:30 am and 1–8 pm.

DIRECTIONS   See Hook 'n' Ladder Deli, below.

HOOK 'N' LADDER DELI, *Exit 59, Fredonia*

Before they went to work on the White Inn, Professors Palmer and Bryant honed their carpentry skills on Fredonia's old firehouse, converting it to offices and a little eatery now called the Hook 'n' Ladder Deli. This one-woman operation has a European feel that emanates from the cook/owner, Marguerite Beichner, a lovely Dutch woman who learned the restaurant trade in Holland. Her fine cooking and her encouragement of strangers to mingle make for delightful light meals and friendly company. And the prices are most reasonable.

The Hook 'n' Ladder is a bright and clean little place with outdoor tables during summer, when fancy ice cream delectables are added to the regular quiche and sandwich menu. Even without ice cream, Marguerite's desserts are special. She bakes cookies, pies, muffins, cobblers, baklava, and other treats year round. Her huge chocolate chip squares are as tasty as they are large.

For sandwiches, Marguerite always has pastrami, salami, turkey, roast beef, and corned beef ($1.75–$1.95), but the biggest seller is the veggie sandwich—cream cheese, cucumbers, shredded carrots, tomato, and alfalfa sprouts ($1.50). You can choose among several breads, including pita that Marguerite bakes herself. There are also dozens of gorgeous cheeses on display; many make their way into Marguerite's beautiful quiches. She also finds time to make chili and spinach pie, which go for $1.75 with salad, and side dishes like German potato and macaroni salads.

For any meal, the Hook 'n' Ladder Deli makes a fine hunger

extinguisher. But don't expect a firehouse motif. The food is too important here to compete with the decor.

HOURS   Mon. & Tue. 9 am–6 pm; Wed.–Sat. 9 am–8 pm; closed Sun.

DIRECTIONS   From Exit 59 follow signs for Fredonia, turning left at light onto N.Y. 60 South. In 0.6 mile turn right onto U.S. 20 West. Go 1.3 miles on U.S. 20 and you'll see the **White Inn** on your right. For **Hook 'n' Ladder,** continue 0.2 mile and turn right onto Park Place at the far side of the square. Go 1 short block to stop sign. In front of you is the firehouse; the deli is to the left.

THE BARK GRILL, *Exit 60, Westfield*

The Bark Grill and the Café de Paris (page 137) in Syracuse compete for honors in the hard-to-believe category. Whereas Café de Paris is set in a used-car lot, the Bark Grill is in a residential neighborhood that has seen better days. Whereas the Café has been painted electric purple outside, this restaurant is paneled inside with great slabs of crusty old bark. Moreover, they're both French restaurants with far-flung reputations for excellence.

In this case, the restaurant's renown has spread as far as Pittsburgh, Cleveland, and Buffalo, from which gastronomes regularly come to dine. Participants in the Chautauqua Arts Festival find a meal at the Bark Grill as essential as practicing scales. *Gourmet* and *Bon Appétit* have both featured dishes from this oddball little place.

For lunch, we tried the mushroom casserole ($3.75) and found it worthy of its acclaim. A mélange of wonderful flavors, it had us guessing as to their identity. Chef John Pereira revealed that it had white wine, lemon juice, a number of herbs, and five different cheeses, but he would go no further. So we gave up the hunt and rested content to savor this delight in ignorance.

Also served at lunch are veal or seafood crêpes ($4), quiche ($3.50), shrimp and scallop brochettes ($4.50), eggs Benedict ($4.50), and some dishes that aren't French at all ("Sorry, this

isn't Manhattan"), including standard American sandwiches ($3.50–$4).

But dinner is exclusively haute cuisine; compared to lunch, it's exclusively priced too. Most entrées are $10–$15 with salad, potato, vegetable, and fresh-baked rolls. There is a strong emphasis on table service and flambéed dishes. Tournedos flambé in pepper sauce is the pride of the house, but you can also order veal Oscar, duck à l'orange, coquilles St. Jacques, or grilled loin of lamb with herb butter. Everything is cooked to order and, except for wintertime asparagus, all ingredients are fresh. Happy to oblige, the chef will put together any dish for which he has the ingredients, and he is often called upon to do so by vegetarian diners.

Despite the exotic, slightly bizarre atmosphere provided by the bark-covered walls, this restaurant has touches of elegance, with its white tablecloths, burgundy napkins, and flowers in bud vases. Nobody seems to know how the bark got there, but nearly everyone in town knows that the Bark Grill was once a speakeasy. Just a block from the train depot, it served conductors and passengers who would dash down for a quick tipple. Maybe the bark helped them think they were off in the woods and so less likely to be caught.

HOURS Lunch: Tue.–Fri. 11:30 am–2 pm. Dinner: Tue.–Thu. 5–9 pm; Fri. & Sat. 5–10 pm (open one hour later in summer). Closed Sundays, Mondays, and the first two weeks of January.

DIRECTIONS From Exit 60 follow signs for Westfield, turning left and driving 1.2 miles to the first light (Clinton St.). Left on Clinton until it ends, and then left onto Pearl St. Go 2 blocks to a fork. Bear right onto East Pearl and you'll see the sign "Bark Grill Parking" on right; restaurant is across the street.

Pennsylvania

VIV'S COUNTRY RESTAURANT, *Exit 7, Erie*

If you ask the people at the Pennsylvania Tourist Bureau where to eat, they'll tell you about all the McDonald's and Burger Kings and Perkin's Pancake Houses their area is blessed with. But if you press them for something local and homey, they're all agreed—Viv's is the place.

Owned by a lively little Italian woman, Evelina Vivarelli, Viv's serves up corned beef hash with two eggs for breakfast ($1.89); ham, bacon, or mushroom omelets are $2. There's an eggless breakfast too: cubes of baked ham and mozzarella cheese, served with home fries ($2.50).

Soups are all homemade, and we quite enjoyed our pea soup, boldly flavored with sizable chunks of bacon and ham. Sandwiches are as cheap as 80 cents for a chili dog or 85 cents for a burger; the high is a BLT at $1.75. Heros and meatball grinders get up to $2.50.

At dinnertime, Viv is true to her ethnicity. Italian dinners like gnocchi or homemade linguini with meatballs, salad, and bread are $3.25. American dinners (fried chicken, liver and onions, meatloaf, etc.), served with potato or pasta, vegetable, and bread, run $3.50 to $4.10.

Viv seems to have taken a lesson from the popular brick-plants-and-oak cafés, though her place is hardly of that sort. She serves fried mushrooms, zucchini, and cauliflower as appetizers (85 cents to $1.25), and we expect that she'll soon add fried potato skins and carrot cake to the menu.

HOURS   Every day 6:30 am–9 pm (closes at 8:30 if slow).

DIRECTIONS   From Exit 7 turn left if eastbound, right if westbound, onto Route 97 North. In about a mile the road forks; bear right, staying on 97 North, and you'll see the restaurant just after the fork, on the left.

LANDWEHR HOUSE, *Exit 3, Girard*

Sandwiched between a Pizza Hut and a Wendy's on Girard's fast-food alley, the Landwehr House is easy to miss altogether, and even if you spot its red brick and white trim, you'll probably mistake it for a suburban motel. In reality, the building is an antebellum mansion housing a labyrinthine network of rooms and corridors, some of which once harbored slaves en route to Canada via the Underground Railroad. There are several dining areas in the house in its current incarnation as a German restaurant, and one of them has the comfortable but not overly fancy feel of a family living room—which is what it was in the past.

We'd like to go on and rave about the magnificent food emanating from the Landwehr's kitchen, but what we found was a mixed bag. The sauerbraten was dry and rather bland even though we were assured that it had been done the right way— marinated for five days at room temperature.

The apple crumb pie, however, was delicious—moist inside, crunchy on top, flavorful throughout. Mrs. Swanson peels fresh apples every morning, and we heard that not only the apple pie rates sky-high; pecan, fresh strawberry, and banana coconut cream are especially popular. Soups too—chicken noodle, vegetable beef, and lentil—are homemade from scratch. Maybe it was just a bad day for sauerbraten.

In addition to sauerbraten, the Landwehr House's German dinner specials include a wurst platter (knockwurst, bratwurst, and brunenwurst) and rouladen (round steak stuffed with pork sausage and sage dressing), both at $8.25. The other house favorite is Lake Erie perch, lightly battered and fried, and served as a lunch entrée ($5.75), dinner entrée ($7.95), or sandwich ($2.25). "Once you've eaten it, you'll never settle for what they have out there," declared one satisfied customer with a bouyant sweep of her arm toward Main Street's lineup of fast fooderies. At the Landwehr, other lunch entrées run $4–$6; sandwiches, $1–$2.25. The lunch menu is available at dinnertime if you're willing to forgo the cozy dining room for an orange booth in the coffee shop out back.

We were told that the waitresses were soon to start wearing peasant outfits. For authenticity, we guess.

HOURS   Mon., Wed. & Thu. 11:30 am–8 pm; Fri. 11:30 am–10 pm; Sat. noon–10 pm; Sun. noon–6 pm; closed Tue. In summer, open until 9 pm on Monday, Wednesday, and Thursday; other hours the same.

DIRECTIONS   From Exit 3 turn onto Route 18 North. Go 2.2 miles to a T. Turn right onto U.S. 20 East and go 2.2 miles (through center of town). It's on right, after Wendy's, before Pizza Hut.

I-95

Virginia (Alexandria), Maryland (INCLUDING I-895), Delaware

Virginia (Alexandria)

ABOUT ALEXANDRIA

If it pains you that I-95 doesn't afford access to Washington's marvelous restaurants, despair no longer. Alexandria, Virginia, just ½ mile from the road, is far more manageable, easier to park in, and gentrified enough to boast an entire United Nations of restaurants. It's also picture-pretty, a sort of mini-Georgetown with ancient trees, cobblestone streets, and Colonial-style buildings.

Within eight blocks along King Street we uncovered excellent Jewish, Greek, Italian, Vietnamese, and even Ethiopian restaurants, a trendy fish house, and much, much more. As you descend King Street toward the Potomac, the restaurants get thicker (and the parking worse) until every other renovated building proclaims itself a café, bistro, lounge, or at least a ristorante!

There was no way we could check all this out, and we urge you to park, walk, peek, and pick. (Do the parking away from the river.) We've written up the well-known **Taverna Cretekou** and the less costly **Fish Market.** But by all means consider **Geranio,** a pricey but excellent Italian place; the **East Winds** (Vietnamese); the **Addis,** moderately priced Ethiopian; and **Terlitzki's Jewish Deli.** And check the side streets. Even when just cobblestone alleys, they usually hide some sort of eatery.

TAVERNA CRETEKOU, *Exit 1, Alexandria*

If the flavors here seem hearty but the textures light, it's because this Greek chef was trained in France. Those who have experienced only the heavy sort of Greek cooking will marvel at the subtlety he imparts to the tiropita (feta and cream cheese in pastry) or the roast leg of lamb seasoned with lemon and garlic.

Taverna Cretekou offers a large menu that includes the more common Greek dishes as well as things like taramosalata (red caviar whipped to a light, creamy paste, $3.25) and the tempting exohikon (lamb sautéed in butter with spring onions, artichokes, peas, carrots, pine nuts, casseri, and feta, all wrapped in filo dough and baked to perfection, $9.75).

The atmosphere is as pleasant as the food is delicious. Although the tables are formally set with white and blue tablecloths, the floors are bare, the chairs plain wood, and the windows large. The mood is light and relaxed, and with a patio out back it all adds up to an environment that feels naturally Mediterranean, with nothing overdone.

Dinners are from $8.50 for moussaka to $14.50 for a filet mignon shish kebab. Full lunches run $5 to $7.75, with a meal-sized Greek salad at $4.20. Lighter appetites may want to sample the baby zucchini salad for $2.75.

Whatever your choice, we think you'll like this place. It's been written about again and again. Even the Greek ambassador is rumored to have declared it better than the restaurants of Athens, but we suspect that that was off the record.

HOURS Tue.–Fri. 11:30 am–2:30 pm and 5–10:30 pm; Sat. noon–11 pm; Sun. 11 am–3 pm and 5–9:30 pm; closed Mon.

DIRECTIONS See end of Alexandria entries, next page.

THE FISH MARKET, *Exit 1, Alexandria*

Trendy, noisy, happy, youthful, and spicy pretty much sums up the Fish Market. Its seven small dining rooms carved out of an old warehouse try to offer "something for everyone"—ragtime entertainment, a piano bar, raw bar, and a nearly free lunch in the main bar at "happy hour." The tone is set by the rough-hewn wood and brick, and the place is good-naturedly gimmicky.

The Fish Market makes no concessions to beef eaters. It's all seafood, with prices running anywhere from $1.55 for a "swabby Joe," a fishy Sloppy Joe, to $11.50 for prawns imperial topped with crabmeat. We tried the house specialty, a creamy, chunky seafood stew, full of delicious, tender scallops, chunks of snapper and haddock, clams and oysters ($2.10 for a healthy serving). It was really quite good, but with so spicy an aftertaste it left us gulping water for a full half-hour.

Most entrées are standard seafood items at about $7.50; $5.50 for lunch. A wide assortment of appetizers and sandwiches makes for a multitude of inexpensive possibilities.

You'll get your money's worth in any case, and you can see the Potomac for free. The shoreline is just a block or two away.

HOURS Mon.–Sat. 11:15 am–2 am (limited menu after 12:15 am); Sun. 11:15 am–12:30 am.

DIRECTIONS FOR ALEXANDRIA RESTAURANTS
Take Exit 1N onto U.S. 1 North. Go six lights (0.6 mile) to King St. For **Terlitzki's Jewish Deli,** turn left on King and go 3 blocks. For all the others, turn right on King. One and a half blocks will bring you to **Taverna Cretekou,** on the right (818 King St.). **East Winds** is directly across the street. Go 1 more block down King for **Addis** and **Geranio,** also on the right. The **Fish Market** is 5½ blocks farther down King (105 King St.), on the left, at the corner of Union St. Park as soon as possible after turning onto King.

Maryland (including I-895)

MICHAEL'S, *Exit 15B, Largo*

The I-95 part of the Capital Beltway goes through Prince Georges County, Maryland, poor relative of Montgomery County and the northern Virginia suburbs. It's to the latter that the Washington moneybags have gone, and with them, alas, the interesting restaurants. All the same, if you stick to steaks and the simpler things of life, you'll do well enough at Michael's, an innocuously Colonial restaurant just a stone's throw from the Beltway.

Michael Tsourounis is a big man with big heart—and honest. He doesn't claim to be the best—just to satisfy the needs of his area, and this he does with Cretan pride, determined that his restaurant be the best of its kind.

There was Romaine among the iceberg lettuce, for example, and if the dressings were merely acceptable, at least the tomatoes were red and ripe in mid-March. Your steak will be cut to order; your crabcake, all backfin meat.

The menu is American, with dinners running from $6.95 for a chopped sirloin to $12.65 for a prime rib (the house specialty). Lunches are around $4.50 ($2.25–$3.85 for sandwiches).

HOURS   Mon.–Fri. 11:15 am–10 pm; Sat. 4:30–10 pm; closed Sun.

DIRECTIONS   Exit 15B will put you on Route 214 West. Go about ¼ mile. On the left.

LEDO RESTAURANT, *Exit 25, College Park*

Our friends in faraway western Pennsylvania had a glazed, nostalgic look in their eyes as they recalled Ledo's pizza from their days at the University of Maryland. They'd "walk a mile," they said, for a Ledo's pizza, and often did.

Well, we'd walk half a mile. It was a good pizza, with a crisp crust, flavorful sauce, and thick slices of pepperoni—far superior to the usual highway fare and worth the 3½-mile drive it takes to reach the Ledo. But we tend to be picky about pizza and just couldn't give Ledo's our highest rating.

There's much more to the Ledo than pizza, however. It's a full Italian restaurant with a good selection of sandwiches and American dishes. And though it's collegiate in spirit (crowded and happily noisy at lunchtime), the clientele was older than we'd expected. A very pleasant place, all in all, tastefully but unpretentiously decorated, light and lighthearted.

Lunches go from $1.95 for soup and salad to $3.95 for lasagne. Italian dinners (the usual) are $4.25 to $7.95; American dinners (also the usual) run about $1.50 higher. Pizzas are $2.65/$3.75/ $6.25, with a dozen add-on options.

HOURS Mon.–Thu. & Sat. 9 am–1 am; Fri. 9 am–2 am; Sun. 9 am– midnight.

DIRECTIONS Take Exit 25 for U.S. 1 South (College Park). Go 1 mile on U.S. 1 and bear right onto Route 193 West (signs for U. of Md.). Go 2½ miles along the edge of the campus to a small shopping center on the right. It's in there.

GAVRILLE'S, *Exit for Route 216, Laurel*

* *Color, not cuisine*

If a simple sandwich and a milk shake will do, then do it at Gavrille's. Leave the hectic highway and step into the quiet world of Christina Gavrille, whose eyes twinkle with mischief when she says, "I know people don't like to be seen buying liquor on Main Street."

Not a whole lot happens at this onetime liquor store, now crammed high up its pink walls with drugstore items, art supplies, and toys. The telephone booth is the original mahogany one, lined with pebbly gray-green sheet metal; the display cases are wooden too, and the counter, where you can see it beneath the candy bars, is marble. They'll make you up a sandwich for under $1.85, and there's a soda fountain for dessert—sundaes for 85 cents, lemonade for 45 cents.

That's it, except for the few tables, and one is usually occupied by Christina and her brother Nick. The place has been in their family since 1910, and they sit here chatting with old friends when business allows, which seems to be more often than not. Since they live right upstairs, the store is really just an extension of their living room.

Theirs is the talk of people who've lived 70 years on Main Street—about watching friends pass away, of Christina's wishing she had studied anthropology (she once heard Margaret Mead), of having won the daily double at the Laurel raceway. She expresses her philosophical views in lilting Southern tones.

161

"Don't put old people on the shelf," she says, and "Don't live by the clock."

No one in Laurel does.

HOURS   Mon.–Fri. 9:30 am–8 pm; Sat. 9:30 am–6 pm; closed Sun.

DIRECTIONS   From the Route 216 Exit (Laurel) go south on 216 about 1½ miles to second light (Main St.). Left on Main, 0.3 mile; it's on your left.

KING'S CONTRIVANCE, *Exit for Route 32, Columbia*

There's little doubt that the best roadside food between Baltimore and Washington is found at the King's Contrivance, a French restaurant emphasizing Maryland seafood. Sorry, no steamed crabs. Here it's more like *la chair de crabes Dewey*—lump crabmeat with mushrooms and green peppers glazed in a sherried fish sauce ($8.95)—or *cassoulette de fruits de mer*—lobster, shrimp, crabmeat, and scallops, simmered in white wine, garlic butter, tomatoes, and herbs ($10.25).

The King's Contrivance is a trifle (or should we say a "truffle"?) contrived itself. Columbia is a suburban town erected from scratch as a planned community, and the restaurant, though a very pleasant place, feels a bit as if it filled a box labeled "fine restaurant" on some city planner's map. The building is an old mansion, but the conversion and renovation were so complete that it feels as new and as spanking clean as the white linen on the tables.

The food *is* good, overseen by a chef from Grenoble who came to Maryland by way of the Savoy and Roosevelt hotels. At lunchtime you can sample his labors for as little as $3.75 (quiche Lorraine or an omelet). For $4.75 you get a spinach and mushroom salad dressed with raspberry vinegar, lemon juice, and olive oil. Entrées go up to $8.50 for roast sirloin. Or you might enjoy the paper-thin slices of raw sirloin for $4.85 or the lightly curried crabmeat on rice for $6.50.

HOURS Lunch: Mon.–Fri. 11:30 am–2 pm. Dinner: Mon.–Sat. 5:30–9:30 pm; Sun. 4–9 pm.

DIRECTIONS Take the exit for Columbia marked "Route 32." Do not confuse this with the other Columbia exit a few miles north. Go to stop sign at end of long ramp and turn left onto Route 32. Go 2½ miles to a small sign for the restaurant and turn right. At next stop sign turn right. It's ¼ mile to restaurant, well marked by signs.

ABOUT BALTIMORE

The sleeping giant of the East Coast has awakened, thanks to its colorful Mayor Schaeffer and his pet project, Harborplace, an urban renewal delight that includes dozens of restaurants and the new National Aquarium (in which the mayor took a dip, as promised in the event of late completion).

Unfortunately, all this plus Little Italy and Corned Beef Row are smack in the heart of downtown. The difficulty is that I-95 and the Harbor Thruway go through the southern and eastern parts of town, the latter too industrial and the former too impoverished to offer much good eating.

But we couldn't let you pass Baltimore without recommending one true Baltimore crab house, **Gunning's,** which we found near I-95 just south of the Harbor Tunnel. And two of the town's most famous older restaurants are in East Baltimore, halfway between downtown and the highway: **Haussner's,** loved for its art collection as much as for its German-style food, and **Olde**

Obrycki's, a crab house with class and full restaurant fare to boot. You'll have to deal with city traffic for any of these, but you'll also get a look at life in Baltimore's older ethnic neighborhoods, complete with row houses and the famous marble steps.

A final point: I-95 enters Baltimore from the east and leaves it from the southwest, but its two ends don't meet in the middle. They are connected by the Harbor Tunnel Thruway (I-895), which we have treated as if it were part of I-95 itself. Confusing, but we're glad they didn't tear out the heart of the city to build more highways.

GUNNING'S CRAB HOUSE, *Canton Avenue Exit & Exit 13, Baltimore*

Gunning's is the perfect place for Baltimore steamed crabs. After all, this is largely a town of ethnic neighborhoods, modest row houses with marble steps, local taverns, and crab houses (which are almost as common as the bars). Gunning's combines all this in one spot, and its excellent, peppery steamers have won it a city-wide reputation.

The formstone exterior and sheet-paneled walls of this neighborhood eatery will clue you to expect nothing fancy. Tearing apart crabs at the table and flinging the innards aside is a pretty gutsy, lusty way to eat. No one dresses up here to bash away at piles of crustaceans on the brown-paper tablecloths.

You can get them year round, imported from Louisiana or North Carolina when the true Maryland crab is out of season. But they'll always be encrusted with red pepper, black pepper, and a host of pungent secrets, and they'll always be steamed the old-fashioned way, over burners in enormous pots, not with live steam, which blows the spices off. When the crab juice and the peppery coating mix on your fingers and all this gets communicated to the sweet meat of the crab (and to your beer glass), then you'll understand what the Baltimore crab cult is all about, and you'll never again think of those long-legged things from Alaska as crabs.

There *are* tamer ways to eat crabs at Gunning's. In the delicious, spicy crab soup, for example ($1.65 a bowl), or in the equally good crabcakes. These are less spicy, moist, and rich, made only from the backfin meat, not the cheaper, dryer stuff from the claw (you've got to watch out for that!). There are soft-shell crabs too—in sandwiches ($3.65) or by the platter ($9.15)—as well as crab fluff, crab imperial, and fried hard crab.

Gunning's *does* have noncrab dishes—all kinds of seafood, in fact, at reasonable prices, and even such other things as kosher hot dogs, hamburgers, and sauerbraten with dumplings. But crabs are what it's all about here, and if you haven't experienced this regional wonder, you owe yourself a try. We know of no one who doesn't love them, not even Alaskans!

HOURS   Mon.–Sat. 11 am–1 am; Sun. 11 am–11:30 pm.

DIRECTIONS   Northbound: Stay on I-95. Do not follow I-895 to Harbor Tunnel. Take Canton Avenue exit. Turn right at end of ramp and go 3½ fast miles through six lights. This is Canton Ave., which turns into Patapsco Ave. The seventh light is Hanover St. Right on Hanover for 6 short blocks. Gunning's is on the left. (Reenter I-95 North by reversing southbound directions, below. Entrance is only 7 blocks from the restaurant.)

Southbound: Shortly after going through Harbor Tunnel take Exit 13 and bear right at end of ramp. Go 1 block to light and turn left onto Patapsco Ave. Go 1 block to Hanover St., turn right, and go 6 short blocks to the restaurant, on the left. (Reenter I-95 South by reversing northbound directions, above.)

Entering I-895

HAUSSNER'S, *Exits for Eastern Avenue & O'Donnell Street, Baltimore*

Haussner's has very good food at moderate prices, but the real reason to visit this local institution is the art. The restaurant is decked out in elaborately framed, floor-to-ceiling paintings on every inch of wall space. And where there's not a painting or a table, there's a statue, etching, or at least a knickknack of some sort. It's 19th-century stuff mostly, collected by the Haussners over a 30-year period. And even if it's not of the highest caliber, it's great fun. To quote a poet laureate of Maryland:

> *Oh what a rare and heavenly treat,*
> *Whenever you're hungry and long to eat,*
> *To go to Haussner's—and what a sight,*
> *The paintings, the sculptures, all so bright.*

Well, not great poetry either, but in the right spirit! This lavish array of color against the plain wood chairs and white tablecloths produces a uniquely enjoyable environment in which to sample the large menu. You can choose from virtually any American dinner, Maryland specialties like crabcakes or crab imperial included. These run as high as $16 or as low as $5.50. But don't overlook the baked rabbit with spaetzle ($8.25), pigs' knuckles with sauerkraut ($5.95), paprika schnitzel ($10.95), or the knockwurst, bauernwurst, bratwurst, or sage sausage ($5.95).

Obviously you can enjoy Haussner's atmosphere for a little or a lot. You can even get a sandwich, with French fries or a cold vegetable, for a mere $1.95. Ox tongue is $2.95; raw beef with onions, $3.95. Gorgeous desserts from Haussner's bakery will end any meal with a flourish.

Come for the art, or come for the food. Haussner's will please you either way.

HOURS Tue.–Sat. 11 am–11 pm; closed Sun. & Mon. No reservations, but frequent lines.

DIRECTIONS Northbound: After going through Harbor Tunnel, take Exit 2 (O'Donnell St. West). Go 0.2 mile to second light (Ponca St.). Right onto Ponca and go 0.4 mile to first light (Eastern Ave.). Left onto Eastern and go 0.9 mile to Clinton. It's on the corner, on the right (3244 Eastern Ave.).

Southbound: After passing exit for Baltimore Beltway (Exit 2/I-695), bear right, following signs for East Baltimore and Harbor Tunnel Thruway. Take the Eastern Ave. Exit, 1 mile after Thruway leaves I-95 proper. Bear right for Eastern Ave. westbound (Highlandtown). Right onto Eastern and go 2.1 miles to Clinton. It's on the corner, on the right (3244 Eastern Ave.).

OLDE OBRYCKI'S, *Exits for Eastern Avenue & O'Donnell Street, Baltimore*

People come from all over town for crabs at Obrycki's. The place used to be a down-to-earth affair located in an East European working-class neighborhood. It moved only a few blocks when it occupied its newly renovated pair of town houses, but the atmosphere changed to warm Colonial and the restaurant got "olde" in the process.

Actually the new decor is very nicely done, featuring a wonderful old bar and several small, intimate dining rooms. And the crabs are as good as ever. But now Obrycki's is a full restaurant specializing in seafood, with dinners in the $9–$14 range. If you've had enough of steamed crabs, soft crabs, crabcakes, and crab soup, then try the tuna chowder or oyster tidbits. But if you're looking for Baltimore's famous decapods at dinnertime, Obrycki's refined environment will let you do it with as much elegance as this kind of eating allows (see Gunning's, page 164, for a description of how it's usually done).

So serious is Obrycki's about its local specialties that they're open only during the Maryland crab season, mid-April to October. No imported substitutes here!

HOURS Open mid-April to October only. Tue.–Fri. 11:30 am–2:30 pm and 5–11 pm; Sat. 5–11 pm; Sun. 4–9 pm; closed Mon. Steamed crabs during dinner hours only.

DIRECTIONS Follow directions for Haussner's (above), but continue past Haussner's on Eastern Ave. about 1.2 miles to Broadway. Turn right onto Broadway and go 3 blocks to Pratt St. Right on Pratt. It's 1 block up, on the right (1729 E. Pratt St.).

Return to I-95

NEW IDEAL DINER, *Exit 5, Aberdeen*

Several things distinguish the New Ideal from your run-of-the-mill stainless-steel eatery. First there's the crab soup, which was surprisingly good—spicy, full of crabmeat in a hearty stock. Then there's the sparkly glitter in the green pinstriping that runs around the diner. We hadn't seen that little touch before, and we were equally pleased by the 1952-vintage Venetian blinds that nicely soften the feel of things within.

We don't know whether it was the soup or the stripes that

launched the New Ideal on its TV career, but the makers of Sunbeam and Blue Ribbon bread thought the diner special enough to star in more than one commercial. Its fame doesn't rival that of Rosie's Diner in Little Ferry, New Jersey, scene of the Bounty paper towel commercials (see page 190), but we're not complaining. We were looking for local color more than notoriety.

Since good things don't come cheap, you'll find some prices at the New Ideal a bit higher than the diner average. Maryland specialties like soft-shell crabs and crabcake dinners are $7.95 and $7.50, respectively. Others are $3.95–$7.75, and $1.50 higher for the full-course treatment. Sandwich prices are more in line, and that good crab soup is $1.10 a cup.

HOURS   Every day 6 am–10 pm.

DIRECTIONS   Northbound: Turn right at Exit 5, following signs for Aberdeen. Go 0.2 mile to a light and turn right. ■ Go 0.2 mile to junction with Route 132 and turn left. Follow 132 for 1½ miles to light at U.S. 40. Right onto U.S. 40. Go 0.1 mile; it's on the right.

Southbound: Left at Exit 5 and go 0.4 mile to a light. Turn right, then as above from ■.

RIVER CITY ICE JAM, *Exit 6, Havre de Grace*

* *Color, not cuisine*

Havre de Grace (HAV-a-dee-grace, in the local dialect) ought to have good restaurants. It's a fine old town located at the junction of the Susquehanna River and Chesapeake Bay, a spot of unparalleled importance for the entire region.

It is the Susquehanna's sweet waters that lower the salinity of the upper bay. This in turn makes Maryland's blue crab the world's tastiest, even if biologists cannot distinguish it from its cousins in North Carolina and Louisiana. (Settle for the cousins if you have to. Maryland crabs are in short supply, and even in Baltimore these reasonable facsimiles are used during the off-season or when there just aren't enough of the real thing to go around. But for Lord's sake don't think those overgrown daddy-longlegs from Alaska are really crabs!)

To return to Havre de Grace: Although you can watch the river meet the bay from Main Street, there's not an inviting restaurant to be found, not even a crab house, except for the River City Ice Jam, which is actually a kids' ice cream parlor, very pleasantly done up in second-grade Crayola, stuffed animals, and bentwood chairs. It's got a fenced outdoor patio that affords a view of both the river and Main Street—a nice spot to cool off with a 50-cent cone ($1.35 for three dips). There are charbroiled burgers for 99 cents, and 14 sandwiches too.

Actually it looks as if Havre de Grace's dearth of full-fledged eateries will soon be remedied. A place called the Rogers House was abuilding right on Main Street, and it appeared to be aiming for excellence. We heard, however, that construction had been held up, so whether it will exist when you arrive we do not know. (Pray for low interest rates!)

HOURS   Tue.–Thu. 11 am–8 pm; Fri.–Sun. 11 am–9 pm; closed Mon.

DIRECTIONS   From Exit 6 turn right if northbound, left if southbound, onto Route 155 East. Follow 155 about 1.6 miles to U.S. 40. Cross U.S. 40 and continue on 155 for 1.3 miles to a right turn under an iron bridge. Take this right and then go straight into town 0.3 mile to Congress Ave. Left on Congress and go 1 block. It's on the corner, on the left.

NORTH STREET HOTEL, *Exit 9, Elkton*

* *Color, not cuisine*

If you'd like as cheap a lunch as can be had, and in the atmosphere of an old hotel/barroom, then check out the North Street in tiny downtown Elkton. It's been in the Nicholson family since 1919, when the law required a building to have at least ten hotel rooms before the authorities would license a bar on the premises. The rooms disappeared with the triumph of tolerance over temperance, but not much else has changed. The result is a delightfully funky neighborhood tavern, patronized by a courthouse crowd at lunchtime and local folks at night.

You can tell it's different before you go in. The large windows are bordered in neon, with pleasant little curlicues of color off in the corners. Inside, the floors are bare and the ceiling yellow. The varnish on the ancient wooden booths is worn bare, and the bar itself is glass block, topped with wood, and illuminated by a marvelous Art Deco fixture that looks as if it had been swiped from an ocean liner. The bentwood chairs seem to have grown there, cigar smoke wafts through the air, and there are three video games. For life at the headwaters of the Chesapeake Bay, this is the place to go.

Of the 24 simple sandwiches the North Street offers, eight are under $1; clubs soar up to $1.90. Hot sandwiches are a few cents more, and the most expensive item on the menu, a crabcake platter, is $2.50. Not bad, but no one is pretending that the North Street Hotel is a fine restaurant. Come for the color, not the cuisine.

HOURS Mon.–Sat. 10 am–6 pm for meals. Later for bar only. Closed Sundays.

DIRECTIONS From Exit 9 turn left if southbound, and bear right if northbound, onto Route 279. Go 2 miles to a light and turn left. Follow the road over the bridge and the restaurant will be just past the second light, on the right.

HOWARD HOTEL, *Exit 9, Elkton*

The North Street isn't the only World War I–vintage hotel now serving little Elkton as a restaurant and bar. Half a block away, the Howard displays pictures of Eisenhower and Taft addressing the throng from its balconies back in its spiffier days. Recently, the small restaurant has been refitted in a clean, plain version of barnboard with red-checked vinyl tablecloths, and according to everyone we asked, it's *the* place for steamed crabs in the Elkton area.

Or in any other area, even Baltimore, according to chef Mel Woolsey. Coauthor Weiner's Baltimore chauvinism was offended, he being a native son, but the matter couldn't be put to the test since the steam pots hadn't been fired up for the day. But we did try a spicy crabcake which the Baltimore authority grudgingly admitted was "okay," even if he wouldn't concede that it was "the real thing."

With objectivity so clearly impossible, we can only report that the crab soup (a mere 50 cents a cup/95 cents a bowl) is made from scratch; the at-least-acceptable crabcake sandwich is $2.45; soft-shells with cole slaw are $4.75; and steamers—the peppery, gutsy, lusty king of the Maryland crab cult—are anywhere from $10 to $18 a dozen. But do check out the Howard's all-you-can-eat steamed crab special ($9) from May to September. That's a good deal, since it's not hard to go through more than a dozen if they're running small and you've a strong stomach (in more senses than one, since, properly eaten, steamed crabs are disemboweled at the table and the chaff flung to one side, but not before its juices cover the fingers, which then transfer the succulent flavors to the meat).

With such refined delights in mind, it seems sacrilegious even to mention such things as hamburgers ($1.10), club sandwiches ($2.85), spaghetti with salad ($3.80), or fried chicken ($3.30). But these things are on the menu, along with shrimp, scallops, and a New York strip steak.

More in the local spirit is the fact that all the clams are opened on the premises, and on Wednesday nights from May to September crabmeat finds its way into the spaghetti sauce.

HOURS   Mon.–Wed. 11 am–9 pm; Thu.–Sat. 11 am–10 pm; Sun. 1–10 pm.

DIRECTIONS   Same as for North Street Hotel, above. It's ½ block farther down the street, on the right.

Delaware

ABOUT NEWARK

For the trouble of a 5-minute drive into this pleasant university town you can have your choice of a diner, a brick-plants-and-oak café, or Newark's best, **Goodfellow's,** a quiet, tasteful place with an eclectic international menu. The three restaurants come in three price ranges, of course, and all are on Newark's Main Street, home turf of the University of Delaware's "Fight'n Blue Hens." (In Wilmington the chemical industry reigns supreme. But south of the Chesapeake and Delaware Canal, poultry is Delaware's biggest product, and Frank Perdue rules instead of the DuPonts.)

There's another choice at Exit 1. You can go the other way, toward Glasgow, and find the **Glass Kitchen,** a place that was very "moderne" in 1952—cheap and decent today.

GOODFELLOW'S, *Exit 1, Newark*

Goodfellow's is an excellent place for something out of the ordinary at prices that won't leave you broke. It's an elegant little gourmet restaurant with a European feel and very good cooking. Consider a lunch of scallops-and-mushroom strudel, for example ($3.95), or roast beef on French bread with Cajun gravy ($3.75). Perhaps a shrimp-and-cucumber omelet ($3.50). Even the humble tuna salad comes dilled, with potatoes, tomatoes, hard-boiled egg, and red onion ($3.50).

Not posh, Goodfellow's is still quite graceful, with its white tablecloths, fresh flowers, and light, airy mood. Dinners are in the same vein as the lunch entrées and run from $7.95 to $12.50. But whenever you stop by you'll find it a refreshing break from the drive.

HOURS Lunch: Tue.–Thu. 11 am–2:30 pm. Dinner: Mon.–Sat. 5–10 pm. Closed Sundays.

DIRECTIONS See end of Newark entries, page 174.

JIMMY'S DINER, *Exit 1, Newark*

Jimmy's is a spanking-clean stainless-steel diner with curtains, great prices, decent food, and a crowd much classier than the usual diner clientele. Professorial types with natty, well-trimmed beards and herringbone jackets occupy many of the booths at lunchtime, joining only a sprinkling of students and workers. For 45 cents we had a good-as-anywhere fried egg sandwich. The chicken salad was acceptable, and we loved the three-pronged milk-shake machine in pink enamel. Sandwiches go up to $2.50 for a club; dinners run from $1.95 for fried haddock to $7.95 for a 16-ounce T-bone. Most are around $3.50, and another $1.75 will get you soup, salad, beverage, and dessert.

Perhaps the spiffy tone at Jimmy's stems from the owner himself. He's the only diner man we've seen who wears a suit to work (dark double-breasted pinstripe), and it's with great dignity that he takes your check on the way out.

HOURS Mon.–Thu. 6 am–8:30 pm; Fri. 6 am–9 pm; Sat. 6 am–8 pm; closed Sun.

DIRECTIONS See end of Newark entries, page 174.

KLONDIKE KATE'S, *Exit 1, Newark*

The name pretty much tells you to expect a brick-plants-and-oak café. And it's a handsome one, collegiate variety, with lots of wood and stained glass, noisy when full, youthful and friendly. The food is good, but not great, and the menu is typical of BPOs—burgers ($2.95), Reubens ($3.75), quiche ($3.50), spinach salad ($2.95), potato skins ($1.25), and soup ($1.25). We decided to test a more substantial meal of spareribs, which seemed

173

a bargain at $4.95, and found them more sweet than spicy, but quite nice all the same.

And Kate cheerfully turned down the music when we requested it.

HOURS Mon.–Thu. 11 am–10 pm; Fri. & Sat. 11 am–midnight; Sun. 11 am–3 pm (brunch) and 3–10 pm.

DIRECTIONS FOR NEWARK RESTAURANTS

From Exit 1 turn right onto Route 896 North. Go 2½ miles, past the stadium and the Chrysler plant, over the bridge and three lights to Delaware Ave. Turn right onto Delaware. For **Jimmy's Diner** take the second left (Haines) and go 1 block to Main. It's on the corner, on the left, with parking in the rear. **Klondike Kate's** is ½ block down Main, to the right. For **Goodfellow's** take the third left off Delaware Ave. and park before reaching Main. It's on Main, ½ block to the right.

THE GLASS KITCHEN, *Exit 1, Glasgow*

'Twas here, before the coming of I-95, that the Weiner family used to stop en route from Baltimore to Atlantic City. So to it we returned, for sentimental if for no other reasons.

But there are others. Good solid food for one (though nothing very special) and modest prices for another. Also it's a good chance to see what "modern" meant in 1952 when this long, low, and very plain building was erected. Nothing's changed, and the glass-enclosed kitchen is still there out amidst the booths and tables. (If the truth be known, the heavy cooking is actually done in back. And the publicly visible kitchen has glass on two sides only.)

Then there's U.S. 40 itself, one of the country's oldest highways, the original link between the East Coast and the frontier of western Pennsylvania, now an underutilized four-laner demoted to local traffic. It never recovered from the advent of I-95, but it's still got the kind of life that used to line the highways. You might want to drive it for a few miles before rejoining high-speed I-95.

We should mention the eight club sandwiches on the Glass Kitchen's menu ($2.75 tops), but there's a lot more to be had than bread stuffers. About $4.50 will get you a pork chop or fried flounder platter. Another $1.35 converts the platter to a full-course dinner.

And do check out the restaurant's logo. It depicts a fat chef, rounded as a '50s sofa. In one hand he holds aloft a steaming platter, while in the other there's a cleaver, partially concealed behind his back. His eyes have a demonic look above the chubby smile, and his intentions are anything but clear.

Not a compelling reason to go out of your way, granted, but the sort of thing that sticks in a child's memory.

HOURS　Mon.–Thu. 11 am–8 pm; Fri.–Sun. 11 am–9 pm.

DIRECTIONS　From Exit 1 turn onto Route 896 South toward Glasgow. Go almost 3 miles to U.S. 40 and turn right. It's 200 yards, on the left.

HADFIELD'S CARRY-OUT SEAFOOD,
Exit 5, New Castle

This is your last chance for steamed crabs if you're headed north. If southbound, it's your first crack at the Chesapeake Bay specialty, but you probably ought to wait until Baltimore to taste this spicy wonder, encrusted in a thick peppery goo and properly washed down only with great quantities of good beer. (Neal, who grew up in Baltimore, insists that there, and only there, can the real thing be had.) In the meantime try any of five kinds of clams. Hadfield's has littlenecks, topnecks, cherrystones, chowders, and Ipswich at $1.50–$2.50 a dozen. There are mussels at 80 cents a pound and oysters, fried or, as the natives love 'em, on the half-shell with a dash of Tabasco and a squeeze of lemon. You can also choose from a beautiful display of fresh fish and then watch them bread and fry it right before your eyes. Or make an entire meal of a pint of Philadelphia snapper soup (rich—with a dash of sherry) or Manhattan clam chowder ($1.25 each).

Despite the name, you won't have to carry out your choice. They've got a few indoor picnic tables at Hadfield's. When they call you by your first name, you pick up your order and share a table with whoever happens to be there. That could be just about anyone. Though Hadfield's trade is mostly local folks, we found ourselves next to a New York couple who have made it their southbound watering hole for years.

It was from the New Yorkers that we learned writer Henry Miller's theory of restaurant locating—look for a dumpy place that's crowded. We think that's better advice than the outdated truck-driver theory. Hadfield's was indeed crowded, and although it's plasticky and fluorescent, it isn't exactly dumpy.

Still, Henry would have liked it.

HOURS   Tue.–Thu. & Sun. 10 am–9 pm; Fri. & Sat. 9 am–10 pm; closed Mon.

DIRECTIONS   From Exit 5 get onto Route 141 South, toward New Castle. Go 1½ miles to U.S. 13 and turn right. It's ¼ mile down U.S. 13, on the left.

NEW CASTLE FARMERS' MARKET AND AUCTION, *Exit 5, New Castle*

* *Color, not cuisine*

On weekends you might enjoy this rural Lower East Side where you can stroll past hundreds of the earthiest little enterprises selling everything from clothing and black velvet paintings to haircuts. There's food too, and it's all lodged in a mammoth concrete-block building painted with countless signs now faded to near illegibility.

At one end is booth 401, which offers barbecued turkey legs

for $1.99, chicken at $1.99 a pound, and chicken wings for 30 cents apiece. They weren't bad, those wings, but not the best either.

At the other side of the building was the more promising Norm's BBQ Heaven, which offered "food with soul," specializing in "celestial chicken and ribs." Unfortunately, Norm's had just changed hands, and the soul food had degenerated into mere hot dogs and hamburgers. But the turnover is fast here. By the time you arrive Norm may be back.

He may have already returned, in fact, if it's the same fellow who runs Norm's Big Dipper, "home of the monster shake." At least the prose style is the same. But in any case you'll find all sorts of eateries between the two barbecue stands—doughnut joints, French bread, bagels, health food, and a booth run by Stolzfus of Intercourse, Pennsylvania. They specialize in Pennsylvania Dutch bacon and sausage, the latter coming with sage in 50-pound mounds or stuffed into 10-yard casings. We assume they'll sell you less, but you'll have to cook it at home.

HOURS   Fri. & Sat. 10 am–10 pm; Sun. 10 am–6 pm; closed Mon.– Thu.

DIRECTIONS   From Exit 5 get onto Route 141 South, toward New Castle. Go 1½ miles to U.S. 13 and turn right. It's about 0.8 mile down U.S. 13, on the left.

THE CRAB SHAK, *Exit 5, New Castle*

This place used to be ruggedly authentic, with newspapers for tablecloths and a great reputation for crabs. Now it's been renovated into a low-lying, barnboard affair with dropped ceiling, wall paneling, and a few nautical touches. Not that bad, really, but nothing you haven't seen a hundred times before. Good local seafood is the specialty, and if Hadfield's and the Farmers' Market sound too rugged, the Crab Shak is a good alternative.

There are chowders and crab soup at lunchtime (75 cents/ $1.25), sandwiches, including crabcakes and soft-shell crab ($2.25–$4.50), and entrées from $4.50 to $6. Dinners are mostly

$10–$16, 90 percent of them seafood, with a few steaks and chops. Most of the many wines are sold at only $1 over retail.

HOURS   Summer: Mon.–Thu. 11 am–10 pm; Fri. 11 am–11 pm; Sat. 1–11 pm; Sun. 1 pm–1 am.
Winter: Tue.–Thu. 11 am–9 pm; Fri. 11 am–10 pm; Sat. & Sun. 3–10 pm; closed Mon.

DIRECTIONS   Take Exit 5 onto Route 141 South, toward New Castle. Go 1½ miles to U.S. 13 and turn right. Go about 1½ miles on U.S. 13 to the restaurant, on the left.

New Jersey

OLD SWEDES INN, *Exit 2, Swedesboro*

Swedesboro is a tiny town just two quick and pretty miles from the turnpike. It has seen better times, but May and Mark Rogers are determined to revive it. They've moved an entire restaurant operation here from Philadelphia, set it up in a well-aged tavern/hotel, and renovated the place themselves. Now they're offering everything from quiche, burgers, and Reubens to escargots, stuffed flounder *en croute,* and tournedos Charon.

It's a good place for a highway stop. The atmosphere is at once dignified and relaxed; despite the white tablecloths, Oriental rugs, and the obvious concern for quality, your traveling clothes will fit right in. Perhaps that's because the homemade renovations, though warm and tasteful, are on the earthy side of refined.

Prices aren't bad either, especially in the lounge, where the refurbishing hasn't been all that extensive. It's still funky, with a red-lit, glass-block bar and carpeted booth seating. Here quiche is only $2.50, as is the cheese, meat, and cracker plate. A hefty cheeseburger goes for $2.50 and the Reuben is a dollar more. (This light menu is available all day.)

Add about $1.50 for the same served in the dining rooms or on the glassed-in porch. There, pleasantly warmed by the sunshine, we tried the fettucini with bacon and cream sauce ($3.95). It was quite good—heartily flavored with an ample dose of garlic. Omelets, spinach salad, eggs Benedict, and eight entrées complete the lunch menu, all comparably priced. Dinners are mostly light continental dishes in the $9–$14 range.

HOURS   Lunch: Tue.–Fri. 11:30 am–2:30 pm. Dinner: Tue.–Sat. 5:30–10 pm; Sun. 4–9 pm. Sunday brunch: 11 am–2 pm. Light menu in lounge at all times.

DIRECTIONS   Left at Exit 2 onto Route 322 West. Go 0.8 mile to light and turn right onto Route 551. Go 1.2 miles to center of town. It's on the right. A pleasant drive through lovely farmland.

OLGA'S DINER, *Exit 4, Marlton*

Lit up like an amusement park, and nearly as large, Olga's is decidedly more than just another gaudy diner. For one thing, its cheesecake and Boston cream pie have won *Philadelphia* magazine's "Best of Philly" awards on more than one occasion. These are produced in an adjacent bakery that offers everything from Danish pastries and Jewish hummentashen to Italian rum cakes and German strudel. (For $3.75 you can buy a 1¾-pound cheesecake so light and smooth it's hard to believe it's sinful.)

But you needn't wait till dessert to sample Olga's good cooking. We tried a veal parmigiana. It arrived huge and golden beneath a light, cinnamon-flavored tomato sauce that gave it a moussaka-like flavor. The Greek potatoes in garlic and oregano butter were excellent, and even the fresh broccoli had real life to it. Somebody's obviously trying to do things right at Olga's, and doing it at only a hair over typical diner prices.

We suspect it's Olga herself. We wish we had met this remarkable woman who first started in the business with a true

lunch-car diner in Camden. Her husband died two months after they opened, but Olga went on alone to make a success of it. Then, with her son, she opened this much fancier place in Marlton. In the meantime she had to do battle with a Michigan-based chain of restaurants, also called "Olga's," which by sheer coincidence just happened to open a branch in nearby Camden, New Jersey!

At Olga's even the glitz is better than average. Crowning the building is a huge red neon sign that shouts "Olga's" in flowing script. The marble façade is lit by the whitest, brightest vapor lamps we've ever seen. Nothing's subtle inside either, but if a bright and plasticky interior can have class, then Olga's has that too!

HOURS   Always open.

DIRECTIONS   Bear left on the Exit 4 ramp onto Route 73 South. Go 3.2 miles to Olga's; it's on the right. Bear right at the light just before the diner and you'll be led right to it.

CAFÉ GALLERY, *Exit 5, Burlington*

What may well be southwestern New Jersey's finest restaurant stands by the banks of the Delaware River just a few miles from Exit 5. Café Gallery is the labor of two couples with a common background in the arts who set out to open a restaurant that "would feed our souls as well as our bodies."

A year's labor converted an old tavern into an elegant French restaurant and art gallery, as handsome a place as you'll find anywhere. The feel is light, clean, and modern; the mood is one of restrained understatement. Quality art fills the dining area as well as the gallery upstairs, and a wall of small-paned windows affords a grand view of the river.

The food is even better. You won't find escargot sandwiches or veal stuffed with kiwi fruit here—just classical French cooking like delicate sole Veronique or sirloin with a full-flavored pepper and Burgundy sauce. "We're not trying to reinvent the wheel. We just want to make a round one," states chef and part-owner

Jim Fisher. And so they have, with as much attention to presentation as to preparation.

Dinner entrées run from about $10 to $13.50. There are a dozen of them, augmented by as many as a dozen other specials that depend on what looks best at the market. We found monkfish in lobster sauce and rabbit stew along with such regulars as braised pork loin in champagne, shrimp thermidor, and broiled trout with almond butter.

Lunchtime offers gazpacho, onion, and soup du jour ($1.50–$2.25); six salads ($2.75 to a high of $5.25 for shrimp); omelets ($3.75); sandwiches with a French accent ($3.75–$5.50); and a variety of entrées around $5.50.

It was a goal of the couples who created Café Gallery to prove "there is life in New Jersey south of Exit 8." That they've done, and made it a good life to boot!

HOURS   Lunch: Mon.–Sat. 11:30 am–3:30 pm. Dinner: Sun.–Thu. 5–10 pm; Fri. & Sat. 5–11 pm. Buffet: Sun. 11:30 am–3 pm.

DIRECTIONS   From Exit 5 turn left onto Route 541 North for Burlington. Go 3.8 miles to junction with U.S. 130. Cross 130 and continue straight about 0.7 mile. It's the last building before the river, on the right.

BURLINGTON DINER, *Exit 5, Burlington*

A wonderful old-style diner, twice as long as the usual, with a two-tone, op-art mosaic tile floor and real ceiling fans (old black things, not neo-Victorian wood and brass). The Burlington also has the most rounded ceiling we've come across and the tallest display of cigarettes by the checkout counter.

What's more, we found better than average diner food here, starring a very nice chicken escarole soup and excellent sticky buns. The supporting cast delivered mixed performances.

HOURS   Always open.

DIRECTIONS   From Exit 5 turn left onto Route 541 North for Burlington. Go 3.8 miles to junction with U.S. 130. Turn right, and there it is on the corner.

MUFFIN'S
MOUNT HOLLY RESTAURANT AND DELI,
Exit 5, Mount Holly

You'll find good food and moderate prices at Muffin's, a pleasing little place in brick and varnished pine nailed on the diagonal. There are the requisite plants and stained glass too, but the menu goes beyond the usual for a brick-plants-and-oak café —specials like eggplant Gruyère, for example, or roast game hen in orange sauce (only $7.95, with soup or salad, rice, coffee and dessert).

The standbys are there too: deli sandwiches ($2.95), spinach salad, Reubens, fancy burgers (about $3.50), steaks, and seafood ($7.95–$10.95).

With Muffin's comes the bonus of a walk through downtown Mount Holly, which turned out to be a surprisingly fetching town with old brick houses and considerable charm. (You'd never guess it from the turnpike!) Right in its center is the Mount Holly Deli, a very plain establishment, offering breakfast and lunch, one corner of it more a grocery store than anything else.

HOURS   **Muffin's:** Lunch: Mon.–Fri. 11:30 am–3 pm. Dinner: Tue.–Thu. 5–10 pm; Fri. & Sat. 5–11 pm; Sun. 3–8 pm. **Deli:** Mon.–Fri. 6 am–4:30 pm; Sat. 6 am–2 pm; closed Sun.

DIRECTIONS   From Exit 5 turn right onto Route 541 South, toward Mount Holly. Go 2.8 miles. **Muffin's** is on the right, with parking in the rear. **Deli** is 2 blocks farther, at the foot of the street.

GOLDEN COACH DINER, *Exit 8, Hightstown*

Just a mile and a half from Exit 8 is the best diner food we've come across, if you can call veal Marsala, Hungarian goulash, pickled herring and chopped liver mere "diner food." But the prices are certainly diner prices. For $5.45 we got a huge portion of juicy, tender bluefish. With it came not only the usual two vegetables (unusually well prepared), and not only a sampling of pasticcio, knish, and spinach-pie appetizers, but also unlimited access to a fine salad bar with feta cheese, great pickled herring, and chopped liver as good as Aunt Sadie's.

The menu at the Golden Coach is an enormous mélange of continental, Greek, Italian, Jewish, and American dishes—the apparent result of Greek owners and a Jewish neighborhood not far from cosmopolitan Princeton University. It's hard to believe that all this could be carried off with success, and we won't say that the sauce meunière was the best we've ever tasted. But it was very good, and so was everything else. At $5.45, who's going to quibble? How they do it, we don't know, but perhaps it has something to do with Peter Zoumas driving to Philadelphia three times a week for grocery shopping, assuring freshness and the lowest possible prices.

Not everything is cheap, however. Dinners do go up to $13.70, and the sandwiches run a bit high. The bargains are to be found in the specials, so study the menu well.

The diner itself is a new, Greco-glitzy affair, with no fewer than four kinds of stone on the exterior and five kinds of tile behind the counter. The wrought-iron stools are painted gold, and the architect didn't miss a single chance to work in an arch or two. It's pleasant enough, in its way, and endearing, even if it goes beyond the bounds of restrained good taste.

HOURS   Always open.

DIRECTIONS   From Exit 8 bear left in the ramp for Hightstown and onto Route 33. Go 0.6 mile and turn left at the railroad bridge. One block to the light, and then turn right. Follow the road 0.9 mile to U.S. 130. Turn left on 130. It's on the left, 200 yards up the road.

JAMESBURG QUALITY BAKERY, *Exit 8A, Jamesburg*

A perusal of Jamesburg restaurants did not reveal anything likely to tickle the taste buds of central New Jersey gourmets. There is **Collura's Italian American Restaurant,** serving three meals a day. Two eggs, home fries, toast, and coffee are only 95 cents, and the decorations seem to have been priced accordingly.

But if a sandwich or light snack is all you require to fuel your tank and push on to D.C. or N.Y.C. or wherever, you can find it at the Jamesburg Quality Bakery. "Quality," of course, is a subjective term, and while we wouldn't call this the pinnacle of patisseries, it is certainly a better than average bake shop with a wide selection of nicely crusted breads, rolls, muffins, pastries, doughnuts, cookies, and cakes.

What's more, there is a deli counter where cold cuts are sliced to order. The bakery doesn't make sandwiches, but since it sells sliced bread and rolls, who's going to stop you from putting two and two together, and washing it all down with some juice or milk from the dairy case?

You can't sit here to eat, but there's a pleasant little park on the lake, just two blocks away.

HOURS   Tue.–Fri. 6:15 am–7 pm; Sat. 6:15 am–6 pm; Sun. 7 am–3 pm; closed Mon.

DIRECTIONS   From Exit 8A turn left (signs for Jamesburg). Go 2½ easy miles until just before the road crosses the railroad tracks. Turn left here (W. Railroad Ave.), go 2 short blocks, and you'll see the bakery on your left. (Collura's is directly across the tracks.)

BOSKO'S DINER, *Exit 9, South River*

* *Far, but cheap; local color*

Although it's only about 35 miles from Manhattan, South River seems to be a town that Megalopolis forgot. Not that it's exactly rural, but the signatures of modern suburban life seem to have missed South River. No shopping plazas, no fast-food strips —just gritty little houses and garment factories along the salt marsh. South River feels like a hard-working midwestern town totally indifferent to East Coast glamour.

185

But South River folks aren't indifferent to Bosko's Diner. Everyone's life crosses it—three times a day for some. Almost everyone you'll see here lives or works in town. If you're willing to drive the 10 minutes it takes to find this hidden outpost, the honest, wholesome food is likely to bring you back again.

The cole slaw is among the best we've found, freshly made each day from great big shreds of cabbage and a sweet, tasty dressing. The secret to its success is said to be in the unrevealed vinegar-to-sugar ratio. As a side order, it costs only 35 cents.

All the fish served at Bosko's (Thursdays and Fridays only) is fresh, and cooked to order. Even though fish sandwiches aren't on the menu, one was cheerfully provided on a hard roll, just for the asking ($2). We found the fish light and flaky, almost grease-less. A fish platter with potatoes and vegetables is $3.75; most of the 20 or so other dinners run $2.95 to $3.35.

Bosko's is located so close to the salt marsh that it has a backyard of reeds and sedges. Unfortunately, the windows don't look out on this estuarine setting, but inside, the rose-colored ceiling emanates a warming glow. Alfrieda, the waitress, calls everyone "hon" or "love," and she even sings impromptu verses as she speeds about.

It's the real thing.

HOURS   Mon.–Sat. 5 am–7 pm; closed Sun.

DIRECTIONS   From Exit 9 enter Route 18 East (signs for South River). In 0.9 mile there is another sign for South River which takes you through a jughandle. Follow South River signs another 0.9 mile to the first light and turn left onto Prospect St. Go 1½ miles on Prospect as it curves, until it ends at a T. Turn left and make an immediate right. Go 0.2 mile; Bosko's is on the left, not to be confused with a less distinguished diner just before it. A bit tricky, to be sure, but if you've read this far you can do it.

CARVAJAL MEXICAN RESTAURANT,
Exit 11, Perth Amboy

Carvajal is the epitome of what we visualized in our most hopeful moments when we started looking for roadside eateries —excellent, local, close to the exit ramp (although it's a long ramp), and tucked away where nobody would ever look. Finding it, however, was another matter.

For one thing, Carvajal is neighbor to no ordinary interstate but the nightmarish New Jersey Turnpike. The city is industrial Perth Amboy, the kind of place everybody knows about and nobody visits. But we'd heard Perth Amboy had a great Mexican restaurant, and we set out to find it. Braving the labyrinth of cloverleafing exit ramps, we took wrong turns right and left, and each time were delivered into a new network of asphalt spaghetti. Eventually we conquered the maze, and the explicit directions given below will spare you our misadventures.

The most amazing thing about Carvajal is that it's just half a block from the bottom of the last ramp. From the head of Goodwin Street, there's no mistaking it, a stucco Latin temple that leaps off the sidewalk in an otherwise drab residential neighborhood.

Discouraged by its outward signs, we took a closer look and saw that Carvajal is not the presumptuous palace of some bigtime restaurateur, but the innocent effort of a single immigrant couple trying to make a go of it entirely with their own hands.

The Mexican food that Natividad ("Nat") and Olga Carvajal have brought to Perth Amboy is a mix of three cuisines: the peasant cooking of Nat's native Michoacán province; the gourmet Mexican cuisine he studied at Mexico City's Academia Gastronomica Cuisina; and the taco/tostada/enchilada dishes that are usually passed off for the whole of Mexican cuisine.

So it is that here you can go Tex-Mex with guacamole and a taco ($6.50 to $7 at dinner) or you can expand your horizons to include Michoacán dishes like camarones a la Veracruzana (shrimp with tomato sauce) or pollo en salsa de Gaujillo (chicken with hot sauce). These run $7.50 to $10.50.

But if you want to see Nat shine, order one of his gourmet specialties, all flambé affairs cooked from scratch at tableside. *Camarones en salsa gastronomica,* for example, is a stunning presentation of shrimp with garlic, onion, parsley, mushrooms, wine, cognac, and a special sauce ($13.95). We couldn't decide which we liked better—eating it or watching Nat's symphony of allegro movements as he prepared it.

Nat himself is most proud of the one gourmet dish that isn't served aflame. It's a paella with chicken, pork, lobster, shrimp, clams, scallops, chorizo, and pimientos ($27.90 for two, maybe even three or four). We didn't have the good fortune to try it, but we'll definitely be back.

Lunch at Carvajal is strictly Mexican-American ($3.50 for tacos, chili rellenos, etc.; $4.50 for a combination plate). But if you can't come back at dinnertime and lunch is not too busy, you might persuade Nat to wheel out the camping stove and set the cognac bottle pouring.

HOURS   Lunch: Tue.–Fri. 11 am–3 pm. Dinner: Tue.–Fri. 5–10 pm; Sat. 4–11 pm. Closed Sun. and Mon.

DIRECTIONS   From Exit 11 follow signs for U.S. 9 South. Go about 2 miles and then bear right, following signs for Smith Street/Keasbey. In ½ mile the road forks; go right for Perth Amboy. In 0.2 mile more, road forks again; bear left for Fayette St. In 1 mile you'll come to a stop sign at Fayette. Cross it and you're on Goodwin St. Go ½ block; it's on your right. Return to highway the way you came—signs make it easy.

SZECHUAN GARDENS, *Exit 11, Woodbridge*

Where it cuts through New Jersey's malodorous sea of refinery tanks that dot the landscape like gargantuan checkers, the New Jersey Turnpike is probably the most despised stretch of road in America. Each year, millions of drivers and passengers suffer this transportation nightmare without benefit of nose plugs, earphones, or tunnel-vision goggles.

Imagine how much more bearable the turnpike torture could be if it were broken up with a bit of Oriental tranquillity. How about a good, quiet Chinese restaurant? We found one, and it's only about three minutes from the turnpike exit—not half as long as it takes to get in the rest-room door at the Vince Lombardy Service Area when it's crowded.

Considering where you've just been, you'll actually welcome Szechuan Gardens' dropped acoustic-tile ceiling. The warm tones of red and beige, the Chinese bas-relief, the carpet and tablecloths are all manna to the weary turnpike traveler. Even the Oriental Muzak is a relief.

If you have to get right back on the highway for another battering, Szechuan Gardens' quick luncheon menu promises to feed you in a jiffy. Served with soup and steamed rice are 15 Hunan and Shanghai selections, all $3.75. Or, for those with a taste for the familiar, there are combination plates of the chow mein/spareribs/moo goo gai pan variety, each served with egg roll and fried rice (most, $3.50–$3.95).

Dinner also offers a choice between Chinese-American and the real thing—Hunan, Szechuan, or Shanghai style. It was suggested that chow sam sen would be a good dish for the Szechuan greenhorn because the zingy spices are used in moderation. We tried it and enjoyed the jumbo shrimp, sliced pork, and white-meat chicken cooked with snow peas, bamboo shoots, and baby corn cobs, but found ourselves yearning for a stronger dose of heat. It costs $6.95; many dinner entrées are less, and portions are ample.

Szechuan Gardens has no liquor license. We witnessed a seated guest storm out in an uproar because he couldn't order wine. The host politely explained that a liquor store practically next door had a wide selection, including one wine especially good with Chinese food. We pass this wisdom along so you'll know before you sit down.

HOURS Sun.–Thu. 11:30 am–10:30 pm; Fri. & Sat. 11:30 am–11:30 pm.

DIRECTIONS From Exit 11 follow signs for U.S. 9 North. It's about 2.7 miles of easy driving to the Caldor Shopping Center, on your right. Restaurant is at far side of plaza.

ROSIE'S DINER, *Exit 18, Little Ferry*

Rosie's may well be the most famous diner in the world. Its fame comes not from food but from show business. This is where Nancy Walker stars as Rosie the diner waitress who wipes up countless spills with Bounty paper towels. Bounty's TV commercials have heaped such fame upon the diner that it recently changed its name from the Farmland Diner to Rosie's.

Rosie's stardom extends beyond paper towels. It has been a set for Sanka, Clorets, Pepsi, and Body-All commercials. Even Ethan Allen furniture has been advertised here, even though no one knows quite why. With each commercial, a swarm of technicians and celebrities descends upon the diner bearing lights, cameras, and sound equipment. Groupies and autograph seekers trail in too, and guests from as far as California have come here just to have their pictures taken with Ralph Corrado, the owner.

That's quite a bit of hoopla for a small-town diner. Why? And why this diner in particular? Our guess is that since diners are pure Americana, any product advertised in one must appear somehow better, purer, more American. And Rosie's is the perfect diner for a TV crew because it's well preserved and, most important, well proportioned. The prodigious 30-foot width is the largest we've seen in an old-time diner, and it's just what a crew needs to maneuver its gear.

With all this show biz hype, Rosie's could probably get away with serving cardboard chops and mud pie, but in fact the food is quite decent. On weekends, goulash is the featured item. We'd hesitate to compare it with that of Boston's Café Budapest, but it was certainly respectable—a large portion served on a bed of wide egg noodles with peas (overcooked) for $3.75. Liver and onions (also $3.75) is a big seller every day of the week; Ralph slices it so thick that he calls it "liver steak." A two-egg breakfast with potatoes and toast is $1.40; sandwiches run $1.45 to $2.25. Rosie's special is called the "Quicker Picker Upper"; it's a bacon-topped hamburger with French fries, cole slaw, and pickle for $3.

Commercials aside, Rosie's is a great place for a half-hour's rest. The old patterned tile floor is a work of art, and we loved the sky-blue color of the curtains, ceiling, and tables. (The color scheme, we heard, changes with every new commercial.) You won't be disappointed with Rosie's unless you're counting on seeing Rosie herself. Chances are, she's lunching at Café Budapest.

HOURS   Always open.

DIRECTIONS   Northbound: From Exit 18 follow signs for Route 46 West/Hackensack. Go about ¾ mile on Route 46 West, until the traffic circle. Rosie's is on the circle.

Southbound: From I-95 take exit labeled "Route 46/Teaneck Rd./The Ridgefields" (last exit before toll). Follow signs for Route 46 West. In 0.8 mile you'll reach a traffic circle, and there you'll see Rosie's.

New Jersey, New York

New Jersey

ROSIE'S DINER, *Exit for Route 46 West, Little Ferry*

You may not realize it, but you've probably seen this diner on TV a dozen times. See page 190 for a full description.

DIRECTIONS If approaching from I-95 South, I-80, Palisades Parkway, or the George Washington Bridge, look for signs to Route 46 West. Do not enter the New Jersey Turnpike, but take Route 46 to the traffic circle that's about 1 mile west of the Turnpike entrance. Rosie's is on the circle.

(If approaching from I-95 North, use northbound directions given on page 191, because I-95 North is the New Jersey Turnpike at this point.)

ABOUT FORT LEE

You don't have to schlep into Manhattan for a World's Fair of ethnic dining. Fort Lee, New Jersey, a culinary oasis at the foot of the George Washington Bridge, is far more convenient for anyone passing by. We feature Fort Lee's Armenian and Japanese restaurants but encourage you to explore the town in search of cooking from other ports. If, for instance, you have an uncontrollable craving for bagels and whitefish, you'll find a kosher restaurant/deli across the street from the two restaurants we have reviewed.

HONDA JAPANESE RESTAURANT, *Exit for Fort Lee*

With the recent establishment of American headquarters for numerous Japanese firms, Bergen County has become something of a Little Tokyo, quite white around the collar. So much the worse for General Motors, but so much the better for highway dining. Fort Lee's classy, glassy Main Street is home not only to Furomuto Realty and the Nan-Han Gallery but also to a couple of excellent Japanese restaurants, Noshiro and Honda. They are similar in so many respects—both with sushi bars, almost identical menus, and comparable prices—that we decided to pick just one. We preferred the clean, modern lines of Honda, but you may wish to spend about $2 less and eat at Noshiro. From what we've heard, the food is equally good.

Honda has the light, open feel of an Oriental gallery: white walls with blond wood trim, rice-paper lanterns, shoji panels, and well-framed modern Japanese art instill a relaxing, dignified effect. On one side of the front room is the tatami dining area, where guests must remove their shoes to sit on straw mats and dine on tables just inches above the floor.

There are conventional chairs too, and seats at the all-important sushi bar, where white-capped chefs deftly wield glistening knives to cleave raw tuna, snapper, bass, and abalone. When the tender morsels are served by themselves, humped on the plate like diving porpoises, they are called sashimi; when molded over ovals of pressed rice, they are known as sushi. We tried combination plates and adored both preparations, especially when made with the surprisingly delicious and smooth red tuna. If that wonder had anything in common with the stuff in supermarket cans, we never found it.

At lunchtime, sushi and sashimi combinations run $6–$7. A sushi dinner is around $10. Other lunch combinations, such as tempura and gyoza (dumplings) with soup, salad, and fried rice, are around $5.50. The tempura is a deep-fried marvel of shrimp, broccoli, and mushrooms in a light, golden batter.

For American-sized appetites, a six-course meal is always available for $14; if that's not enough food, you may opt for the seven-course dinner at $18. Or, in the $9–$12 range, you can settle for four-course austerity, choosing entrées like salmon teriyaki, seafood sukiyaki, or beef negimaki (filet mignon wafers enveloping green onions in rice-wine sauce).

Whatever you order, it will be a feast for the eyes as well as the palate; like all fine Japanese restaurants, Honda pays considerable attention to the presentation of food and garnishes. Each plate is a splendid still life, almost too beautiful to eat.

HOURS   Tue.–Fri. noon–2:30 pm and 5:30–10:30 pm; Sat. 5–11 pm; Sun. 4:30–10 pm; closed Mon. (Noshiro is open Mondays, however.)

DIRECTIONS   See end of Fort Lee entries, page 195.

THE MEDITERRANEAN ARMENIAN RESTAURANT, *Exit for Fort Lee*

Care for a dish of harpout kufta? Perhaps a little kouzou kerzartma on the side? If you have developed a taste for such Armenian delicacies or would like to (it's not hard at all), we commend to you the Mediterranean Armenian Restaurant in Fort Lee.

Tucked behind a former storefront on Fort Lee's Main Street, this is a friendly, informal family restaurant that feels Middle Eastern through its subdued Islamic tone, not overdecoration. And, of course, through the spirit of its owners, Ruth and Harry Artinian.

When Harry left Syria in 1976 he had been holding down three jobs at the same time, and was therefore well prepared for the restaurant business, which, he says, is only slightly more demanding. Harry is a polite and gentle host who greets at least half the customers by name, while his wife, Ruth (who prepares everything from the hummus to the pastry), is a buoyant woman with dancing eyes and upbeat confidence. When we told her how we adored her zesty, zingy broiled chicken, for example, she raised one arm with a flourish, backed into the kitchen, and in one phrase sang out the secret: "Eleven different spices."

The chicken ($7.95) truly was a masterful transformation of what might have been an ordinary dish, but we equally enjoyed the kouzou kerzartma, an unbelievably tender lamb shank baked in tomato sauce with garlic, green pepper, onion, lemon juice, and Armenian spices ($8.25).

All dinner entrées, which range in price from $6.95 to $9.75, are served with vegetables and rice pilaf. If the thought of rice pilaf suggests something out of a box, a forkful of Ruth's tender grains studded with pine nuts, almonds, and pistachios will do away with that idea forever.

Although it would take many days of dining out to sample (and pages to describe) the nine different entrées and eleven appetizers served here, you can get a shot at many of them in one lunch. Every weekday, an array of appetizers and a variety of salads and meat dishes are spread out in an all-you-can-eat buffet for the remarkable price of $3.95. Try to find that in Manhattan!

The Mediterranean Armenian Restaurant is definitely a place to expand one's culinary consciousness, and no one should be put off by the exotic names. Since few of the customers are Armenian or Syrian (most are Jewish, in fact), every dish is described on the menu in plain English. When you know that it's really just a meatball of spiced ground beef, pine nuts, and onions encased in cracked wheat, not even harpout kufta sounds terribly foreign.

HOURS   Lunch: Mon.–Fri. 11:30 am–2:30 pm. Dinner: Mon.–Thu. 4–10 pm; Fri. & Sat. 4–11 pm. Closed Sun.

DIRECTIONS FOR FORT LEE RESTAURANTS

Northbound (actually heading east): While approaching the George Washington Bridge on I-95, take a local (not express) lane. Just before the bridge, take exit labeled "Palisades Pkwy/Fort Lee/Routes 9W & 46." From ramp go straight for 0.4 mile to the fourth light, and turn right onto Lemoine Ave. In 0.2 mile turn right at the light onto Main St. In half a block, **Mediterranean Armenian Restaurant** is on your left, then **Noshiro,** and a block farther, on the same side, is **Honda.** Public parking in lot across from Honda.

Southbound (actually heading west): Take upper roadway of George Washington Bridge (very important). Immediately after bridge (just after exit for Palisades Parkway), bear right, following sign for "Fort Lee/ Routes 67 & 9W." Ramp splits; bear right for Lemoine Ave. At stop sign turn left to light. Left at light onto Lemoine. Go 0.3 mile, to the second light, and turn right onto Main St. In ½ block, **Mediterranean Armenian**

Restaurant is on your left, then **Noshiro,** and a block farther, on same side, is **Honda.** Public parking in lot across from Honda.

New York

PHIL'S LUNCHEON, *Exit 16, New Rochelle*

The weather-worn storefront of Phil's Luncheon matches the neighborhood it's in, but once inside you'll find a heartwarming small-town lunchroom. Even if it doesn't shine with pristine perfection, we wouldn't want to change very much except maybe to restore the scuffed floor and let in some more light. But the mahogany counter, the wall moldings and intricate trim, the ancient tin ceiling (not ordered from a design catalog), and the old ice cream fountain hark back to the heyday of luncheonettes. Now that they are an endangered species, old-fashioned lunchrooms win nostalgia points. It's too bad that, like health, one rarely appreciates these things until they start to go.

But it's not strictly a yen for the ambience of the past; we're just as interested in the kind of plain but honest cooking that can still be found in places like Phil's.

The owner of Phil's (whose name is Steve) puts up a roast beef or turkey every day. When you walk in and ask for a sandwich ($2.25) or dinner plate ($3.50), you know you're not about to be a victim of food processing, portion control, or mass production. Steve simply ambles back to the warming oven, pulls out his roast, and slices off your portion. When you order a hamburger ($1.15), he grabs a handful of fresh-ground beef and slaps it into a patty. The production experts at McDonald's would cringe. We cheer.

Steve also makes his own chicken, egg, tuna, and salmon salads (sandwiches $1.25–$1.75). His chicken rice and split pea soups are homemade too, but a few soups are not; it's best to ask.

Originally, Phil's was strictly a soda fountain. Although Steve continues to sell ice cream scoops (55 cents) and shakes ($1.25), he's cut back on his operation and can offer only two flavors, vanilla and chocolate. He hasn't cut back on quality, however: the ice cream is still homemade.

HOURS   Mon.–Sat. 7 am–7 pm; Sun. sometimes 7 am–noon, sometimes not at all (sounds authentic, eh?).

DIRECTIONS   Northbound: From Exit 16 bear right. In 0.2 mile, at light, turn right onto North Ave. ■ Immediately on your right is a small parking lot. Park, then continue walking along North Ave. for about 1 more block. Phil's is on the left side of the street.

Southbound: Exit 16 puts you on a traffic circle. Go halfway around and bear right for North Ave. In ¼ mile you'll reach the light at North Ave. Turn right, then as above from ■.

CHINATOWN DINER, *Exit 19, Harrison*

How many Chinese restaurants do you know that serve three meals a day? How many sell miniature bottles of wine (as on airplanes) for a dollar? Where two people can walk away from dinner stuffed, with change from a $10 bill in hand? And if you do know one like that, is it in an old diner? No doubt about it, the Chinatown Diner is one of a kind.

The diner itself is a remnant of the '30s. The only thing Chinese about its decor is the scattering of bamboo wall hangings (for sale at $3.95). The pink tile floor, gay curtains, and colorful tablecloths all but hide the grime of a long and greasy history. Even though the housekeeping isn't exactly fastidious, this is one of the cheeriest diners we've seen.

The owner, Poshen Pea (Anglicized from Pei so you'll know how to say it), is a short, impish man, a beaming Oriental hobbit in a Yankees cap, who greets all his guests at the door as if they'd been there yesterday. In about 30 seconds, newcomers feel like regulars.

Unfortunately, after all this buildup, we have to tell you that the wonton soup tasted like tap water. Later, we heard that the hot and sour soup is the one to try. In any case, our meal improved considerably from there on.

The egg roll was exceptionally crisp, stuffed with large chunks of obviously fresh ingredients. For a main dish, we ordered shrimp with cashews. It was an enormous mound of food, with fried rice, for just $3.95. Hardly subtle in its spices or exotic vegetables, and not the pinnacle of Chinese cuisine, it was nevertheless a respectable dish with an abundance of nicely browned shrimp, diced fresh peppers, carrots, bamboo shoots, and water chestnuts. All had been bought at a Chinese market in Manhattan the day before. No MSG here, and its absence can be detected by a certain clarity of flavor. Mr. Pea's native province, Hupei, is known for its noodle dishes, and the Chinatown Diner's noodle soups are a meal in themselves (all $3.95, like most main dishes on the menu).

In addition to Chinese food, the mimeographed menu offers conventional American breakfasts, sandwiches, and hot plates. Like the Oriental specialties, these are priced about as low as they can go. Perhaps it's because they charge for tea and fortune cookies that the Peas can keep prices so reasonable. We laid our dime on the counter and grabbed a word of wisdom on the way out. The little slip read, "You have made an unwise investment."

It must have meant the wonton, because the rest of the lunch was worth every penny.

HOURS   Tue.–Fri. 6:30 am–9 pm; Sat. 7 am–9 pm; closed Sun. & Mon.

DIRECTIONS   See Jillyflower's, below.

JILLYFLOWER'S, *Exit 19, Harrison*

If you were to design a restaurant as the Chinatown Diner's antithesis, you'd probably come up with something like the place that's only a few doors away, Jillyflower's.

By no means is Jillyflower's a diner but a carefully conceived blend of deep-hued brick, wood, and carpeting, with pink and green accents. The fine modern art arranged tastefully on the wall is not for sale, but if it were, it would cost a lot more than $3.95. Eating here isn't cheap (your $10 bill might buy two appetizers, but don't expect much change), and there certainly aren't any bottles of wine for a dollar. (For $3, though, you can have a

glass of Clos du Bois California Chardonnay 1979.) The bill of fare, attractively printed on heavy textured stock, is limited to a manageable number of appetizers and entrées. And quite unlike the Chinatown Diner, whose name tells all, the appellation of this restaurant is a puzzle. Even those who know that a jilly-flower is a kind of New York State apple, and also an English flower, aren't likely to conjecture from the name that this is a French restaurant.

We're not sure just why Jillyflower's three owners named their place as they did, but we know that the restaurant has quickly soared to prominence in Westchester County's epicurean circles. Scarcely two months after it opened, *The New York Times* reviewed it and titled the piece "Seven Weeks Old but Making News."

The news, of course, is that the food is delicious. We have wistful memories of the scrumptious scallop salad that preceded our meal. It was a creamy mélange of scallops and mushrooms with strips of colorful vegetables. Just as good was the entrée of mushrooms, chicken, and duck livers that had been sautéed with shallots and sauced with a veal stock, then added to al dente pasta for a sprightly blend of subtly contrasting flavors and textures.

Entrées here run $4.50 to $7.50 at lunch, $8.25 to $18 at dinner. You could easily spend much more, and do much worse, in Manhattan. As one of the owners told us, almost with embarrassment, Jillyflower's is said to be where Westchester's "beautiful people" congregate. She wasn't sure she liked it, but admitted it was true.

HOURS   Lunch: Mon.–Fri. noon–2:30 pm. Dinner: Mon.–Thu. 6–9:30 pm; until 10 on Fri. and 10:30 on Sat. Closed Sun.

DIRECTIONS   From Exit 19 follow signs for Harrison, which direct you onto Theodore Fremd Ave. Turn left on Fremd and go 0.8 mile. Fremd Ave. becomes Halstead Ave. but that shouldn't worry you. **Jillyflower's** and **Chinatown Diner** are both on your left, across from the railroad station. Easy parking at the station.

New York Route 17 (Quickway)

New York

TRUFFLES, *Exit 70N, Johnson City*

Here's a place that would be worth going out of your way for, but if you're on Route 17 it's barely 30 seconds off the highway.

At the front of the large room, Truffles is a gourmet store/bakery/deli selling just about everything imaginable that's good to eat: cheeses (82 of them), meats (about that many), candies and chocolates from all over the world, cookies and cannoli shells, croissants, rolls, and bread baked on the premises, crackers and cream puffs, Danish and bagels, pasta and pâté, jams and jellies, coffees, teas, and spices, even scintillating salads, like pineapple-chicken with broccoli in cream sauce or vegetables with pasta and garlic sauce.

If you can plot a direct course through this orgy of gustatorial delights, proceed to the restaurant at the rear. It is done up tastefully, not intimate but joyful, light, and bright, with clean modern lines and sensual paintings of food on the walls. Most striking are the fire-engine-red designer chairs that look like high-tech transmogrifications of a chain-link fence. To our surprise, they were superbly comfortable.

Everything found in the gourmet shop can be brought to your table, but the restaurant's menus are also worthy of inspection. From the sandwich list we ordered a masterful combination of cheese, pastrami, and turkey with cole slaw and Russian dressing on excellent rye bread. Our jaws strained to accommodate this monster, but the taste made it worth our effort. At $4.25, this was the highest-priced sandwich; others start at $2.50. For $2.25 we also had a huge bowl of clam chowder beside a fresh croissant; the chowder was delicious, not suffering at all from the restaurant's landlocked location.

While the sandwich menu is available all day, a dinner menu also appears at around 5 PM. It has six daily specials (most at $5.95), featuring items like linguini with clam sauce, stuffed cabbage, veal and peppers, some kind of interesting salad, and a cheese platter (with six cheeses, fruit, and French bread).

Behind all this gourmet goodness we suspected a good story, and we were right. Co-owner Barry Gray once ran a fancy cookware shop downtown. To effectively use his own merchandise he took up gourmet cooking but soon tired of trips to New York City for supplies. "Someone ought to open a gourmet shop," he lamented until he tired of crying and did it himself.

Two years of research preceded Truffles. Barry and his partner Bob Flynn knew what they liked, but not where to get it or how to make it. One weekend, questing for the perfect dill pickle, they drove 150 miles, all in Manhattan. Finally, they found their Grail—in Brooklyn. In Chicago, they once came upon an unparalleled chocolate-chip cheesecake. To divine the recipe, they actually sent the cake off to a laboratory for chemical analysis!

If you need a bread-and-butter gift for whomever you are visiting, you'll have no trouble at all finding the bread, the butter, and anything to go in, on, or beside it.

HOURS   Store: Mon.–Sat. 9 am–9 pm; Sun. 9 am–5 pm. Restaurant: Mon.–Sat. 11 am–8:30 pm; Sun. 11 am–4:30 pm.

DIRECTIONS   Exit 70N puts you on a feeder road that takes you to a light in front of the Oakdale Shopping Center. Don't enter shopping center but turn right at light onto Harry L Drive. At the next light turn right into the Giant-Oakdale Plaza. It's next door to the Giant Supermarket, an unlikely location, but don't be put off. Less than 1 mile total.

NUMBER FIVE
WHOLE IN THE WALL, *Exit 4S, Binghamton*

See pages 85 to 87 for descriptions of these easily accessible restaurants, one a natural foods eatery, the other a gourmet steakhouse. Since Route 17 is concurrent with I-81 in this stretch, exit numbers are the same, and directions are identical no matter which of the two roads you are driving.

CRANE'S RESTAURANT, *Exit 84, Deposit*

Every once in a while we find a gem of a restaurant in a residential neighborhood, close enough to the highway for convenience yet too far for anyone to chance upon it. Crane's is just such a discovery.

No suburban beefhouse this. It's been around since 1937, when it was a popular resting spot for travelers on the main route between New York City and Buffalo. Now all intercity traffic flies by on the four-lane Quickway, and only local folks know about Crane's.

It's a dinner-only, family-style, meat-and-potatoes place serving well prepared, reasonably priced entrées ($6.95 and up, including soup, homemade bread, salad, and potato). There's fish, shellfish, and poultry as well as steak, but on a Saturday night you might feel a little bit out of place if you don't order prime rib.

Inside, little has changed in nearly half a century. Though very clean and well kept up, Crane's still has the old dark-stained plywood that somehow looks a lot less like plywood than today's product, and a decorative molding strip dotted with coat hooks that haven't budged in 45 years.

Hanging above the hooks is owner John O'Conner's prized collection of military memorabilia—rifles, pistols, bayonets,

bolos (Spanish-American War swords), and other relics that he
has been garnering from veterans since he was knee high. Many
were retrieved from local barns, attics, and tool sheds, and they
go back to the Civil War, as does some of the military art John
has collected, including two Currier and Ives originals. On one
wall are issues of *Stars and Stripes* with banner headlines like
"INVASION!" "HITLER DEAD," and "NAZIS QUIT!!!"

Not generally drawn to military displays, we nevertheless
found Crane's a fascinating place. If you go there, be sure to talk
to John about his hobby; he's extremely friendly and happy to
share his enthusiasm.

HOURS   Tue.–Thu. 5–9 pm; Fri. & Sat. 5–10 pm; Sun. 2–8 pm;
closed Mon.

DIRECTIONS   Eastbound: From Exit 84 turn left onto Routes 8 and
10 North. In 0.8 mile you will cross over a bridge and come to a blinking
light. ■ Go straight through the light and in 0.2 mile turn left at the traffic
light onto Second St. Go ½ mile; Crane's is on your left, just before the
Chrysler dealer.

Westbound: From Exit 84 turn right onto Routes 8 and 10 North. In ½
mile you'll cross over a bridge and come to a blinking light. Then as
above from ■.

LA SALETTE, *Exit 87, Hancock*

* *Untried, but likely*

Hancock is where the east and west branches of the Delaware
River become one. Pitched like a tepee on a high nub of land, La
Salette offers a great view of the entire valley. A ski chalet–style
building with plastic tablecloths, Muzak, and dark-stained post
and beam casings, La Salette's finest visual point seems to be its
view. Unfortunately, the panorama is visible only from the bar.

The restaurant is on a golf course, and the small family-style
trattoria downstairs is meant to serve golfers and anyone else
who drops by. The menu is inexpensive and limited—five pasta
dishes with tomato sauce ($3), pizza ($3), heros ($2), and a few
American standbys like burgers and hot dogs. But they're prob-

ably all you need for a quick lunch stop; you'll find the unpretentious ambiance down here in keeping with the menu—simple but adequate.

Upstairs, the menu gets more ambitious, and more expensive. For $8–$10, you can order frogs' legs Provençale, chicken Cordon Bleu or, a favorite, escargots Bourguignonne. Pasta dishes like spaghetti with clam sauce are somewhat lower priced (around $6), and steak and seafood dishes get up to $13 or so. Chef John Carlo Costanzo, who worked for 20 years on the Italian Line, wanted to show us his stuff, but we were in the neighborhood at the wrong time of day so we had to pass up the opportunity. Let us know what you find.

HOURS Winter: Sun.–Fri. 5–10 pm; Sat. 5–11 pm. Upstairs dining room open only on Friday and Saturday in winter. Summer: Lunch: every day 11 am–2 pm. Dinner: Mon.–Fri. 5–10 pm; Sat. 5–11 pm; Sun. 2–10 pm.

DIRECTIONS Eastbound: From Exit 87 turn right at stop sign. Go 1 block and turn right onto Route 97 North. Pass under highway and 0.1 mile later turn right onto Golf Course Drive. Go ½ mile and it's on your left at Hancock Golf Course.

Westbound: From Exit 87 turn right and go 100 feet to Golf Course Drive. Turn right, go ½ mile, and it's on your left at Hancock Golf Course.

ANTRIM LODGE HOTEL, *Exit 94, Roscoe*

If you read this anytime between April Fool's Day and the end of September you can be certain that, no matter how foul the weather, a contingent of hardy New Yorkers in waders and insulated underwear will be standing up to their hips in frigid water, flinging, with the aid of a flexible stick, tiny hooked wisps of feathers, fur, and tinsel into a stream. Some will be performing this rite in the Beaverkill and Willowemoc Rivers, especially at one of the rocky pools near the town of Roscoe. And of those who choose Roscoe's waters for their fishing, it's a sure bet that virtually every one will conclude his day at "Keeler's Pool," the affectionately named dining room of the Antrim Lodge Hotel.

Opened by Anna Mae Keeler's grandparents, this four-story red-clapboard Victorian hotel has been host to fishermen, hunters, and summer people since 1890. On any summer evening it is redolent with talk of water levels, temperatures, the ones that got away, and—often enough—the one that didn't. On the varnished walls of the dark, low-ceilinged taproom are mounted fish, painted fish, and framed displays of artificial flies that are rumored to catch real fish. An hour in the Antrim Lodge, and you'll have some fish stories of your own.

You may also have some food stories, for Anna Mae's husband, Doug, is revered for his cooking by the Beaverkill's anglers. Of course, the best thing he can possibly cook is the trout you bring him yourself, still pulsing and wriggling. But if you don't happen to have a meal flapping about in the back seat, try one of Doug's wonderful sandwiches, especially the roast beef or turkey. Yes, he roasts the beef and cooks the bird himself, and at lunchtime you can get a real stack of it, along with potato salad and pickles, for $3.25.

Unless it's particularly busy in the evening, Doug will be happy to fix you a sandwich at dinnertime even though none are on the menu. You may be even more tempted by what is on the evening slate: complete dinners, with entrées like boneless stuffed chicken breast ($8.50), pan-fried mountain brook trout amandine ($9.75), or broiled ham steak Hawaiian ($9.85). Some items may be frozen; if that is important to you, ask. Prime rib and lobster tail are big favorites here, selling for $10.90 and $17.50 respectively, à la carte.

A delightful alternative to the expensive Catskill resorts whose brassy billboards have assailed you for the past 50 miles, the Antrim Lodge Hotel also offers rooms at rates as low as $11 for a single, year round. If you want to know whether to bother packing your rod and reel, phone ahead—Doug keeps track of what's biting and where.

HOURS   Dec.–Apr.: Tue.–Thu. 5–9 pm; Fri. & Sat. 5–9:30 pm; Sun. noon–9 pm. Apr.–Nov.: Lunch: Tue.–Sat. noon–2:30 pm. Dinner: Tue.– Sat. 5–9:30 pm; Sun. noon–9 pm. Closed Mondays all year.

DIRECTIONS   Eastbound: From Exit 94 turn left, pass under highway, and immediately turn left again. It's 1½ short blocks down, on the right.

Westbound: From Exit 94 turn left, go 0.2 mile to light, and turn left onto Broad St. Go 1 long block and turn right (you'll see a sign for the lodge). It's 1½ short blocks down, on the right.

ROSCOE DINER, *Exit 94, Roscoe*

In the parking lot you can see the salmon-colored bumper stickers that they give away inside: MEET ME AT THE "FAMOUS" ROSCOE DINER. We're not sure why it's famous but we do know that the Roscoe is a favorite midway stopping point for thousands of college students on their way from the metropolitan New York area to Cornell, Syracuse, Harpur, Elmira, and Ithaca. In his college days, David stopped here frequently during such jaunts, mostly because he knew no alternative. Had he been so enlightened, the Roscoe Diner wouldn't have won out over the Antrim Lodge (above), but the diner does have the unarguable advantage of never closing.

It's not that the food is bad here (the homemade vegetable beef soup was quite good, in fact), but the decor is nothing we haven't seen before—all too often, in fact. Like so many Greco-glitzy diners, every square inch of the Roscoe, even the rest rooms, has been covered with tile, ersatz brick, stucco, or fake timbers.

Although the menu is extensive, prices are somewhat higher than what they might be for this kind of place: $1.75 for a hamburger, $3.95 for a roast beef or turkey sandwich, $4.95 for salad plates, and $5.25 to $7.50 for dinner entrées. Two eggs, home fries, and toast go for $1.75 (coffee extra). But, as we said, it never closes.

HOURS   Always open.

DIRECTIONS   Eastbound: From Exit 94 turn left, pass under highway and through the center of town to the first light. Turn right, go 0.2 mile, and it's on your left.

Westbound: From Exit 94 look right. Can't miss it.

PIONEER DINER, *Exit 104, Monticello*

* *Not great, but low-priced*

In the heart of the borscht belt—the Catskill's Jewish hotel district—this stainless-steel diner serves equal numbers of local customers and city visitors. Owner Dave Buchsbaum, a New York native himself, says he can tell them apart with a short glance down the long counter. "The city people eat twice as much," he claims, and although he doesn't know why that is, his waitress suggests that the fresh air gives urbanites a hearty appetite.

To satisfy that appetite, Dave advances America's love affair with food patties served on a bun. He has almost a dozen so-called "burgers," from hamburgers, Swissburgers, and Reuben burgers to chicken burgers, fish burgers, shrimp burgers, and pizza burgers. Other than shape and low price ($1.20 to $1.85), most of these have little in common with their chopped-beef ancestor. Most are a compressed food product that is frozen and then deep-fried. Still, thanks to Ronald McDonald perhaps, they are fun for kiddies of all ages.

Breakfast is always inexpensive at the Pioneer—two eggs, home fries, and coffee go for a mere $1.19, as does French toast with the morning brew. When we were there, lunch specials consisted of chili dogs (95 cents), chili con carne ($1.50), and sausage and pepper heros ($1.85). Dave had just added borscht

to his menu, following an editorial writer's gripe that it was almost impossible to find a bowl of beet soup in the borscht belt. While well intentioned, Dave's effort doesn't gain our plaudits: commercially bottled borscht is what he serves—the very product, ironically, that ruined the reputation of what was once rightly regarded as a delicious soup.

Dave saw us to the door and proffered a good-humored parting message: "I still say the city people eat more!" Leaning out behind him, his waitress piped in, "It's the country air!"

HOURS   Sept. to mid-June: Sun.–Wed. 6 am–8 pm; Thu.–Sat. 6 am–midnight. Mid-June to Sept.: Mon.–Sat. 6 am–midnight; closed Sun.

DIRECTIONS   Eastbound: From Exit 104 go straight through light and in 0.1 mile you'll see it on the right.

Westbound: From Exit 104 follow signs for Route 17B West/Raceway. At end of ramp turn left at light and in 0.1 mile you'll see it on the right.

KAPLAN'S
BAGEL BAKERY
STOLLMAN FISH COMPANY AND DELI
Exit 105A, Monticello

Monticello is the gateway to the borscht belt, and the eating you find here is largely of one ethnicity. Walking along Broadway, you can pop into any of several places that would be at home on Brooklyn's Canarsie Street. There's **Kaplan's,** a large kosher deli-restaurant that was in the throes of changing ownership when we tried to visit. The **Bagel Bakery** spreads cold cuts, tuna salad, or chopped liver on its delicious breadstuffs. Predictably, there's also a Chinese restaurant, the **Canton.**

Our favorite was **Stollman Fish Company and Deli,** which is manned by several jovial, grandfatherly men happily slapping slices of Hebrew National meats on challah, rye, or rolls ($1.95–$2.69). You can follow your sandwich with rugalech, hummentashen, or tarts from Reissman's kosher bakery in Brooklyn, or with a beautiful navel orange that cost just 10 cents when we were there. But it's harder to find a place to sit—Stollman's has

209

no tables or chairs. When we expressed our disappointment, one of the men pulled an empty milk case out from behind the counter. "So sit," he chanted. "Sit, sit."

DIRECTIONS   See **Larry's Luncheonette,** below.

LARRY'S LUNCHEONETTE, *Exit 105A, Monticello*

Have you ever wondered where everyone who lives in a resort area like Monticello goes in the wintertime? Larry's Luncheonette is the answer. It's as local a restaurant as they come —the regulars even sign their names to the counter stools!

But don't worry—you can find a place to sit at one of half a dozen small Formica tables backed up against the cheerful yellow-plaid wallpaper. You may be surprised—we were—to find on each table a "tea list" of herbal, black, and blended teas. Sandwich offerings are written on paper plates that dot the sky-blue tiles behind the counter: liverwurst, salami, corned beef, etc., $2.30 to $3.

There is also homemade soup fresh each day (65/85 cents) and soup-and-sandwich lunch specials: turkey breast for $3.19, shrimp salad for $2.99.

HOURS   Mon.–Fri. 6 am–3 pm; closed Sat. & Sun.

DIRECTIONS   Exit 105A puts you on Route 42 South. In ½ mile you come to a light. Turn right onto Broadway. In 0.1 mile, St. John St. is on your left. Turn here for **Larry's Luncheonette** or continue straight down Broadway about ¼ mile for **Stollman's, Kaplan's, Bagel Bakery,** etc.

DANNY'S, *Exit 113, Wurtsboro*

Danny's is a sandwich restaurant and taproom in what once was a grand old Victorian hotel replete with porch, balconies, cornices, gingerbread, and mansard roof. But don't expect the quiet elegance of a country hotel now. Danny's is nice enough, but in a loud sort of way. Perhaps they'll have turned down the radio by the time you arrive.

Roast beef, corned beef, ham and Swiss, liverwurst, shrimp or chicken salad, $2 to $2.85; hard roll or tomato, 25 cents extra. That's the menu, almost in totality. Draft beer, 35 cents. Can't beat that these days.

On the knotty pine walls hang a few deer trophies and a far greater number of softball trophies. If you're thinking of going into the restaurant business, check out the scallop-edged tables; it's a trick we hadn't seen before.

HOURS Every day 11 am–3 am.

DIRECTIONS From Exit 113 turn left if eastbound, right if westbound, onto Route 209 North. Go 1.3 miles to the first light. Look across the intersection and you'll see it.

FORT WESTBROOKVILLE INN,
Exit 113, Westbrookville

* *Untried, but likely*

The Fort Westbrookville Inn serves dinners only, Wednesday through Sunday. Unfortunately, we arrived in time for lunch on Monday and that meant a long wait before we'd be served. We couldn't manage it, so we'll have to take the word of Renee Vorbach of the *Newburgh Evening News,* who wrote to us with rave reviews of this restaurant, especially its spinach salad and house dressing.

These come with an $11.95 fixed-price dinner that also includes relish tray, your choice of soup or appetizer (salmon mousse, caviar, artichokes vinaigrette), entrée, dessert, and coffee. The main course could be roast duckling, Wienerschnitzel, filet of sole amandine, or roast loin of pork with sauerkraut and German fried potatoes. Had our timing been luckier, however, we'd have gone for "pesce del Forte"—fresh mussels, shrimp, cod, and Italian sausage on linguini with the Fort's own sauce, a blend of marinara and garlic butter. (Just thinking of it brings forth tears of regret.)

The building is a handsome stone fort dating from 1750. We couldn't get its story, but what we could see looking through a window was absolutely charming—a low, intricately detailed ceiling, old wooden chairs, white tablecloths, fireplaces, nifty little staircases here and there—just about everything you'd hope for in a country inn.

HOURS   Wed. & Thu. 5–9 pm; Fri. & Sat. 5–10 pm; Sun. 2–9 pm; closed Mon. & Tue.

DIRECTIONS   From Exit 113 turn right if eastbound, left if westbound. Go 5½ miles on Route 209 South. It's on the right.

EL BANDIDO, *Exit 122, Middletown*

This place has that north-of-the-border Mexican look—fake stucco, dark-stained wood, Mexican bric-a-brac, posters of revolutionaries, and bouncy Latin music. It's not elegant or authentic, but with subdued lighting, soft carpeting, and comfy chairs, it makes for a nice break from the drive, and maybe you're just not in the mood for chicken soup.

Except for the specials, the cuisine is typical Tex-Mex—nachos, guacamole, quesadillas as appetizers ($1.95 at lunch, $3 at dinner), black bean soup ($1.25 at lunch, $1.75 at dinner), and the typical combination platters. We tried one that included a chili relleno, a taco, and an enchilada ($4.95 at lunch, $7.25 at dinner). Everything was quite acceptable but nothing especially outstanding.

More exciting were the specials: flautas (pastrylike tortillas filled with beef or chicken), chicken in pumpkin-seed sauce, Mexican-style shrimp and fish filet with tomato sauce and olives. At lunch these run from $3.50 to $5.75; at dinner, $6 to $10.

As a bonus, you get a culinary map of Mexico printed on the menu. It might interest you to know, for example, that camarones come from Nyarit and ceviche from Guerrero, near Acapulco.

HOURS   Every day 11 am–midnight.

DIRECTIONS   From Exit 122 turn left if eastbound, right if westbound, onto Middletown Rd. (County Road 67). Go 1.1 miles; it's on the right.

GASHO OF JAPAN, *Exit 131, Central Valley*

See page 99 for a description of this impressive variation on the Japanese steakhouse theme.

DIRECTIONS   From Exit 131 turn left onto Route 32. In 1.6 miles, after passing through Central Valley, you'll find it on your left.

Taconic State Parkway

(INCLUDING SAW MILL RIVER PARKWAY)

New York

Saw Mill River Parkway

CANTINA, *Exit for "Restaurant in the Park," Ardsley*

When we saw the sign "Restaurant in the Park," we did not expect to find a handsomely renovated 200-year-old granite-walled tavern perched over a serene lake. Even less did we expect this restaurant to offer quality Mexican food, pleasantly and efficiently served by snazzy, vested waiters.

With such a bucolic setting, only the pricier-than-usual lunch menu betrays Cantina's location, just 6 miles north of New York City. Most lunches run $5 to $6, although burgers with French fries are available for a little less. With a few exceptions, it's standard Tex-Mex fare, and a tabletop card affords the uninitiated a vocabulary lesson in basic Mexican food terms (their meaning in New York, at least; don't expect them to work in Los Angeles).

At dinnertime, two-item combination plates cost $5.95; three items, $7.50. Most beef, chicken, and seafood entrées and casseroles run $7.50 to $10.95.

V. Everett Macy Park dates to the pre-Revolutionary era, and Woodlands Lake has been used as a mill pond since the days of the Dutch. In its time, it has powered not only a grist mill, but a lumber mill and cider press as well. We had a bit of fun imagining the old mill workers trying burritos and tostadas.

HOURS Sun.–Thu. 11:30 am–10:30 pm; Fri. & Sat. 11:30 am–midnight.

DIRECTIONS On Saw Mill River Parkway, between Ardsley and Elmsford, watch for signs saying "Restaurant in the Park." Follow the signs, and you're there in two seconds.

214

VENUTI'S DELI, *Exit for N.Y. 119 East/Elmsford*

In a hurry? Want to grab something to eat in the car? How's roast beef, rare and juicy, with lettuce, tomato, and mayo, on a hard roll?

For convenience, price, and quality, you could do much worse than Venuti's Deli on Elmsford's Main Street. Venuti's has all the usual sandwiches and a few not-so-usual ones—about two dozen altogether, including roast pork, prosciutto, olive loaf, and spiced ham. But here, roast beef is king, and ours was indeed royal.

Sandwiches run $1.25 to $2.50, and grinders ("wedges," in the vernacular) are a lot bigger without costing a lot more. Tell them to lay it on thick and they'll do it. Cole slaw and other deli salads too.

HOURS   Tue.–Sat. 8 am–7 pm; Sun. 9 am–7 pm; closed Mon.

DIRECTIONS   Northbound: From Saw Mill River Parkway, use exit for N.Y. 119 East/Elmsford. Bear right onto N.Y. 119 East. Go through one light, then 1½ short blocks; it's on the left (23 Main St.).

Southbound: From Saw Mill River Parkway, use exit for N.Y. 119/Elmsford. Bear right; go 0.2 mile and turn right onto N.Y. 119 East. Go through one light, then 1½ short blocks; it's on the left (23 Main St.).

Taconic State Parkway

TRAVELER'S REST, *Exit for N.Y. 134, near Millwood*

Since the '30s, Traveler's Rest has been a favorite weekend retreat in the lower Hudson Valley. It no longer operates as an inn, but the dinner-only German restaurant is still going strong.

Inside the doorway, you can look at a black-and-white photo of the simple cottage that once was Traveler's Rest. Success has obviously gotten hold of Traveler's Rest. It is homey no more, having sprouted a regal canopy leading to a new, marble-faced wing. But this ludicrous exterior can easily be forgotten when you sink into the genuinely plush, dark-wooded dining area overlooking extensive, meticulously landscaped grounds, complete with waterfall, manicured gardens, and a full-time gardener who keeps every shrub in line.

The menu is extensive too—about 25 entrées. Ever since the Langner family took over 20 years ago, the continental cuisine has inclined toward German specialties, most notably the Jaeger schnitzel—baby milk-fed veal in white cream sauce with Swiss mountain mushrooms. Kasseler rippchen (smoked pork loin) and roulade of beef with spaetzle (German noodles) are two other favorites, but if your taste yearns for more familiar fare, you'll find rack of lamb, beef Wellington, baked stuffed shrimp, and the like. There are also some excellent appetizers, including smoked trout, escargots, various herring preparations, and a Cumberland liver pâté. And oh, what desserts! No matter what entrée you choose, you can order it à la carte ($10.50–$12) or as a complete dinner ($3 more).

Because reservations are advised on weekends (phone 914-941-7744), and meals are cooked with deliberation, this restaurant may not fit into your travel schedule. But if you like German cuisine and can find the time to visit, you'll probably find it an ideal traveler's rest.

HOURS   Mon., Wed. & Thu. 5–9:30 pm; Fri. & Sat. 5–10 pm; Sun. 1–9 pm; closed Tue.

DIRECTIONS   If northbound, take exit for N.Y. 134 and turn right onto N.Y. 134 East. If southbound, bear right onto N.Y. 134 East. Go 2 miles to a T junction. Turn right onto Route 100 South. You'll see the restaurant on your right in about ¼ mile.

YORKTOWN FISH MARKET INN,
Exit for U.S. 202, near Peekskill

"Are they putting us on, or is this the real thing?" we wondered as we walked by the market baskets of beautiful breads and shining produce, past the retail fish counter stocked to the gills, and through the double doors that lead to the large dining room. The Hudson Valley just can't compete with wharfside Manhattan for seaside atmosphere, we knew, yet this place felt genuine. It was difficult to accept a landlocked lighthouse for a building, or sawdust on the wooden floor, yet we found that the waxed-paper place mats and vinegar bottles set on red-checked tablecloths gave the Yorktown Fish Market Inn a gusty, gutsy feel we instantly liked. Adding to the charm were menus peremptorily scrawled across brown wrapping paper, a fire in the old stone fireplace, and informally dressed, nonuniformed waitresses.

The food fit right in. It's all fish, all fresh, and all extremely well prepared. Naturally, the menu changes with the tides, but what we saw was probably typical. There was a surprisingly large bowl of Manhattan-style seafood chowder (swordfish, clams, shrimp, and vegetables) for the surprisingly small price of 75 cents. In addition to steamed mussels ($2.75 for a pile of them), there were three fish entrées at $3.75—halibut steak, sea trout filet, and monkfish. Monkfish, a vogue item in seafood circles, is a firm-fleshed fish, aptly called "poor man's lobster." We enjoyed it thoroughly.

At dinnertime, the menu—still hand-written and presented on an easel—retains its midday simplicity. The higher prices ($7–$10) are for complete dinners, including salad, bread, a vegetable platter, and fresh fruit dessert. A few sauced dishes are added to the selection, as are some additional fish specialties like tilefish or golden snapper (a cold-water denizen that feeds on lobster).

The Yorktown Fish Market Inn is in every way a delightful seafood restaurant. The only thing lacking is the sound of the surf; we're thankful that they haven't tried to put it in.

HOURS   Sun.–Thu. 10 am–10 pm; Fri. & Sat. 10 am–midnight.

DIRECTIONS   See **Crompond Diner,** below.

CROMPOND DINER, *Exit for U.S. 202, near Peekskill*

Locally, the Crompond is affectionately known as "Pete and Ray's," and that affection runs deep. On the diner's 25th anniversary in 1981, the owners showed their gratitude for a quarter-century of local support by lowering prices to 1945 levels. For a full week, coffee was 15 cents, pie 25 cents, and complete dinners just $1.10. Customers lined up around the block.

Prices are back to normal now, but they aren't tough to manage. An unassuming two eggs, home fries, toast, and coffee breakfast is just $1.25. Every day, two lunch specials—entrée, potato, and vegetable—go for $3.25. Soup is 65 cents a bowl.

But the Crompond is not only reasonable, it's high quality too. The French fries are fresh and cut to order; we saw several parties who had come in strictly for their regular French fry fix. Others came over to Pete Cacchioli, a warm, affable host, to rave about the previous night's dinner—roast duckling, salad, soup, vegetables, and homemade bread—all for $6.25. Another good dinner choice is the seafood crêpe with crab legs, shrimp, scallops, and mushrooms; with side dishes, it costs just $5.75. But Pete believes that his best value is chicken in the basket: half a fried chicken with French fries and salad for $5.50. It's enough for two, and it is so popular as a take-out item that he had an aluminized box custom-made for the purpose.

The Crompond is in a Jewish neighborhood, so you'll find creamed herring on the menu. Cream cheese and Nova Scotia lox on bagel go for $3.25; a lox and onion omelet is $3.85.

The diner itself is a lovely De Raffele model, made in New Rochelle, New York. The company still makes diners, Pete told us, but "you see one and you've seen them all." Although the distinctive purple window shades of this one are a bit garish, the pink and white arched ceiling and textured stainless-steel walls are pert and pretty. The original fluorescent lights have been replaced with more subdued bonnet lamps, but other than that, the main part of the diner is unretouched.

Don't leave the Crompond without trying the delicious apple dumplings that Pete makes fresh each day from Rome apples and serves with hot rum sauce ($1.25). And ask him about the time his son's college admissions counselor in Delaware, knowing only the town the boy came from, recommended a diner up that way because it served the world's best apple dumpling.

HOURS   Mon.–Thu. 6 am–1 am; Fri. & Sat. 6 am–2 am; Sun. 6 am–10 pm.

DIRECTIONS   From exit for U.S. 202/Peekskill/Yorktown Heights, turn left if northbound, right if southbound, onto U.S. 202 West. In 1¼ miles you'll see the **Yorktown Fish Market Inn** on your left, and ¼ mile farther, on the same side, the **Crompond Diner.**

THE BACK COURT, *I-84 West Exit, Fishkill*

It's only about 10 minutes out of your way to this handsome, up-to-date restaurant in a most unusual setting; see page 94.

DIRECTIONS   From the Taconic, enter I-84 West. Then follow directions found on page 95.

THE OVERSTUFFED DONUT,
Exit for N.Y. 52, East Fishkill

* *Not great, but never closed*

This unspectacular restaurant is in an area where little else is open late at night. It seems a hybrid of Friendly's Ice Cream (counter design) and Dunkin' Donuts (snack offerings), with a definite inheritance from your basic village lunchroom (breakfast and sandwich menu).

Perhaps it's worth a visit just to note the bizarre, bright-red ceiling fan that looks as if it were made out of lawn furniture. If you are luckier than we were, you'll learn its origin—our server seemed not to know, or care.

Prices aren't bad—most sandwiches and burgers run $1.30–$1.75; a bowl of soup is 99 cents; a three-egg "overstuffed" omelet with home fries goes for $3.25; dinner platters are $3.95.

HOURS   Always open.

DIRECTIONS   From exit for N.Y. 52/Fishkill/Carmel, turn left onto N.Y. 52 West. Restaurant is on the right, just past the junction with N.Y. 376, 1 mile from the exit.

RESTAURANT IN THE PARK,
Exit for James Baird State Park, Pleasant Valley

Perhaps you've traveled the Taconic a dozen times, each time passing the entrance to James Baird State Park without once venturing a gander. Even when famished, you've ignored the official-looking restaurant sign. After all, on the gastronomic ladder there aren't many rungs lower than park concession food.

You're forgiven, but please reconsider.

The Restaurant in the Park is no smoky-grill hot dog stand, its floor sloppy with spilled Cracker-Jacks. Once it was, until Joe Baldwin took over. A graduate of the Culinary Institute of America, he balked at the idea of short-order cooking. But he did want to retain quick meals for people on the go, so now he offers the best of both worlds: quality fast food and a selection of gourmet dishes too. Everything is made from scratch; the entire menu (breakfast included) is available all day, and prices are remarkably reasonable. What more could a traveler want, especially when the restaurant is set in 700 lovely acres of woods and fields, cross-country ski trails, and a golf course.

Aptly, it has the feeling of a lodge: knotty pine walls, wooden tables, and mate's chairs lend a relaxing ambiance. A nice touch are the two chaise longues in the corner by the fireplace; our favorite spot, though, was the bricked dining terrace overlooking a rolling fairway.

When we stopped by, the day's special was quiche Lorraine with choice of soup or salad ($3.25). The quiche was good, and the navy bean soup was especially noteworthy. Cooked with chunks of top round, it had a delightful—but not overpowering—smoky flavor. We also tried a tossed salad (95 cents) and enjoyed its creamy house dressing.

Most sandwiches are $2–$2.50, although a humble hot dog can still be had for $1. A particularly appealing item on the menu's low-cost page is the beef barbecue. We didn't try it, but neighboring diners lustily attacked the four-rib servings well doused in a dark brown sauce ($3). They reported it as excellent.

Most entrées (served with potato, salad, and vegetable) run $8–$9. You can enjoy double-thick stuffed pork chops, beef Bourguignonne, brook trout meunière, or veal scallops, but the chef would probably want to show off his chicken à la James Baird. A variation on chicken Divan, the poultry is served with a supreme sauce over broccoli or asparagus—whichever is in season.

HOURS   Second Saturday in April to first Tuesday in November: Mon.–Fri. 8 am–8 pm; Sat. & Sun. 6 am–9 pm. First Tuesday in November to second Saturday in April: open only Friday, Saturday, Sunday, and on school holidays, 9 am–8 pm.

DIRECTIONS   About ½ mile north of N.Y. 55, you'll see signs for James Baird State Park Restaurant. Follow them, and you'll be there before you can say the park's name three times.

COTTONWOOD INN,
Exit for U.S. 44, near Washington Hollow

We had a pleasant surprise at the Cottonwood Inn because we let the restaurant's looks prejudice our expectations. Not that it was unattractive—it is quite pleasant and comfortable, in fact. But the inside of this lovely old house has been decorated in Ethan Allen Colonial—the decor so often chosen for uninspired "family" restaurants.

It seems this restaurant was once owned by a German woman, and when she sold it, her secrets came with the property. Now that's an old saw, but we soon discovered that she must have been an excellent recipe writer. The sauerbraten we had here was among the best we've tasted—tangy yet tender and altogether pleasing. "We put it in on Monday and pull it out on Friday afternoon," said manager Steve Slansky, referring to the five-day marinating process that true sauerbraten demands. Many places, he told us, just use pot roast and at the last minute bathe it in a vinegar and raisin gravy.

We also tried—as a sizable appetizer that could have been a main course—quiche Lorraine ($1.25), and it too was excellent.

221

Though the Cottonwood is less than 2 miles from the Taconic, travelers often don't know it's there, and Steve feels it imperative to keep up quality and portion size in order to maintain a local clientele. On weekdays during the months of November, January, February, March, July, and August, he offers dinners that include entrée, salad, soup, bread, and coffee for just $5.95. Entrées are likely to be beef Bourguignonne, stuffed trout, or chicken breast stuffed with rice. Regular dinner prices are $7–$11, but portions are so large that two people often share a meal.

At midday, you can get complete luncheons with American-style entrées for $5–$7.50, salads for $4–$5, or homemade soup with sandwich or quiche for $2.50–$4. If the dinner we enjoyed was any indication, the lunches should be ample and satisfying.

HOURS   Lunch: Mon.–Sat. noon–3 pm. Dinner: Mon.–Fri. 5–9 pm; Sat. 5–10 pm; Sun. noon–8 pm.

DIRECTIONS   From exit for U.S. 44/Poughkeepsie/Millbrook, turn right if northbound, left if southbound, onto U.S. 44 East. After about a mile, the road forks. Bear right, staying on U.S. 44. You'll see the Cottonwood on the left, ¾ mile past the fork.

WEST TAGHKANIC DINER,
Exit for N.Y. 82, West Taghkanic

This is a clean and pretty Mountain View diner, sky blue and white inside, shiny stainless steel outside. It's almost—but not quite—visible from the Taconic, and you can't miss its neon Indian chief as soon as you turn off the highway.

Joan Diande is hostess and chef; true to her name, she specializes in Italian dishes. Mostaccioli (outsized macaroni) and sausage is one of them—$5.25, with bread and salad. Joan also makes a dandy minestrone soup with some unexpected ingredients like chickpeas (70 cents a cup, and only a nickel more for a bowl).

You can also get hamburgers, sandwiches, and salad plates here, all reasonably priced. The Taghkanic Club is a triple-decker with fresh turkey, crisp bacon, lettuce, and tomato. With French fries and cole slaw, it's $5.25. A bowl of chili—hotter than it is wonderful, but certainly passable—is $1.50. The bread pudding (90 cents) was creamy and chunky, obviously homemade.

If it be your pleasure, you can buy bottled beer or wine by the glass to go with your meal.

HOURS   Opens 7 am every day; closes 8 pm on Mon., Wed. & Thu.; 3 pm on Tue.; 11 pm on Fri.; 9 pm on Sat.; 10 pm on Sun.

DIRECTIONS   From exit for N.Y. 82/Hudson/Ancram, bear right if northbound, left if southbound, onto N.Y. 82 North. It's the first building on your left.

VILLAGE BAKERY, *Exit for N.Y. 217, Philmont*

How often do the alluring charms of bakery-case beauties prove to be just crust deep? More often than not, in our experience. It won't happen at the Village Bakery. Here, Joel Gordon cooks up breads, rolls, cookies, Viennese-style pastry, Danish, tortes, and turnovers that are every bit as good to the tooth as they are to the eye.

You can pick up your pastry at the counter, pour yourself a cup of coffee or herb tea (just 25 cents), and sit at one of the butcher block tables by the window.

Or, you can lean on the counter and chat with Joel, who is genuinely friendly and loves to talk about the fine points of baking. He considers it something of a mission to show people how good food can be without "seducing them," as he says, with lots of butter or sugar. The absolutely scrumptious rum-raisin cheese squares we tried attest to that, as do the date-nut cookies and three-grain sourdough loaf we took home.

When baked goods are made from freshly milled flour, Joel believes, they have a much longer shelf life than run-of-the-mill products. His flour comes from one of the nation's oldest organic farms and is milled no more than seven days before he digs his fingers into it. He has also found that super-fresh ingredients allow him to cut down considerably on salt without anyone crying "Bland!"

Inevitably, says Joel, he's moving into the restaurant business. At the time we visited, he had taken the first step by offering full breakfasts, with some nice touches that only a baker could provide. And, on Saturdays, he serves pizza, available in your choice of three doughs—white, whole wheat, or rye. By the time you get there, it's quite possible that there will be quiche, homemade pasta dishes, and perhaps a daily lunch. A sidewalk café may also be under way. Whatever Joel gets into, it's sure to be good, and you'll probably enjoy the peaceful small-town setting as well.

HOURS   Tue.–Fri. 6 am–6 pm; Sat. 6 am–8 pm; Sun. 6 am–1 pm; closed Mon.

DIRECTIONS   From exit for N.Y. 217/Philmont, turn left onto N.Y. 217 West. In 1.8 miles, it's on your left.

CHIEF TAGHKANIC DINER,
Exit for N.Y. 295, East Chatham

* *Not great, but very close*

This spotless, cheerful diner is as bright and colorful as they come. The menu has no surprises, though, and it seems a bit on the expensive side, as diners go. If you want something more interesting, try Jackson's Old Chatham House (below), but for a quick stop you couldn't find anything closer to the highway than the Chief Taghkanic. You'll see his headdress before you're off the ramp.

HOURS   Every day 7 am–8 or 9 pm.

DIRECTIONS   From N.Y. 295 exit turn right if northbound, left if southbound, and you'll see it, almost immediately, on your left.

JACKSON'S OLD CHATHAM HOUSE,
Exit for N.Y. 295, Old Chatham

See page 127 for a description of this charming old public house. It's a few miles out of the way, but the drive through Shaker country is superbly scenic.

DIRECTIONS   From exit for N.Y. 295 turn right if northbound, left if southbound, onto Route 295 East. Go about 2½ miles and turn left at sign for Old Chatham. Take this winding road 3.2 miles and you'll see it on the right.

Atlantic City Expressway

New Jersey

ABOUT ATLANTIC CITY

Atlantic City. You've heard about it, read about it, seen movies about it. Perhaps you've even dreamed about it, the boomtown, big-bucks, fast-lane home of croupiers and slot machines, the casino city that never sleeps.

Go ahead, feed a quarter to the one-armed bandit. If you've any quarters left by the time you're played out, you need only trot up a flight of stairs from the casino at **Harrah's** to the lavish buffet where the odds of walking away satisfied are considerably higher.

But if you'd rather avoid temptation altogether, we commend to you **12 South,** a purveyor of modern American cuisine that is two full blocks away from the nearest blackjack table.

In Atlantic City, parking can cost as much as lunch, but we've kept that in mind. Both of these restaurants have free parking lots for customers.

---

12 SOUTH, *Exit 1, Atlantic City*

If you listen to National Public Radio's "All Things Considered," you already know about 12 South. Having caught that 1980 series on the birth of a restaurant, we were madly curious to see how the youngster turned out.

It's a modern American café with turn-of-the-century decor—

brass rails, etched glass, tulip light fixtures, mirrors, cushy booths, polished mahogany, and a bar made from old mantelpieces. We couldn't understand why, with so many tasteful touches and fine antiques (some rescued from buildings demolished for the casinos), they papered many of the walls with old newspapers.

Still, it's a welcome contrast to the severe, contemporary look of the casinos. It's also relaxed. We saw a well-coiffed starlet in mink back to back with a fellow wearing blue jeans and running shoes.

And the food is good, quite good in fact. Portions are large, and the menu has some unusual possibilities. To be sure, you can get the sandwiches, gourmet burgers, and spinach salads (most, $3.50–$4.50) that are the signature of this kind of BPO café. But you can also get pasta frittata, the house specialty ($5.25). It's an outsized omelet filled with spinach, mushrooms, and spaghetti in marinara sauce. Sounds like an odd marriage, but it works.

Tempura—batter-dipped, deep-fried vegetables—is light and lovely here ($3.95); you might do better in the finest Japanese restaurants, but not much. For $3.95, you can also get a large basket of fresh, crisp vegetables served up with any of several dips (how does tangy onion with sherry sound?). Baby back ribs are barbecued over an open pit and served by the slab ($10.50). There are also fresh seafood, steak, and poultry entrées. Almond broccoli chicken ($10.50), in white wine sauce on a bed of fettucini, tempted us plenty, but the frittata and tempura had done us in.

If you've just scored a big win, you can wash all this good stuff down with a bottle of Dom Perignon. It's $115, but in Atlantic City everyone will understand.

HOURS Every day from "11 to 7," which in this town means 11 am until 7 am (i.e., closed only between 7 and 11 in the morning, although the bar stays open then, just in case you hit the jackpot).

DIRECTIONS See Harrah's, below.

HARRAH'S BUFFET, *Exit 1, Atlantic City*

Harrah's calls itself "The Other Atlantic City"—more because of what's outside than in. Located at the foot of the Brigantine Bridge, Harrah's is several miles from the casinos that crowd Atlantic City's famous Boardwalk. Inside, it's got the same jazzy look as its competitors, but it also has a buffet the others don't match.

To get there, you walk from the high-rise parking lot, over a pedestrian bridge, down the stairs, and into the casino itself. It's a cavernous, darkish room, a sea of gaming tables and slot machines, each silently manned by hunched bodies divorced from every thought in the world but one. Above their heads, giant electronic numerals tick off the steadily rising jackpot. It was $62,000-something when we headed for the restaurant.

Here, the tone is lighter, brighter, softer; the jackpot comes in the form of food—a limitless buffet of over fifty items from fruits to fish, including greens and salads of every kind, meats hot and cold, breads and rolls, cheeses and cakes. If you could hoard food internally, you wouldn't have to eat again for a year.

It isn't gourmet, but it's lavish and luscious for this kind of mass meal buffet. The price is $8.75 at lunch, $12.75 at dinner. That may sound a bit steep if you only want a nibble, but it's not bad, really, for all that you can eat in a town where a tuna salad sandwich can easily cost over $5.

All in all, Harrah's Buffet is a good deal, the only sure bet in the place.

HOURS   Open every day. Lunch: 11:30 am–5:30 pm; dinner: 5:30–11 pm.

DIRECTIONS   When the Atlantic City Expressway ends, you are fed into Missouri St. Signs for **Harrah's** are clear until you see its looming presence; free parking for three hours. For **12 South,** take Missouri to the third possible left and turn here onto Pacific (it comes after Arctic and Atlantic). Four blocks on Pacific brings you to Indiana. Left on Indiana. Restaurant is on the left side of the street; free parking down the alley across the street.

GIACOMO'S VINEYARD,
Exits 12W & 17, Egg Harbor City

If you're heading east, you're almost in Atlantic City by the time you get here, but you won't find prices like these on the Boardwalk. Giacomo's Vineyard is a former hotel, now an apartment house, in a low-keyed residential neighborhood. Eclectically funky, the small dining room boasts a genuine old-time tin ceiling, imitations of imitation Tiffany lamps, metal chairs, a few arches here and there, and trellises of two-by-fours draped with plastic grapes. (They probably don't come from the Renault Vineyard around the corner, where you can take a tour and taste the wine for $1.) It's so fake that it's camp.

There's nothing camp about Giacomo's cooking, though. He makes everything right here, even the pasta. Ravioli or ricotta gnocchi costs $5.50; ziti in meat sauce, also $5.50; fettucini Alfredo, $7.50. The lasagne we tried ($6.50) was quite good, well stocked with sausage, ground beef, and ricotta. Veal dishes, steaks, and seafood get more expensive, most $7.50 to $12, some higher.

Giacomo's appetizers are especially popular, and if you ask you'll find that he's happy to turn an appetizer into a meal in a very affordable way. A hefty pile of steamed mussels in red or white sauce, for instance, is $3.95. Add a side of spaghetti and it's $4.95. With bread and salad too, you're up to $5.95 and you won't go away hungry.

HOURS Tue.–Thu. 4–9:30 pm; Fri. & Sat. 4–10:30 pm; Sun. 4–10 pm; closed Mon.

DIRECTIONS Eastbound: From Exit 17 turn left onto Route 50 North for 2½ miles to the White Horse Pike. Right on the pike for 0.3 mile to St. Louis Ave. Left on St. Louis for ½ mile. It's on your right.

Westbound: More difficult. From Exit 12W turn left and go 2.1 miles to light. Left onto Route 563. Go 1.8 miles to light at White Horse Pike. Left on pike and go 2.7 miles to St. Louis Ave. Turn right, go ½ mile, and it's on your right. This is a bit tough because the expressway engineers decided not to let westbounders off at Exit 17. Sorry.

WILLIAMSTOWN DINER, *Exit 38, Williamstown*

The sign outside says "Broasted Chicken." Inside, you can get your chicken broiled or roasted. Maybe if you order half of each and eat them together, you'll have yourself a broasted chicken.

It seems that "broasting"—whatever that is—was once the specialty here. Nowadays, the large stainless-steel diner is better known for its cherry cheesecake ($1.10) and its snapping turtle soup (75 cents a cup/$1.10 bowl). They were out of cheesecake when we stopped in, but we were able to try the soup. Tasty, if somewhat gelatinous, the concoction had a pleasantly pungent bite to it (certainly more pleasant than the bite of the turtle before he's made into soup).

The rest of the menu is standard diner stuff, and everything is homemade. Especially popular are Italian dishes like rigatoni and seafood specialties like fresh flounder (fried or broiled, stuffed or not), crabs, and oysters. Most dinners here run $4–$6 à la carte, $1 more if complete. But for a bargain, you can't beat the sandwich special: a bowl of soup, cheese steak (shredded steak with melted cheese on a toasted roll), French fries, and coffee for $2.60. Considering that our *cup* of snapper soup was truly bowl-sized, we imagine that a bowl of it is beyond measure.

HOURS Always open.

DIRECTIONS From Exit 38 turn right if eastbound, left if westbound, following signs to Williamstown. In about 1½ miles turn right at traffic light onto Route 42 North. In 0.1 mile, the diner is on your left.

Garden State Parkway

New Jersey

ABOUT CAPE MAY

After a visit to Cape May, other seaside resorts feel like miniature golf—fun perhaps, but pallid next to the real thing. The whole town is on the National Historic Register, and it is the ultimate expression of the gingerbread ethic in America. Beneath mansard roofs, jigsawed rickrack adorns gables and porticoes, and fussy paint jobs show it off without a trace of modesty. Everywhere you look, inns, guesthouses, and small hotels line the tree-shaded streets. In season, restaurants crop up like zucchini.

We give you three. The **Mad Batter** serves some of the finest food we've found anywhere. The **Chalfonte Hotel** means superb Southern cooking the way it's meant to be. And the **Lobster House Coffee Shop** is where Cape May's working folks go, any time of the year.

THE MAD BATTER, *end of parkway, Cape May*

Our reaction to this place is captured in the ruddy-faced jubilance of the *bons vivants* in Renoir's "Luncheon of the Boating Party," a print of which hangs in the Mad Batter's dining room. If you've got a corpuscle of hedonism in your veins, take the time to sit on this restaurant's ocean-breezed veranda and treat yourself to a meal as memorable as Cape May's gingerbread architecture.

We first tried the potage Crécy, a subtle blend of carrots, herbs, and cream, seasoned perfectly to elevate the humble root to regal stature. Our passions aroused, we tried another soup, a propitious marriage of homemade chicken stock, heavy cream, diced fresh mushrooms, and sherry. They call it cream of mushroom, but it bears little resemblance to what those words usually call to mind.

We even managed an appetizer—suppa de clams, half a dozen steamed littlenecks atop a smooth marinara so good we unabashedly finished it with our spoons.

Getting down to real business, we perused the day's entrées. Regretfully, we passed by such temptations as duck fermière (duck pieces braised in white wine with leeks, garlic, peas, and carrots), angelfish sauté (with snow peas and carrots in a sweet-and-sour sauce), and pollo mimosa (chicken breasts sautéed with artichoke hearts, capers, white wine, and light cream). Instead, we fell headlong in love with the Batter's crab roulade—fresh backfin crab, onions, spinach, and ricotta cheese wrapped in filo dough and baked to perfection. Tender, yet ever so lightly crunchy, the dish is a symphony of flavors and textures.

To all of this culinary excellence, add a picture-perfect setting at the Carroll Villa Hotel: candlelight, bud vases, harpsichord music, a warm and knowledgeable staff, outdoor seating on the street-side veranda or the garden-side terrace, and a handsome dining room with well-framed art and just enough curlicues to remind you of its origin. With the recent spate of brick-plants-and-oak cafés freshly adorned by pressed-tin ceilings, Tiffany-style lamps, and advertising mirrors ordered from design catalogs, it's pure delight to see Victoriana without cliché. For a restaurant that could hold its own against Manhattan's finest, the Mad Batter happens to be ludicrously low priced. Catch this: On weekdays during the off-season (April to mid-June and Labor Day to mid-October), a full-course breakfast/brunch is $3.25; lunch, $4.25; and dinner, $10.50. Even at its priciest, à la carte dinner entrées run $7 to $13 or so.

HOURS Open first Saturday of April to mid-October, every day 8 am–2:30 pm and 5:30–10 pm.

DIRECTIONS See end of Cape May entries, page 235.

CHALFONTE HOTEL, *end of parkway, Cape May*

If you had a grandmother who was a superb Southern cook, a meal at her place would be like eating at the Chalfonte. A 75-year-old Virginia lady named Helen Dickerson has been "grandmother" to the Chalfonte's guests for over 35 years. Before that, her mother filled the role. Now her daughter and granddaughter help out. That's four generations of Dickersons in the same kitchen.

Cape May is the queen of Jersey's seaside resorts, and the Chalfonte is her crown jewel. The frilly L-shaped Victorian structure wrapped with two-story porticoes is preserved by a grant from the National Parks Service. Up to 225 guests can be accommodated in the 103 rooms. At mealtimes, they eat at long galley tables where they are joined by restaurant guests. The hostess introduces neighbors as they are seated, so don't come for intimate or anonymous dining. At the back of the room sit the Satterfields, the Chalfonte's keepers since 1910. And Helen Dickerson feeds them all.

Everything, absolutely everything, is made from scratch. Even the mayonnaise. Helen once tried it out of a jar but she didn't like it. That was the closest the Chalfonte has come to serving a processed food.

Fried chicken is served at dinner on Sunday and Wednesday. Roast lamb on Monday. On Tuesday and Saturday roast beef is featured; on Thursday, country ham and turkey; on Friday, crab-cakes. Bluefish almost every day. Everything comes with all the trimmings: spoonbread, Helen's famous dinner rolls, and tossed salad with Dot's (her daughter's) French dressing. Bread pudding for dessert. Fixed-price dinners are $11.95.

The Chalfonte also serves a sumptuous morning meal ($5.25) that makes you wonder why you've been eating just fried eggs, home fries, and toast all these years. Here, breakfast consists of eggs, fried fish, spoonbread, homemade biscuits, juice, and coffee or tea.

Spoonbread, by the way, is a type of cornbread baked in a casserole. You have to try it.

There are no recipes, and if there are any measuring cups in the kitchen at all, they're never used. Helen just knows how to do it, and it always comes out right.

HOURS   Open Memorial Day weekend and from mid-June to Labor Day. Mon.–Sat. 8:30–10 am and 6:30–8:30 pm; Sun. 8:30–10:30 am and 2–3 pm.

DIRECTIONS   See end of Cape May entries, page 235.

LOBSTER HOUSE COFFEE SHOP,
end of parkway, Cape May

The Lobster House is a sprawling dockside complex that includes a take-out stand, fish market, gift shop, and a large, always crowded restaurant. It's the first commercial establishment of any kind after you cross the Cape May Canal, and it seems to nab tourists the way Cape May's fishermen nab flounder.

We were delighted to find, on the lee side of the restaurant, a less crowded and more genuine coffee shop that exists only to serve the clammers, scallop men, and other workers of the town. There's no view to speak of from the coffee shop and not much of what some call atmosphere, but we liked it just fine—plain people eating good food served by waitresses who mark their orders on paper napkins and call everyone "hon."

You can get soups, including chowder and snapper (that's snapping turtle), for 75 cents or $1.25. Platters like fresh flounder, deviled clams or crabs, and veal cutlet run $4.50 to $5.75, and most sandwiches cost $1.45 to $1.80; shrimp and lobster salad are $2.95, but on the day we stopped, a lobster salad sandwich with a cup of soup was the special—just $1.95. Another special, surprising perhaps, was ham and cabbage, with carrots, potato, and rolls, for $3.95.

Orange juice is squeezed before your eyes here, and even though from your seat in the coffee shop you cannot see the fishing boats hauling in the day's catch, you can top off your meal with a stroll out onto the dock. It's got the same view they pay for with big bucks in the restaurant.

HOURS   6 am–10 pm, every day but Christmas.

DIRECTIONS FOR CAPE MAY RESTAURANTS
When the Garden State Parkway ends, it becomes Route 109 South and crosses the Cape May Canal. Almost immediately after the bridge, you'll see the **Lobster House's** large sign on your left. For the other two restaurants, continue straight ahead (Lafayette St.).

For **Chalfonte,** turn left in 1¼ miles onto Franklin. Go through one light to stop sign. Turn right at stop sign onto Columbia. Go 1 block and turn left onto Howard. You're in front of it (301 Howard St.).

For the **Mad Batter,** continue along Lafayette for an additional 2 blocks, until it ends at a T. Turn left here onto Jackson and go about 2 blocks. The restaurant is on your left, in the Carroll Villa Hotel, half a block before the ocean (19 Jackson St.).

12 SOUTH
HARRAH'S BUFFET, *Exit 38, Atlantic City*

If you're driving the Garden State, hungry and with a little time to kill, and you don't mind a 10-mile detour, you might like to try eating in Atlantic City. You could leave with more than a full stomach, or less. See pages 226 to 228 for descriptions of two Atlantic City restaurants.

DIRECTIONS   From Exit 38 enter Atlantic City Expressway eastbound. From there, see page 228 for directions to restaurants.

SMITHVILLE INN, *Exits 48 & 50, Smithville*

The "Towne of Historic Smithville" is a primped-up complex of shoppes selling everything from candles to condominiums. It looks as if it's trying to be Williamsburg but comes off more like Disneyland.

The towne's focal point is the Smithville Inn, which, unlike its neighbors, has actually been here since the 18th century (most of the other buildings were moved to Smithville in the 1970s). And, in fact, once you're inside the inn and past all the hoopla, it's actually quite nice, with white tablecloths, spindle-backed chairs, antiques, lamplight, and classical music.

For lunch, there are three separate menus offered in three different rooms. For a sit-down lunch in the dining room ($5–$6), you can get American dishes like old-fashioned chicken shortcake or fare with a continental touch such as eggs Benedict or chicken-apple crêpes. The "Pony Express Luncheon" in the tavern features sandwiches, quiche, and chef's salads ($3–$4.50). And, if you want to eat as the inn's 18th-century guests never did, help yourself to the buffet of 50 hot and cold items ($8.95).

At dinnertime, valet parking is instituted, the "proper attire" sign goes up, and prices jump considerably ($13.95 for the buffet, $12 and up for entrées, no more sandwiches). If this sounds like too much, or if you hated the sound of the place to begin with, drive on to the Oyster Creek Inn, where they would probably serve you in cut-offs and a T-shirt.

HOURS   Lunch: Mon.–Sat. 11:30 am–2:30 pm. Dinner: Mon.–Fri. 4–9 pm; Sat. 4–10 pm; Sun. 2–9 pm. (In summer, dinner runs until 10 pm Monday to Saturday; until 9:30 on Sunday.)

DIRECTIONS   See Oyster Creek Inn, below.

OYSTER CREEK INN, *Exits 48 & 50, Leeds Point*

* *Far, but worth it*

It's only 7½ miles from here to Atlantic City as the dinghy rows, but it's a thousand life-styles away. At the Oyster Creek Inn, you'll find the clammers and scallop men and fishing boat captains to whom casinos and night life are as foreign as Antarctic penguins. We watched them steer their dories to the dock and, in four quick steps, bound inside.

If you come by car, you'll find the Oyster Creek Inn at the end of Moss Mill Road, a narrow, winding lane through woods and salt marsh. The road itself is only 2½ miles long, but by the time you reach the end you've given up hope of finding anything to eat unless you catch it yourself. Once you see the inn, you probably won't even care about its food because you're so delighted that such a neat old place could still exist.

It's a low-lying, shake-covered building with wings that stick out at odd angles, each opening onto a dock on Oyster Creek. The interior is simple but pleasant, with mounted fish on wooden walls, and baskets of oyster crackers on every table. In good weather, grab your crackers and a drink and take them out onto the dock to watch the boats in the creek, the people who operate them, and the birds of Brigantine National Wildlife Refuge on the other side.

Actually, we were a little disappointed with our overfried combination plate. But based on the many rave reports we received before and since, we suspect that our experience was unlucky and uncommon. On the positive side, our crabcakes were delicious—chock-full of fresh crabmeat, not those bready lumps so often passed off for crabcakes that ought to be called fried turkey stuffing. And the creamy clam stew served here (more like chowder than stew to us New Englanders) was rich, smooth, and tasty.

Dinners, including salad, potato, slaw, and beverage, run $5.50 to $10.50. Our combination plate—with fish, scallops, shrimp, crabcake, and deviled clam—was $9.50.

One other thing you should know about Oyster Creek Inn: its setting is also home to the "Leeds Devil," a Loch Nessian creature that has inspired two poems, several artists' renderings, and a TV movie that was filmed right at the inn.

Down near the point
Where the reeds are highest,
That's where the devil conjures the slyest.

Now you've been warned
Look out for black magic
To laugh or scoff will prove very tragic.

You just might not want to come alone.

HOURS   Tue.–Sat. 4–9 pm (sometimes till 9:30); Sun. 1–9 pm; closed Mon.

DIRECTIONS   Northbound: In their wisdom, the designers of the Garden State Parkway made it impossible to get here conveniently from the northbound lane. Short of an illegal U-turn across the median strip, the best way to do it is to take Exit 50, bear right, cross over the parkway, reenter the southbound lane, and take Exit 48. From there, read on.

Southbound: Exit 48 puts you on Route 9 South. In 4 miles, the **Smithville Inn** is on your right. For **Oyster Creek Inn,** take the first left past Smithville (Moss Mill Rd.). In 1½ miles curve left and drive another mile to the end of the pavement. You're there.

ALLEN'S CLAM BAR, *Exits 50 & 52, New Gretna*

If you've managed to get this far without stopping at a clam bar, this is the one to pick. It is only about 1½ miles from the parkway and three miles from the Great Bay, where oyster and scallop boats come in each day to unload their catch.

The restaurant is not much to look at—inexpensive paneling, Formica tabletops, bare concrete floor. But never mind the floor, look at the man behind the counter. He's husky, hearty-voiced Win Allen, and he'll tell you everything you need to know about shucking oysters. He's the New Jersey State Oyster Shucking

Champion, having extracted, cleaned, and presented on the half-shell, two dozen gritty-shelled bivalves in 1 minute 29 seconds. If that doesn't sound impressive, try to shuck one. It might take you 20 minutes!

Once you've had a chance to watch Win pop out oysters with the ease of a child flicking a Yo-Yo, you'll want to sample the product of his labors. For $4.95 you can partake of a full platter of fried oysters with French fries, cole slaw, lettuce and tomato. Other seafood platters (deviled crabs or clams, fried flounder or clams, etc.) run $4 to $4.50. Or, for $2, you can have an oyster sandwich on a hard roll; flounder and clam sandwiches are less.

Win's mother is in charge of the chowder (clam and, of course, oyster), and her recipe is a secret from everyone, even Win! We tried it (75 cents/$1.35) and found it tasty and well stocked with potatoes, onions, bacon, tomato, and herbs. But for unadulterated shellfish taste, try what around here is called stew —no vegetables or seasonings to distract you, just chunky diced clams or oysters in milk and cream with a gob of butter and a dash of paprika.

No matter what you order, you'll get to sample oyster crackers, those hard Brussels-sprout-sized nuggets served around here instead of bread. They come piled in a basket, with fresh-ground horseradish on the side. Yes, horseradish, and it goes straight to your eyeballs. If you mistake the stringy white mass for cole slaw and fork it down, you won't even be able to explain what hit you.

HOURS Winter: Sun. & Tue.–Thu. 11 am–7 pm; Fri. & Sat. 11 am–8 pm. Summer: Open one hour later every day. Closed Mondays all year.

DIRECTIONS Northbound: From Exit 50 bear right onto Route 9 North. In 1½ miles you'll see it on the right.

Southbound: From Exit 52 turn left. In 1.1 miles turn right at T junction and go 0.9 mile, through town, and you'll see it on your left.

"72" FAMILY DINER, *Exit 63, Manahawkin*

* Not great, but always open

This is a small and boxy diner loaded to the grills with stainless steel; it's recently been refurbished with butterscotch booths that manage not to intrude too much on the old-time feel. Unfortunately, the old-time diner taste seems to be absent.

At least they're honest about it. "Uh . . . the soup isn't homemade, but it's pretty good," we were told when we ordered. Inquiring about the chili, we were informed, "It's more or less homemade." We wondered if that meant it was made in the backyard.

Breakfast looks like your best bet here, with a great variety of interesting omelets including asparagus and what's called an "O'Brien"—with potatoes, onion, bacon, and peppers. These run $2.75 to $3.75; simpler egg breakfasts cost less, of course. There are also various egg sandwiches (with bacon, ham, pork roll, or sausage), available throughout the day ($2.25). If you want to try something local, order scrapple—a mush of pork scraps, cornmeal, and seasonings that is molded, sliced, and fried. It's good. More or less.

HOURS Always open.

DIRECTIONS From Exit 63 bear right. In ½ mile you'll see it on your right.

THE SWEET SHOP, *Exit 81, Toms River*

Here's an old-fashioned soda fountain/luncheonette with a few Formica touches. But the terrazzo floor, the cream-colored plaster walls, and much else are still intact, and a just-folks spirit is evident throughout. The menu is typical of this restaurant genre: pancakes or eggs with home fries (just 95 cents!), burgers, and all the sandwiches you could hope for, from pepper steak ($1.45) to pork roll with egg ($1.75) to chicken, egg, or tuna salad. Specials like roast beef sandwich with soup and beverage ($2.50) are posted each day, as are low-priced "student specials." (Toms River High School is around the corner, but they won't turn you down if your locker is elsewhere.)

If you need to plan your route past Toms River, you can pick up a map on the way out the door. They've got quite a selection on every scale, from Ocean County and Atlantic City to the World and the Heavens.

HOURS   Mon.–Fri. 7 am–5 pm; Sat. 7 am–3 pm; Sun. 8 am–noon.

DIRECTIONS   Northbound: From Exit 81 go straight, following signs for Toms River. In 0.4 mile turn left at the first light onto Main St. You'll see its "Breyer's Ice Cream" sign on your right, shortly before the traffic light.

Southbound: From Exit 81 bear right onto Route 9N. In 0.6 mile turn left at the second light onto Main St. It's on the right, shortly before the light —look for "Breyer's Ice Cream" sign.

THE ORIGINAL EVELYN'S SEAFOOD RESTAURANT, *Exit 98, Belmar*

As the story goes (and you know the minute you walk in the door that this place has a good one), Evelyn Longstreet was asked to make sandwiches and chowder for the men building the Shark River Bridge during the bone-chilling winter of '33. Using scrap lumber from the bridge, she banged together a counter at her fish market, moved in a two-burner stove, and went to work. Bridge workers, fishermen, locals, and outsiders caught wind of her ways with a skillet and they started coming in. They haven't stopped yet.

Evelyn's has grown, of course, but despite its obvious success and greatly expanded size, it still has a local flavor. The small tables are set close together under plastic ivy and deepsea dioramas. The friendly waitresses wear black vests, pastel skirts, long white ties, and large round buttons that ask, "Did you know?" Go ahead, bite. The reply will be, "Did you know that we serve seafood on a skewer?" All in all, it's more fun than funk and more homey than hokey.

If Evelyn's is a success, it's because of the food, not the humor. Everything we tasted was excellent, from the moist corn-bread to the sensuously creamy cheesecake (made here, and sold by the pound for home consumption). The broiled bluefish was among the best we had anywhere, not shriveled and dry, but plump and juicy throughout, lightly sauced with lemon and paprika. And enormous! One serving included an outsized filet flanked by another that was half as large. Either piece could have been called a portion at most restaurants. The cole slaw (home-made, of course) had zest.

Evelyn's has a large menu with sandwiches, burgers, quiche, and salads, as well as fish specialties. Our bluefish lunch (with rice and salad) cost just $2.95! At dinner, fresh fish runs $5.25 to $7.50 à la carte, seafood on a skewer (shrimp, scallops, flounder, shrimp teriyaki, and combinations) from $7 to $8.25. On Tuesday through Thursday evenings, Evelyn's offers seashore dinners that include ⅓ pound of peel-your-own shrimp as well as chow-der, entrée, salad, dessert, and beverage for $8.45. It's almost cheaper than catching the fish yourself.

HOURS   Winter: Sun.–Thu. 11:30 am–9 pm; Fri. 11:30 am–9:30 pm; Sat. 11:30 am–10 pm. Summer: Open ½ hour later every night.

DIRECTIONS   See Pat's Deluxe Diner, below.

PAT'S DELUXE DINER, *Exit 98, Belmar*

We don't really recommend Pat's over the superb seafood served at Evelyn's, but like many diners, it has the advantage of long hours (24 each day) and low prices (though a bit higher here than at many of its cousins in lower rent districts). Not that the food is bad—the menu is extensive, soups are homemade, and the fish is fresh and good. But the best thing about Pat's is its view across Route 35 to the Shark River, abundantly populated by cabin cruisers and yachts and charter fishing boats of all sizes.

HOURS   Always open.

DIRECTIONS   From Exit 98 follow signs for Route 38 East. After about 2½ miles of easy driving, pick up signs for Route 35 North. After 1.4 miles on Route 35, **Pat's** is on your right. For **Evelyn's,** turn right 0.2 mile later, just before the bridge, onto 7th Avenue. Cross the tracks and at the light turn left onto Main St. One and a half short blocks and you're there. It's on the left, with parking next door and across the street (free for customers).

MOLLY PITCHER INN, *Exit 109, Red Bank*

"The Molly" is a well-known dining spot on the northern New Jersey shore. It's a Federal-style building with a Greek Revival porch, but the cornerstone tells all—it was built in 1928, not 1828. It's not surprising, then, that there is a strong air of pretense extending right down to the nailed-on beams, the Revolutionary-era maps, and the archaic typeface used on the menu. The view of the Navesink River is charming, if you're lucky enough to get a window seat. We weren't, even though there seemed to be a few empty ones. Still, we enjoyed our lunch, so we won't argue too much with the appointments.

We had a very large Reuben sandwich ($3.75) that was thick and juicy, although there isn't much good to be said about the mushy French fries that accompanied it. Before the sandwich, we'd had a respectable bowl of minestrone soup ($1). In addition to sandwiches ($2.25–$3.75), the Molly Pitcher Inn serves salads and American-style entrées ($4.75–$6) for lunch.

A semi-complete early dinner (5–6:30 P.M.) is just $6.50. If you get there later than that, you'll pay $8 to $12 for most entrées —shrimp scampi, roast duck, prime rib, etc.

HOURS   Mon.–Thu. 7 am–9 pm; Fri. 7 am–10 pm; Sat. 8 am–10 pm; Sun. 8 am–9 pm.

DIRECTIONS   Northbound: From Exit 109 bear left on ramp for Half Mile Road. ■ Go straight through light to end of road. Turn right

243

onto West Front St. Go 1.1 miles, pass under railroad trestle, and immediately turn left onto Rector Place. In 0.2 mile turn gently right. Inn is on your left in 0.1 mile.

Southbound: From Exit 109 turn left. Enter right lane, following sign for Half Mile Road, which takes you around a jughandle. Then as above from ■.

CARVAJAL, *Exits 125 & 129, Perth Amboy*

See page 186 for a description of this most surprising Mexican restaurant in the middle of residential Perth Amboy.

DIRECTIONS Northbound: From Exit 125 turn right, following signs for Perth Amboy. Bear left three-quarters of the way around traffic circle, and head straight out over the old bridge to Perth Amboy (the new one is off to your left). Go 1½ miles to second light past bridge; turn right onto Fayette St. In 0.4 mile you're at Goodwin St. Turn right on Goodwin, and in ½ block it's on your right. Rejoin parkway by crossing Fayette and entering a long ramp that takes you right to it.

Southbound: From Exit 129 follow signs for Route 9. The left lane feeds you into the same access road that the New Jersey Turnpike's Exit 11 lets into, and directions are identical to those on page 188 for turnpike travelers.

SZECHUAN GARDENS, *Exit 129, Woodbridge*

On page 188 there is a description of this quality Chinese restaurant featuring Szechuan, Hunan, and Shanghai cuisine.

DIRECTIONS From Exit 129 follow signs for U.S. 9 North. In about 2 miles U.S. 9 will merge with U.S. 1, and ½ mile later Woodbridge Shopping Plaza is on your right. Look for Caldor sign. Restaurant is at the far end of plaza.

SHORT STOP DINER, *Exit 148, Bloomfield*

The Short Stop is a tiny stainless-steel gem, bejeweled with rainbow stripes outside and a pretty pink terrazzo floor within. We'd have called this nine-stooler the Lionel of diners but we were told that there's another Short Stop half its size in Bellville.

Despite its diminutive size, the Short Stop does a mighty business, serving four to five hundred people a day. Few stay on the premises more than fifteen minutes, perhaps because the diner's motto is "Eat it and beat it." Diners, no doubt, were the first fast-food restaurants and this one has continued the tradition without sprouting arches.

There's no question about the house specialty here—you can read signs about it before you leave your car. For its hundreds of regular customers and thousands of irregulars, the Short Stop is synonymous with "eggs in a skillet." When you order the special, as we did, the short-order cook sets a small cast-iron skillet on a gas burner, plops down a dollop of butter, grabs two eggs from the pile in the display cooler, and cracks them into the sizzling butter. In a few moments, she removes the skillet from the range top and waves it under a broiler. Then the whole affair goes onto a wooden trivet that is placed smack dab in front of you. And that's how you eat it, right out of the cast-iron pan. We're not sure whether eggs cooked this way taste any better than eggs cooked on a grill and served on a plate, but they sure were hot right down to the last bite.

245

Two eggs thus presented cost $1.10. With smoked ham, pork roll, bacon, or sausage, it's $2.15. Three-egg "he-man omelets," with hash browns, lettuce, tomato, toast, and coffee, are $3.35, and a "rib sticker"—half a pound of chopped sirloin with the above fixin's—is $3.95.

That's about it for the menu, except for hamburgers, BLTs, and, of course, "the best cup of coffee in town." They probably couldn't fit any more in.

HOURS   Always open.

DIRECTIONS   Northbound: From Exit 148 go straight to second light. It's on the right.

Southbound: From Exit 148 take the first left, cross under parkway, and look left.

INDEX OF RESTAURANTS AND TOWNS

[When a restaurant carries two separate page references, the first is the description and the second gives driving directions.]

Our best source of leads to worthwhile restaurants is you, the traveler who cares. Please tell us of any you know that lie close to the road, and we'll check them out for future editions in THE INTERSTATE GOURMET series.

Send your suggestions to:

Summit Books
Code ISG
1230 Avenue of the Americas
New York, NY 10020

Restaurant name_____

Near Highway_____

Exit_____

City_____

State_____

Directions_____

_____

Comments_____

_____

_____

_____